W9-AYO-343

WITHDRAWN

CAPITALISM

WITHOUT

CAPITAL

CAPITALISM
WITHOUT
CAPITAL

THE RISE OF THE INTANGIBLE ECONOMY

Jonathan Haskel and Stian Westlake

PRINCETON UNIVERSITY PRESS
Princeton & Oxford

Copyright © 2018 by Princeton University Press

Published by Princeton University Press, 41 William Street,
Princeton, New Jersey 08540
In the United Kingdom: Princeton University Press, 6 Oxford
Street, Woodstock, Oxfordshire OX20 1TR

press.princeton.edu

Jacket images courtesy of iStock

All Rights Reserved

ISBN 978-0-691-17503-4

British Library Cataloging-in-Publication Data is available

This book has been composed in Berling LT Std
and Gotham

Printed on acid-free paper. ∞

Printed in the United States of America

1 3 5 7 9 10 8 6 4 2

CONTENTS

List of Illustrations   vii

Acknowledgments   ix

1 Introduction   1

Part I The Rise of the Intangible Economy

2 Capital's Vanishing Act   15

3 How to Measure Intangible Investment   36

4 What's Different about Intangible Investment?
The Four S's of Intangibles   58

Part II The Consequences of the Rise of the Intangible Economy

5 Intangibles, Investment, Productivity, and Secular
Stagnation   91

6 Intangibles and the Rise of Inequality   118

7 Infrastructure for Intangibles, and Intangible
Infrastructure   144

8 The Challenge of Financing an Intangible Economy   158

9 Competing, Managing, and Investing in the
Intangible Economy   182

10 Public Policy in an Intangible Economy:
Five Hard Questions   208

11 Summary, Conclusion, and the Way Ahead   239

Notes   243

References   253

Index   267

ILLUSTRATIONS

Figures

Figure 1.1. "Intangibles" references in scientific journals   6

Figure 2.1. Intangible and tangible investment over time, United States   24

Figure 2.2. Intangible and tangible investment over time, UK   25

Figure 2.3. Intangible and tangible investment in Europe   26

Figure 2.4. Intangible and tangible investment in Europe and the United States   26

Figure 2.5. Intangible and tangible investment as shares of country GDP   27

Figure 2.6. Intangible and IT investment   29

Figure 2.7. Intangible intensity in manufacturing and services   31

Figure 2.8. Tangible and intangible investment and regulation   32

Figure 2.9. Intangible investment and government R&D spending   33

Figure 2.10. Intangible investment and trade restrictiveness, 2013   34

Figure 5.1. Real investment as a percentage of real GDP   92

Figure 5.2. Long-run real interest rates for the United States and UK   93

Figure 5.3. Measures of profits and profit spreads   95

Figure 5.4. Labor productivity spreads   95

Figure 5.5. Growth of labor and multi-factor productivity   96

Figure 5.6. Investment/GDP ratios with and without new intangibles   103

Figure 5.7. Intangible intensity and change in productivity spread   106

Figure 5.8. Intangibles and R&D capital services growth: all countries   107

Figure 5.9. Multi-factor productivity and intangible capital
  services growth   108

Figure 5.10. Multi-factor productivity and R&D capital
  services growth   109

Figure 5.11. Output growth with and without intangibles   117

Figure 6.1. Inequality in median annual earnings
  between high school and college graduates   121

Figure 6.2. Inequality between the generations, UK   122

Figure 6.3. Income shares of the top 1 percent in
  English-speaking countries   128

Figure 6.4. Rises in house prices for selected US cities 137

Figure 6.5. Rises in real house prices for UK regions,
  1973–2016   138

Figure 6.6. "Openness to Experience" and voting
  to leave the EU   142

Figure 9.1. "Management" and "Leadership" mentions in
  the *Harvard Business Review*   184

Figure 9.2. The declining informativeness of earnings
  and book value reporting   203

Tables

Table 2.1. Examples of Tangible and Intangible Business
  Investments   22

Table 3.1. Categories of Intangible Investment   44

Boxes

Box 4.1. Knowledge, Data, Information, and Ideas:
  Some Definitions   63

Box 5.1. Productivity and Profitability Explained   97

Box 6.1. Measures of Inequality   119

Box 6.2. An Outline of Piketty's $r > g$ Condition   125

Box 10.1. An Opportunity for Small Nations: or,
  What Should Ruritania Do?   234

ACKNOWLEDGMENTS

This book would be impossible without the years of determined and insightful work by economists and others who glimpsed the beginnings of the intangible economy and sought to understand and to measure it. From the very start, Carol Corrado, Chuck Hulten, and Dan Sichel have been extraordinarily open and generous with their time and advice and have become delightful coauthors and friends. In particular, Carol Corrado has made detailed and invaluable comments on this text.

It is a pleasure as well to thank our various close coauthors over the years, as much of the data and thinking in this book is drawn from our joint work. Particular thanks are due to Tony Clayton of the Office for National Statistics and UK Intellectual Property Office, Peter Goodridge (Imperial College), Massimiliano Iommi (ISTAT), Cecilia Jona-Lasinio (LUISS), Gavin Wallis (Bank of England), Albert Bravo Biosca (Nesta), Mariela Dal Borgo (Warwick), Peter Gratzke (Nesta), Brian MacAulay (Nesta), Martin Brassell (Inngot), Ben Reid (Nesta), and Mauro Giorgio Marrano (Queen Mary).

We are also grateful to the organizations that have funded this work, including the Engineering and Physical Sciences Research Council (EPSRC, EP/K039504/1), the European Commission Seventh Framework Programme (COINVEST, 217512; SPIN-TAN 612774), HM Treasury, and the Agensi Inovasi Malaysia. In particular, much of the cross-country data in this book comes from the COINVEST- and SPINTAN-funded projects with long-standing coauthors Carol Corrado, Massimiliano Iommi, and Cecilia Jona-Lasinio.

Our authorial partnership began with our collaboration on Nesta's Innovation Index, a project that would not have happened without the support of Richard Halkett and Jonathan Kestenbaum of Nesta, John Kingman of HM Treasury, and David Currie, who chaired the advisory board. A commission from Ryan

Avent of the *Economist* gave us the idea of writing something for a wider audience.

We are also grateful to the people who challenged us to think about the broader implications of intangibles for the economy and for society and who patiently commented on drafts. Particular thanks go to Diane Coyle, for her insightful advice and comments throughout the project, and to Alex Edmans, Fernando Galindo Rueda, Neil Lee, Mike Lynch, David Pitt Watson, and Giles Wilkes, who commented on particular chapters, and Simon Haskel, who read the text in its entirety. Other readers and discussants to whom we are very grateful include Hasan Bakhshi, Daniel Finkelstein, Tom Forth, John Kay, Juan Mateos Garcia, Ramana Nanda, Paul Nightingale, Robert Peston, and Bart van Ark. Jonathan thanks his students Hussam Bakkar, Viktor Bertilsson, Shi The, and Xiaoyi Wang, while Stian thanks Nesta's Policy & Research team for their input and support.

Of course, all errors and omissions are our responsibility.

Stian's participation in the project was enabled by a period of leave from Nesta, which would not have been possible but for Geoff Mulgan, who generously granted it, and Louise Marston, who led the team with flair in his absence. Jonathan is grateful for the support of Imperial College and the European Commission-funded SPINTAN project during the writing period. All the while, Gemima King of Nesta and Donna Sutherland Smith of Imperial helped keep the show on the road.

Princeton University Press has been a source of support and encouragement throughout; we are especially grateful to Sarah Caro, Hannah Paul, and Chris Van Horne for their hard work.

Above all, we are grateful to our families for their boundless support and encouragement throughout this project: Stian to Kirsten, Aurelia, and Clara and Jonathan to Sue, Hannah, and Sarah. We dedicate this book, with love, to them.

CAPITALISM
WITHOUT
CAPITAL

1

Introduction

Valuation, the Old-Fashioned Way: or, a Thousand Years in Essex

Colin Matthews was vexed. To have valuers crawling all over his airport was the last thing he wanted. But after three years, it could no longer be stopped.

It was the summer of 2012. For three years he had been fighting the UK competition authorities' attempts to break up British Airports Authority (BAA), the company he ran and which owned most of Britain's large airports. He had exhausted his legal options and was giving up.

So now the men and women with suits and spreadsheets and high-viz vests were going round his airports, working out how much they were worth to potential buyers. Accountants and lawyers and surveyors and engineers measured and counted, and bit by bit, they came up with a value for the whole of Stansted, Britain's fourth-busiest airport, to the northeast of London.

They priced up the tarmac, the terminal, the baggage equipment. There was an agreed value for the parking lots, the bus station, and the airport hotel. There was some argument about the underground fuel pumps, but the calculation was not out of the ordinary for BAA's accountants: the cost of the asset less its depreciation, with some adjustment for inflation. Sure enough, when Stansted was sold in 2013 (for £1.5 billion), the price was pretty close to what the accountants had valued the business at.

In one sense, the valuation of Stansted looked like a quintessentially twenty-first-century scene. There was the airport itself. What could be a better emblem of globalized high modernity than an airport? There was the troupe of accountants and lawyers, those ubiquitous servants of financial capitalism. And, of course, there was the economic logic of the process: from the privatization that put BAA in the private sector in the first place, to the competition policy that caused the breakup, to the infrastructure funds that circled to buy the assets after breakup; all very modern.

But at the same time, the valuation of Stansted was the kind of thing that had been going on for centuries. The business of working out how much something was worth by counting up and measuring physical stuff has a long and noble tradition.

Nine and a quarter centuries before, Stansted, then just another country village, had played host to a similar scene. Reeves and messengers, the eleventh-century forerunners of the accountants and lawyers that had so vexed Colin Matthews, had converged on the place to assess its value for Domesday Book, the vast survey of England's wealth carried out by William the Conqueror. Using tally-sticks rather than laptops, they carried out their own valuation. They talked to people and counted things. They recorded that Stansted had a mill, sixteen cows, sixty pigs, and three slaves. Then they measured what they counted and valued the manor of Stansted at £11 per year.[1]

And although the value they put on the medieval village of Stansted was rather less than the £1.5 billion BAA got for selling the airport in 2013, the reeves and envoys who did the measuring for William the Conqueror were doing something fundamentally similar to what Colin Matthews's accountants were doing.

For centuries, when people wanted to measure how much something ought to be worth—an estate, a farm, a business, a country—they counted and measured *physical* stuff. In particular, they measured things with lasting value. These things became the fixed assets on accountants' balance sheets and the investments that economists and national statisticians counted up in their attempts to understand economic growth.

Over time, the nature of these assets and investments changed: fields and oxen became less important, animals gave way to machinery and factories and vehicles and computers. But the idea that assets are for the most part things you could touch, and that investment means building or buying physical things was as true

for twentieth-century accountants and economists as it was for the
scribes of Domesday Book.

Why Investment Matters

The nature of investment is important to all sorts of people, from
bankers to managers. Economists are no exception: investment oc-
cupies a central place in much economic thought. Investment is
what builds up capital, which, together with labor, constitutes the
two measured inputs to production that power the economy, the
sinews and joints that make the economy work. Gross domestic
product is defined as the sum of the value of consumption, investment, government spending, and net exports; of these four, investment is often the driver of booms and recessions, as it tends to
rise and fall more dramatically in response to monetary policy and
business confidence. The investment element of GDP is where the
animal spirits of the economy bark, and where a recession first
bites.

As a result, the statisticians whose job it is to work out national income have put long and sustained efforts into measuring
how much businesses invest, year after year, quarter after quarter.
Since the 1950s, national statistical agencies have sent out regular questionnaires to businesses to find out how much businesses
are investing. Periodic studies are done to understand how long
particular assets last and, especially for high-tech investments like
computers, how much they are improving over time.

Until very recently, the investments that national statistical offices measured were all tangible assets. Although these investments
represented the modern age in all its industrial glory (in 2015 in
the UK, for example, businesses invested £78bn in new buildings;
£60bn in IT, plant, and machinery; and £17bn in vehicles[2]), the
basic principle that investment was about physical goods would
have made sense to William the Conqueror's reeves.

The Dark Matter of Investment

But, of course, the economy does not run on tangible investment
alone. Stansted Airport, for example, owned not just tarmac and

terminals and trucks, but also things that were harder to see or touch: complex software; valuable agreements with airlines and retailers; internal know-how. All these things had taken time and money to build up and had a lasting value to whoever owned the airport, but they consisted not of physical stuff but of ideas, knowledge, and social relations. In the language of economists, they were *intangible*.

The idea that an economy might come to depend on things that were immaterial was an old one. Futurists like Alvin Toffler and Daniel Bell had begun to talk about the "post-industrial" future as long ago as the 1960s and 1970s. As the power of computers and the Internet became more apparent in the 1990s, the idea that immaterial things were economically important became increasingly widely accepted. Sociologists talked of a "network society" and a "post-Fordist" economy. Business gurus urged managers to think about how to thrive in a knowledge economy. Economists began to think about how research and development and the ideas that resulted from it might be incorporated into their models of economic growth, an economy parsimoniously encapsulated by the title of Diane Coyle's book *The Weightless World*. Authors like Charles Leadbeater suggested we might soon be "living on thin air."

The bursting of the dot-com bubble in 2000 dampened some of the wilder claims about a new economy, but research continued among economists to understand what exactly was changing. It was in this context that a group of economists assembled in Washington in 2002 at a meeting of the Conference on Research in Income and Wealth to think about how exactly to measure the types of investment that people were making in what they were calling "the new economy." At this conference and afterwards, Carol Corrado and Dan Sichel of the US Federal Reserve Board and Charles Hulten of the University of Maryland developed a framework for thinking about different types of investment in the new economy.

To get an idea of what these sorts of investment are, consider the most valuable company in the world at the time of the conference: Microsoft. Microsoft's market value in 2006 was around $250bn. If you looked at Microsoft's balance sheet, which records its assets, you would find a valuation of around $70bn, $60bn of which was cash and various financial instruments.[3] The traditional assets of plant and equipment were only $3bn, a trifling 4 percent of Microsoft's assets and 1 percent of its market value. By the conventional accounting of assets then, Microsoft was a modern-day miracle. This was capitalism without capital.

Not long after the conference, Charles Hulten combed through Microsoft's accounts to explain why it was worth so much (Hulten 2010). He identified a set of intangible assets, assets that *"typically involve the development of specific products or processes, or are investments in organizational capabilities, creating or strengthening product platforms that position a firm to compete in certain markets."* Examples included the ideas generated by Microsoft's investments in R&D and product design, the value of its brands, its supply chains and internal structures, and the human capital built up by training.

Although none of these intangible assets are physical in the way that Microsoft's office buildings or servers are, they all share the characteristics of investments: the company had to spend time and money on them up-front, and they delivered value over time that Microsoft was able to benefit from. But they were typically hidden from company balance sheets and, not surprisingly, from the nation's balance sheet in the official National Accounts. Corrado, Hulten, and Sichel's work provided a big push to develop ways to estimate intangible investment across the economy, using surveys, existing data series, and triangulation.

A Funny Thing Happened on the Way to the Future

And so the intangibles research program developed. In 2005 Corrado, Hulten, and Sichel published their first estimates of how much American businesses were investing in intangibles. In 2006 Hulten visited the UK and gave a seminar on their work at Her Majesty's Treasury, which immediately commissioned a team (that included one of this book's authors) to extend the work to the UK. Work also began in Japan. Agencies like the Organisation for Economic Co-operation and Development (OECD), which were very early on the intangible scene (see, e.g., Young 1998), promoted the idea of intangible investment in policy and political circles, and the idea attracted some attention among commentators and the emerging economic blogosphere. As figure 1.1 shows,

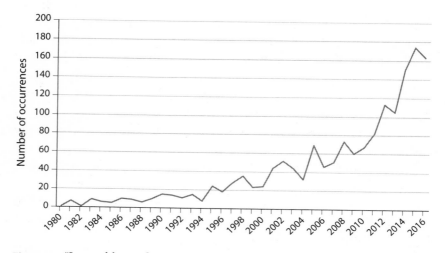

Figure 1.1. "Intangibles" references in scientific journals. Data are the number of mentions of the word "intangible" in the Abstract, Title, or Keyword in academic journals in the field "Economics, Econometrics and Finance" recorded in the database ScienceDirect. Source: authors' calculations from ScienceDirect.

mention of "intangible" became steadily more fashionable even in dry academic journals.

But then something happened that changed the economic agenda: the global financial crisis. Economists and economic policymakers were, quite reasonably, less interested in understanding a purported new economy than in preventing the economy as a whole from collapsing into ruin. Once the most dangerous part of the crisis had been averted, a set of new and rather bleak problems came to dominate economic debate: how to fix a financial system that had so calamitously failed, the growing awareness that inequality of wealth and income had risen sharply, and how to respond to a stubborn stagnation in productivity growth. To the extent that the idea of the new economy was still discussed, it was mostly framed in pessimistic, even dystopian terms: Had technological progress irreversibly slowed, blasting our economic hopes? Would technology turn bad, producing robots that would steal everyone's jobs, or give rise to malign and powerful forms of artificial intelligence?

But while these grim challenges were dominating public debate on economics in op-ed columns and blogs, the project to measure new forms of capital was quietly progressing. Surveys and analyses were undertaken to produce data series of intangible investment, first for the United States, then for the UK, and then for other developed countries. Finance ministries and international organizations continued to support the work, and national statistical agencies began to include some types of intangibles, notably R&D, in their investment surveys. Historical data series were built, estimating how intangible investment had changed over time. And, as we shall see, intangible investment has, in almost all developed countries, been growing more and more important. Indeed, in some countries, it now outweighs tangible investment.

Why Intangible Investment Is Different

Now, there is nothing inherently unusual or interesting from an economic point of view about a change in the types of things businesses invest in. Indeed, nothing could be more normal: the capital stock of the economy is always changing. Railways replaced canals, the automobile replaced the horse and cart, computers replaced typewriters, and, at a more granular level, businesses retool and change their mix of investments all the time. *Our central argument in this book is that there is something fundamentally different about intangible investment, and that understanding the steady move to intangible investment helps us understand some of the key issues facing us today: innovation and growth, inequality, the role of management, and financial and policy reform.*

We shall argue there are two big differences with intangible assets. First, most measurement conventions ignore them. There are some good reasons for this, but as intangibles have become more important, it means we are now trying to measure capitalism without counting all the capital. Second, the basic economic properties of intangibles make an intangible-rich economy behave differently from a tangible-rich one.

Measurement: Capitalism without Capital

As we will discuss, conventional accounting practice is to not measure intangible investment as creating a long-lived capital asset. And this has something to be said for it. Microsoft's investment in a desk and an office building can be observed, and the market for secondhand office equipment and renting office space tells you more or less daily the value of that investment. But there is no market where you can see the raw value of its investment in developing better software or redesigning its user interface. So trying to measure the "asset" that's associated with this investment is a very, very hard task, and accountants, who are cautious people, typically prefer not to do so, except in limited circumstances (typically when the program has been successfully developed and sold, so there is an observable market price).

This conservative approach is all very well in an economy where there is little investment in this type of good. But as such investment starts to exceed tangible investment, it leaves larger and larger areas of the economy uncharted.

Properties of Intangibles: Why the Economy Is Becoming So Different

The shift to intangible investment might be a relatively minor problem if all that was at stake was mismeasurement. It would be as if we were counting most of the new trucks in the economy but missing some of them: an interesting issue for statistics bureaus, but little more.

But there is, we will argue, a more important consequence of the rise of intangibles: intangible assets have, on the whole, quite different economic characteristics from the tangible investment that has traditionally predominated.

First of all, intangible investment tends to represent a *sunk* cost. If a business buys a tangible asset like a machine tool or an office block, it can typically sell it should it need to. Many tangible investments are like this, even large and unusual ones. If you've ever fancied one of those giant Australian mining tractors, you can buy them secondhand at an online auction site called Machinery Zone; World Oils sells gently used drilling rigs; and a business called UVI Sub-Find deals in secondhand submarines. Intangible assets are harder to sell and more likely to be specific to the company that makes them. Toyota invests millions in its lean production systems, but it would be impossible to separate these investments from their factories and somehow sell them off. And while some research and development gives rise to patents that can in some cases be sold, far more of it is tailored to the specific needs of the business that invests in it, certainly sufficiently so to make intellectual property markets very limited.

The second characteristic of intangible investments is that they generate *spillovers*. Suppose you run a business that makes flugelbinders, and you own a tangible asset in the form of a factory, and an intangible asset in the form of an excellent new design for a flugelbinder. It's almost trivially easy to make sure that your firm gets most of the benefits from the factory: you put a lock on the door. If someone asks to use your factory for free, you politely refuse; if they break in, you can call the police and have them arrested; in most developed countries, this would be an open-and-shut case. Indeed, making sure you get the benefit from tangible assets you own, like a factory, is so simple that it seems a silly question to ask. The designs, however, are a different business altogether. You can keep them secret to prevent their being copied, but competitors may be able to buy some flugelbinders and reverse-engineer them. You might be able to obtain a patent to discourage people from copying you, but your competitors may be able to "invent around" it, changing just enough aspects of the product that your patent offers no protection. Even if your patent is secure, getting redress against patent infringement is far more complicated than getting the police to sling intruders out of your factory—you may be in for months or years of litigation, and you may not win in the end. After their world-leading first flight, the Wright brothers spent much of their time not developing better aircraft, but fighting rival developers who they felt were infringing on their patents. The tendency for others to benefit from what were meant to be private investments—what economists call spillovers—is a characteristic of many intangible investments.

Intangible assets are also more likely to be *scalable*. Consider Coke: the Coca Cola Company, based in Atlanta, Georgia, is responsible for only a limited number of the things that happen to produce a liter of Coke. Its most valuable assets are intangible: brands, licensing agreements, and the recipe for how to make the syrup that makes Coke taste like Coke. Most of the rest of the business of making and selling Coke is done by unrelated bottling companies, each of which has signed an agreement to produce Coke in its part of the world. These bottlers typically own their own bottling plants, sales forces, and vehicle fleets. The Coca Cola Company of Atlanta's intangible assets can be scaled across the whole world. The formula and the Coke brand work just the same whether a billion Cokes are sold a day or two billion (the actual number is currently about 1.7 billion). The bottlers' tangible assets scale much less well. If Australians dramatically increase their thirst for Coke, Coca Cola Amatil (the local bottler) will likely need to invest in more trucks to deliver it, bigger production lines, and eventually new plants.

Finally, intangible investments tend to have *synergies* (or what economists call complementarities) with one another: they are more valuable together, at least in the right combinations. The MP3 protocol, combined with the miniaturized hard disk and Apple's licensing agreements with record labels and design skills created the iPod, a very valuable innovation. These synergies are often unpredictable. The microwave oven was the result of a marriage between a defense contractor, which had accidentally discovered that microwaves from radar equipment could heat food, and a white goods manufacturer, which brought appliance design skills. Tangible assets have synergies too—between the truck and the loading bay, say, or between a server and a router, but typically not on the same radical and unpredictable scale.

Conclusion

These unusual economic characteristics mean that the rise of intangibles is more than a trivial change in the nature of investment. Because intangible investments, on average, behave differently from tangible investments, we might reasonably expect an economy dominated by intangibles to behave differently too.

In fact, once we take into account the changing nature of capital in the modern economy, a lot of puzzling things start to make sense. In the rest of this book, we'll look at how the shift to intangible investment helps us understand four issues of great concern to anyone who cares about the economy: secular stagnation, the long-run rise in inequality, the role of the financial system in supporting the nonfinancial economy, and the question of what sort of infrastructure the economy needs to thrive. Armed with this understanding we then see what these economic changes mean for government policymakers, businesses, and investors. Our journey will take us past the appraisers of old into the unmapped territory that is modern intangible investment.

PART 1

The Rise of the Intangible Economy

2

Capital's Vanishing Act

Investment is one of the most important activities in the economy. But over the past thirty years, the nature of investment has changed. This chapter describes the nature of that change and considers its causes. In chapter 3, we look at how this change in investment can be measured. In chapter 4, we explore the unusual economic properties of these new types of investment, and why they might be important.

Investment is central to the functioning of any economy. The process of committing time, resources, and money so that we can produce useful things in the future is, from an economic point of view, a defining part of what businesses, governments, and individuals do.

The starting point of this book is an observation: Over the last few decades, the nature of investment has been gradually but significantly changing.

The change isn't primarily about information technology. The new investment does not take the form of robots, computers, or silicon chips, although, as we will see, they all play supporting roles in the story. The type of investment that has risen inexorably is *intangible*: investment in ideas, in knowledge, in aesthetic content, in software, in brands, in networks and relationships.

This chapter describes this change and why it has happened.

A Trip to the Gym

Our story begins in the gym, or rather in two gyms. We're going to step inside a commercial gym in 2017 and in 1977 and look at some of the differences. As we will see, gyms provide a vivid but typical example of how even industries that are not obviously high-tech have subtly changed the types of investment they make.

Gyms are an interesting place to begin our search for the intangible economy because at first glance there's nothing much intangible about them. Even if you avoid gyms like the plague, you probably have an idea of the sort of things you would find there. Our gym in 2017 is full of equipment that the business needs to run: a reception desk with a computer and maybe a turnstile, exercise machines, some weights, shower fittings, lockers, mats, and mirrors ("the most heavily used equipment in the gym," as one gym owner joked). All this kit is reflected in the finances of businesses that own and run gyms: their accounts typically contain lots of assets that you can touch and see, from the premises they operate in to the treadmills and barbells their customers use.

Now, consider a gym from forty years ago. By 1977 the United States was full of gyms. Arnold Schwarzenegger's breakout movie *Pumping Iron* had just been released, featuring scenes of him training in Gold's Gym in Venice Beach, Los Angeles, which had been established in 1965 and was widely franchised across America. Other gyms contained machines like the Nautilus, the original fixed-weight machine, invented by Arthur Jones in the late 1960s. If you were to look around a gym of the time, you might be surprised to see many similarities to today's gym. Granted, there might be fewer weight machines and they would be less advanced. Membership would be recorded on index cards rather than on a computer; perhaps the physical fittings would be more rough-and-ready, but otherwise many of the business's visible assets would look the same: some workout rooms, some changing rooms, some equipment.

But if we return to our 2017 gym and look more closely, we'll notice a few differences. It turns out that the modern gym has invested in a range of things that its 1977 counterpart hasn't. There is the software behind the computer on the front desk, recording memberships, booking classes, and scheduling the staff roster, linked to a central database. The gym has a brand, which has been built up through advertising campaigns whose sophistication and expense dwarf those of gyms in the 1970s. There's an operations handbook, telling the staff how to do various tasks from inducting new members to dealing with delinquent customers. Staff members are trained to follow the handbook and are doing things with a routinized efficiency that would seem strange in the easygoing world of *Pumping Iron*. All these things—software, brands, processes, and training—are all a bit like the weight machines or the turnstile or the building the gym sits in, in that they cost money in the short run, but over time help the gym function and make money. But unlike the physical features, most of these things can't be touched—certainly no risk of dropping them on your foot. Gym businesses are still quite heavy users of assets that are physical (all of the UK's four biggest gyms are owned by private equity firms, which tend to like asset-intensive businesses), but compared to their counterparts of four decades ago, they have far more assets that you cannot touch.

And the transformation goes deeper than this. In one of its rooms, the gym puts on regular exercise classes for its members; one of the most popular is called Bodypump, or, as the sign on the door significantly puts it "Bodypump®." It turns out the company that runs the gym is not the only business operating in the premises—and this second business is even more interesting from an economic point of view.

Bodypump is a type of exercise called "high-intensity interval training" (HIIT), where participants move about vigorously and lift small weights in time to music, but this description does not do justice to the intensity of the workouts or the adrenaline-induced devotion that well-run HIIT classes engender in their customers. The reason for the registered trademark sign is that Bodypump is designed and owned by the other company at work in the building, a business from New Zealand called Les Mills International.

Les Mills was an Olympic weightlifter who set up a small gym in Auckland three years after Joe Gold opened his first gym in Los Angeles. His son Philip, after a visit to LA, saw the potential for merging music with group exercise: he brought it back to New Zealand and added weights to the routines to produce Bodypump in 1997. He realized that by writing up the routines and synchronizing them with compilations of up-to-date, high-energy music, he had a product that could be sold to other gyms. By 2005 Les Mills classes like Bodypump and Bodycombat were being offered in some 10,000 venues in 55 countries with an estimated 4 million participants a week (Parviainen 2011); the company's website now estimates 6 million participants per week. Les Mills's designers create new choreography for their programs every three months. They film them and dispatch the film with guidance on the choreography notes and the music files to their licensed instructors. At the time of writing, they have 130,000 such instructors. To become an instructor, you have to complete three days of training, currently costing around £300, after which you can start teaching, but to proceed further you have to submit a video of a complete class to Les Mills, which checks your technique, choreography, and coaching.

The things that a business like Les Mills uses to make money look very different from the barbells and mats of a 1977 Gold's Gym. True, some of their assets are physical—recording equipment, computers, offices—but most of them are not. They have a set of very valuable brands (gym customers have been known to mutiny if their gym stops offering Bodypump), intellectual property (IP) protected by copyrights and trademarks, expertise on designing exercise classes, and proprietary relationships with a set of suppliers and partners (such as music distributors and trainers). The idea of making money from ideas about how to work out is not new—Charles Atlas was selling bodybuilding courses a decade before Les Mills was born—but the scale on which Les Mills International operates, and the way it combines brands, music, course design, and training is remarkable.

Our excursion into the world of gyms suggests that even a very physical business—literally, the business of physiques—has in the last few decades become a lot more dependent on things that are immaterial. This is not a story of Internet-driven disruption of the kind we are familiar with from a hundred news stories: gyms were not replaced with an app the way record shops were replaced by Napster, iTunes, and Spotify. Software does not replace the need to lift weights. But the business has nevertheless changed in two different ways. The part that looks superficially similar to how it did in the 1970s—the gym itself—has become shot through with systems, processes, relationships, and software. This is not so much innovation, but *innervation*—the process of a body part being supplied with nerves, making it sensate, orderly, and controllable. And new businesses have been set up that rely almost entirely for their success on things you cannot touch.

In the rest of this chapter, we will look at how the changes in investment and in assets that took place in the gym industry can be seen throughout the economy, and the reasons for these changes. But first, let us look more rigorously at what investment actually is.

What Are Investment, Assets, and Capital?

When we looked at the things that gyms bought or developed to run and make money, we were talking about assets and investments. Investment is very important to economists because it builds up what they call the "capital stock" of the economy: the tools and equipment that workers use to produce the goods and services that together make up economic output.

But "investment," "assets," and "capital" can be confusing terms. Take "investment." Financial journalists typically refer to people who buy and sell securities as "investors," and nervously diagnose the "mood of investors." The same journalist might call a long-term financier like Warren Buffett an "investor" and his short-term rivals "speculators." Someone considering going to college might be advised that "education is the best investment you can make."

The terms "assets" and "capital" are also used in a confusing variety of ways. In his justly famous *Capital in the Twenty-First Century*, Thomas Piketty (2014) defined capital as "all forms of wealth that individuals . . . can own." Marxist writers commonly ascribe to "capital" not just an accounting definition, but an entire exploitative system. "Assets" also have different definitions. Many firms think of their business assets as their stock of plant and equipment. For an accountant, business assets commonly include the cash in the firm's bank account and bills its customers have yet to pay, which don't seem to be machines used in the business production but rather the results of doing that business.

Because of these multiple meanings, and because we'll be coming back to these terms frequently, it will be helpful to establish working definitions for investment, capital, and assets. We will stick to the internationally agreed definition of investment used by statistics agencies the world over when they measure the performance of national economies. This has the benefit of being standardized and the fruit of much thought, and of being directly linked to figures like GDP that we are used to seeing in news bulletins.

According to the UN's System of National Accounts, the bible of national accounting, "*investment is what happens when a producer either acquires a fixed asset or spends resources (money, effort, raw materials) to improve it.*"[1] This is a quite dense statement, so let's unpack what it means.

First of all, let's look at the definition of *assets*. An *asset* is an economic resource that is expected to provide a benefit over a period of time.[2] If a bank buys a new server or a new office building, it expects to get a benefit that lasts for some time—certainly longer than just a year. If it pays its electricity bill quarterly, the benefit lasts for three months. So the server and the building are assets, but neither the electricity nor the fact of having paid the bill is.

Second, consider the word *fixed*. A *fixed* asset is an asset that results from using up resources in the process of its production. A plane or a car or a drug patent all have to be produced—someone has to do work to create something from nothing. This can be distinguished from a *financial* asset, like an equity stake in a public company. An equity stake is not produced (except in the trivial sense that a share certificate might be printed to represent the claim). This means that when economists talk about *investment* they are *not* talking about investing in the personal finance sense, that is, buying stocks and shares. And because they are talking about *fixed assets* they are not talking about the accountancy concept of cash in a company bank account.

Third, there is the idea of *spending resources*. To be deemed an investment, the business doing the investing has to either acquire the asset from somewhere else or incur some cost to produce it themselves.

Finally, there is the word *producers*. National accounts measure *production* by firms or government or the third sector. Production by households (say, doing the laundry or cooking at home) is not included, and so neither is investment by a household, say, in a washing machine or stove. This is a definitional feature of the way national accounts are calculated, and it is one of the reasons people criticize GDP (not least because it is large, and because it excludes from the record a part of the economy that has historically been run primarily by women). Perhaps one day "production" will have a broader definition in national accounts; for our purposes, most of the changes we describe in this book would, we believe, apply to the household sector as well as to so-called producers.

So, in this book when we talk about "investment" we are *not* talking about the buying or selling of pieces of paper on a stock market or households paying university tuition. Rather, we are talking about spending by business, government, or the third sector that creates a fixed (i.e., nonfinancial) asset, that is, resources spent that create a long-lived stream of productive services. We shall call such a fixed asset providing these long-lived productive services "capital." Because both capital and labor produce such productive services, economists refer to them as "factors of production."[3]

Not All Investments Are Things You Can Touch

One of the examples of an investment in the section above was a drug patent, say, one owned by a pharmaceutical company. The pharmaceutical company is obviously a producer, not a household; the company has to expend resources to produce the patent or acquire it; the patent arises from a process of production—in this case, the work of scientists in a lab—and if the patent is any good, it will have a long-term value, since the company can develop it for future use and perhaps sell medicines based on it. The patent is an example of an *intangible* asset, created by a process of intangible investment. So too were the various assets in the gym story, from the gym's membership software to Les Mills International's Bodypump brand. They arose from a process of production, were acquired or improved by producers, and provide a benefit over time.

These kinds of investments can be found throughout the economy. Suppose a solar panel manufacturer researches and discovers a cheaper process for making photovoltaic cells: it is incurring expense in the present to generate knowledge it expects to benefit from in the future. Or consider a streaming music start-up that spends months designing and negotiating deals with record labels to allow it to use songs the record labels own—again, short-term expenditure to create longer-term gain. Or imagine a training company pays for the long-term rights to run a popular psychometric test: it too is investing.

Some of these investments are new technological ideas. Some are other sorts of ideas that have less to do with high technology: new product designs or new business models. Some take the form of lasting or proprietary relationships, such as a taxi app's network of drivers. Some are codified information, like a customer loyalty card database. What they have in common is that they are not physical. Hence we call them *intangible investment*.

Table 2.1 sets out some examples. On the left-hand side are tangible business investments: buildings, ICT equipment like computer hardware, non-ICT equipment, and vehicles. On the right are intangibles: software, databases, design, mineral exploration, R&D, and business processes, for example. These intangibles in the right column are those elements of spending that business and national accountants have been reluctant to count as investment, though, as we shall see, over the last forty years some of them have been included as such.

TABLE 2.1. EXAMPLES OF TANGIBLE AND INTANGIBLE BUSINESS INVESTMENTS

Tangible investments	Intangible investments
Buildings	Software
ICT equipment (e.g., computer hardware, communications equipment)	Databases
Noncomputer machinery and equipment	R&D
Vehicles	Mineral exploration
	Creating entertainment, literary or artistic originals
	Design
	Training
	Market research and branding
	Business process reengineering

Source: Adapted from the System of National Accounts (SNA) 2008, para 10.67 and table 10.2, and Corrado, Hulten, and Sichel 2005. The SNA also includes as tangible assets weapons systems and cultivated biological resources. As intangibles it includes R&D, mineral exploration and evaluation, computer software and databases, and creating artistic originals. The other intangible assets are those set out in Corrado, Hulten, and Sichel 2005.

Intangible Investment Has Steadily Grown

The story of how intangible investment expanded in the gym business is not unusual.

Consider another sector that is familiar to most people: supermarket retail. If you found yourself in a self-service supermarket of forty years ago, it would look dated, but not unrecognizable. Supermarkets then were big rooms full of shelves, fridges, and freezers just as they are now; customers put their own goods in a shopping cart and took them to a checkout to pay; behind the scenes, trucks resupplied the supermarket from central warehouses. Of course, aspects of the tangible assets of a supermarket business have changed since then: the stores have changed shape (some are bigger and outside of town, others are much smaller and in city centers), and the checkouts have more silicon chips in them and some of them are self-service. But these changes are minor compared to the changes in supermarkets' intangible assets. Even in the 1970s bar codes were increasingly being used to keep track of supermarket inventories; as the 1980s and 1990s went on, this gave rise to computerized systems for managing supply chains, significantly increasing the productivity of the sector. Supermarkets began to invest in complex pricing systems; more ambitious branding and marketing campaigns (including launching ranges of own-label products); more detailed processes and systems for staff to follow, backed up by training; and management systems to allow stores and central offices to track performance, balance stock levels, and plan promotions. Alongside this, a host of intangible-intensive businesses have appeared in the sector, ranging from online competitors like FreshDirect and Ocado, which use software to replace stores, to businesses that process information to help supermarkets, such as loyalty data experts DunnHumby and LMUK.

Fast-growing tech companies are some of the most intangible-intensive of firms. This is in part because software and data are intangibles, and the growing power of computers and telecommunications is increasing the scope of things that software can achieve. But the process of "software eating the world," in venture capitalist Marc Andreessen's words, is not just about software: it involves other intangibles in abundance. Consider Apple's designs and its unrivaled supply chain, which has helped it to bring elegant products to market quickly and in sufficient numbers to meet customer demand, or the networks of drivers and hosts that sharing-economy giants like Uber and AirBnB have developed, or Tesla's manufacturing know-how. Computers and the Internet are important drivers of this change in investment, but the change is long running and predates not only the World Wide Web but even the Internet and the PC.

The rise of intangible investment becomes clear if we look at data for the economy as a whole. For some years, economists have been measuring those aspects of intangible capital not in the national accounts and building increasingly accurate estimates of the amount of intangible investment going on. We will discuss the components of this measurement and how it is undertaken in the next chapter, but figure 2.1 shows the general trend.

Even though the economists of the time were not focused on measuring intangible investment, in recent years scholars have been able to reconstruct how much was invested by businesses in intangible assets decades ago.

In the early years, even in the most developed countries, intangible investment was something of a sideshow. As the graph shows, over time this balance began to shift. Intangible investment

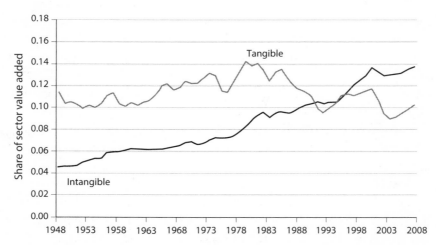

Figure 2.1. Intangible and tangible investment over time, United States. Data are US business investment in intangible and tangible assets relative to US non-farm business sector output, including intangible output. Last datapoint is 2007. Source: Corrado and Hulten 2010, online data appendix.

steadily increased. Tangible investment, as a proportion of the economy as a whole, grew slower and in some cases decreased. In the United States, it looks as though intangible investment got the better of tangible investment by the mid-1990s.[4]

Only in the United States can we go back this far, but for the UK, we have some estimates by Peter Goodridge and his colleagues back to 1992 (Goodridge et al. 2016). They find that intangible investment overtook tangible investment by around the late 1990s (see figure 2.2).

A series of recent EU-funded projects have tried to gather this data consistently across EU countries.[5] The data for the major European economies is set out in figure 2.3 and shows that while intangibles are growing, they have not yet overtaken intangible investment.

If we put all the countries together, we get figure 2.4, which suggests that intangible investment overtook tangible investment around the time of the global financial crisis.

Breaking down the results by country shows that some countries are more intangible-intensive than others. Figure 2.5 shows for countries with available data the shares of GDP accounted for by tangible and intangible investment. The graph is ranked by the share of intangibles. Starting on the left are Spain and Italy. Both have the lowest levels of intangible investment as a proportion

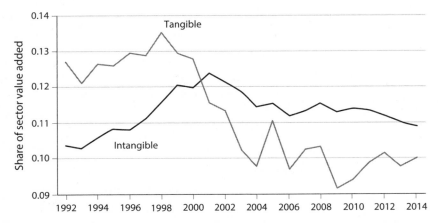

Figure 2.2. Intangible and tangible investment over time, UK. Data are UK market sector investment in intangible and tangible assets relative to UK market sector output, including intangible output. Last datapoint is 2014. Source: Goodridge et al., 2016.

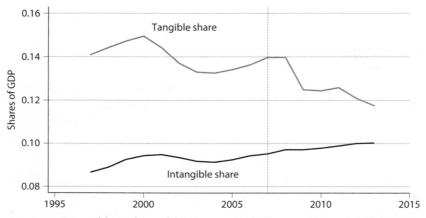

Figure 2.3. Intangible and tangible investment in Europe. Data are EU country whole-economy investment in intangible and tangible assets relative to GDP, including intangible output. Last datapoint is 2013. European countries are Austria, Czech Republic, Denmark, Finland, France, Germany, Italy, Netherlands, Spain, Sweden, UK. Source: authors' calculations based on INTAN-Invest database (www.intan-invest.net).

of GDP and relatively high levels of tangibles—they are tangible-intensive economies. Germany, Austria, Denmark, the Netherlands, and France are next, with low-to-moderate intangible intensity and high-to-moderate tangible intensity; all of them invest more in tangibles than in intangibles. Finland, the UK, the United

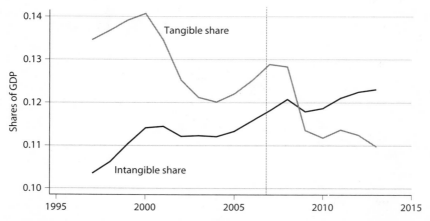

Figure 2.4. Intangible and tangible investment in Europe and the United States. Countries are Austria, Czech Republic, Denmark, Finland, France, Germany, Italy, Netherlands, Spain, Sweden, UK, USA. Source: authors' calculations based on INTAN-Invest database (www.intan-invest.net).

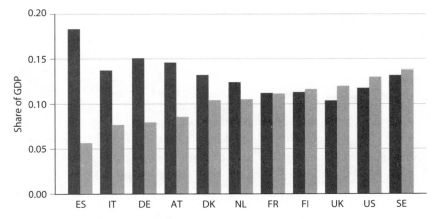

Figure 2.5. Intangible and tangible investment as shares of country GDP (averages, 1999–2013). Data are whole economy, GDP adjusted to include intangibles. Countries are Austria (AT), Denmark (DK), Finland (FI), France (FR), Germany (DE), Italy (IT), Netherlands (NL), Spain (ES), Sweden (SE), UK (UK), USA (US). Source: authors' calculations based on INTAN-Invest database (www .intan-invest.net).

States, and Sweden all have higher intangible than tangible investment intensity.

These differences across countries seem to line up with intuition. Broadly, the Mediterranean countries are at the bottom of the intangible investment pack, with the Nordics, the United States, and UK at the top and the rest of Continental Europe in the middle.

These charts are the result of over a decade of research to codify and measure intangibles. In the next chapter, we'll look at this research and at how these measurements are carried out. But before we do, it is worth giving some thought to the reasons for this long-term increase in intangible investment.

Reasons for the Growth of Intangible Investment

It is not the main aim of this book to explain why intangible investment has undergone such a steady and long-lasting increase: we are more concerned with describing the rise and its consequences for the wider economy. But before we move on to look in detail at how intangible investment has been measured, let us consider some of the likely reasons.

To understand the causes of this remarkable change, we will go back to some of the differences across countries that were hinted at in the earlier figures.

Technology and Cost

It has long been understood that the productivity of the manufacturing sector generally increases faster than that of the services industries, since automation and labor-saving equipment tend to be more useful for manufacturers. Over time, this means that labor-intensive services become more expensive relative to manufactured goods. (In honor of William Baumol's description of this effect, economists call it Baumol's Cost Disease.)

Now, most tangible investments are manufactured (think of the many factories around the world that churn out everything from vans to machine tools to silicon chips). There is certainly a lot of labor involved in tangible investments (laying cables, shop fitting, the whole construction industry), but manufacturing matters too.

Intangible investments, on the other hand, depend much more on labor. Design involves paying designers. R&D involves paying scientists. Software involves paying developers. So over time, we would expect intangible investment spending to gradually rise relative to tangible as Baumol predicted. Some of that rise might be offset by the point, which we look at in detail below, that some intangibles costs are mostly "fixed" or one-off, so this cannot be the whole story, but it is likely to be at least one element of it.

Technology and Productivity of Intangibles

New technology also seems to be increasing the opportunities for businesses to invest productively in intangibles. The most obvious example is IT. Because many intangibles involve information and communication, they can almost by definition be made more efficient with better IT. Think of Uber's organizational investment in building its vast networks of drivers: it would have been theoretically possible before the invention of computers and smartphones (after all, radio cab networks existed), but the return on the investment was massively increased by smartphones, with their ability to connect people quickly and enable the rating of drivers and the metering of rides.

Social technologies have also improved the return on intangible investment. The concept of the corporate R&D lab in nineteenth-century Germany, and its development in both Germany and the United States (intangible investments in the process of producing intangible investments), made commercial R&D more systematic and more worthwhile. The invention and development of systems, such as Kanban, the lean manufacturing technique associated with Toyota, increase the return on organizational investment. Code repositories like GitHub and Stack Overflow and the way they are used are a type of social technology—one that increases the return on software investments by helping programmers collaborate.

Country-by-country data on intangible investment gives us a hint of this. Figure 2.6 shows some correlation between the share of intangible investment in GDP in a country and the share of tangible investment accounted for by IT.

This raises an interesting question: Is it possible that the rise of intangible investment is nothing more than a consequence of improvements in IT? Is the intangible economy a sort of corollary

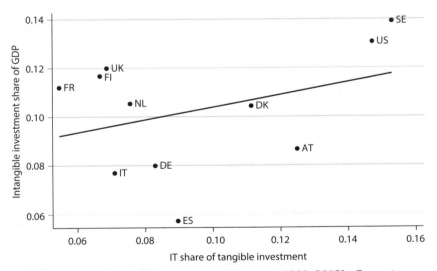

Figure 2.6. Intangible and IT investment (averages, 1999–2013). Countries are Austria (AT), Denmark (DK), Finland (FI), France (FR), Germany (DE), Italy (IT), Netherlands (NL), Spain (ES), Sweden (SE), UK (UK), USA (US). Source: authors' calculations based on INTAN-Invest database (www.intan-invest.net).

of Moore's Law or an epiphenomenon of what Erik Brynjolfsson and Andrew McAfee call the Second Machine Age? It is difficult to prove causality in technological change, but there are grounds to think it is a bit more complicated than that. It is certainly true that some intangibles operate through computers—indeed, for one category of intangibles, software, computers are a necessary precondition. And it seems more than likely that the market size for many intangible assets, such as entertainment, has been greatly expanded by IT.

But it seems unlikely that the rise of computers is the only cause of the intangible economy. First of all, as we saw earlier, the rise of intangible investment began before the semiconductor revolution, in the 1940s and 1950s and perhaps before. Second, while some intangibles like software and data strongly rely on computers, others do not: brands, organizational development, and training, for example. Finally, a number of writers in the innovation studies literature argue that it may be that it was the rise of intangibles that led to the development of modern IT as much as the other way around. The historian James Beniger (1986) argued that modern information technology developed as it did because of an overwhelming need to control production and operations, first on the part of the military, and then in the world of business—by this logic, IT and the research that led to it was shaped by an economy hungry for intangible investment rather than intangible investment happening as a response to the serendipitous invention of various forms of IT.[6]

Industrial Structure

One plausible explanation for the rise in intangible investment is that the balance of what businesses produce has changed. Everyone knows that the output of developed countries, even ones with large manufacturing sectors like Germany or Japan, consists mostly of services. Some of the sociologists and futurists who first heralded the rise of "post-industrial society" were also prophets of what became known as the knowledge economy. Is it true, then, that the modern world is replacing dark satanic mills with service businesses that invest in systems, information, and ideas?

It turns out the evidence is not so clear-cut. Figure 2.7 shows that, in all our countries, the service sector was, in the late 1990s, more tangible-intensive, but this has reversed. Remarkably, the manufacturing sector is more intangible-intensive than tangible-intensive and has grown more so. So, the structure of the economy will affect the relative importance of intangibles, but that effect will change over time. The data for manufacturing should not come as a surprise, since it is likely in part due to globalization. When trade opens up with developing countries, as when China joined the WTO in 2000, developed countries have to further specialize where they have a comparative advantage. The manufacturing businesses that tend to thrive in high-wage economies are ones that invest a lot in intangibles, from the R&D programs of Pfizer or Rolls-Royce to the lean production techniques of the Japanese motor industry. (To the extent that globalization requires the construction of more complex organizations and networks, it could also drive increased intangible investment directly.)

A Changing Business Climate

The years since 1980 have seen a steady relaxation of a whole range of regulations on both products and labor markets in most of the

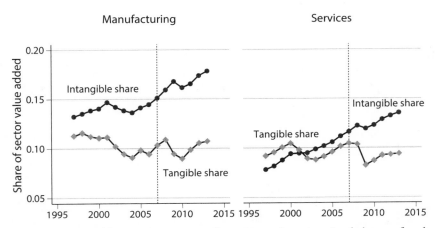

Figure 2.7. Intangible intensity in manufacturing and services (real shares of real sector value added, EU and US, non-farm business). Source: authors' calculations from INTAN-Invest (www.intan-invest.net) and SPINTAN (www.spintan.net) databases.

world's biggest economies. At the same time, most governments on both the right and the left have prided themselves on a degree of business-friendliness that would have surprised politicians of the 1960s or 1970s. Might this have encouraged a long-term rise in intangible investment?

Turning back to the comparison of intangibles across countries, we see some evidence that looser regulation of product markets and labor markets encourages intangible investment. Figure 2.8 shows the share of business-sector GDP accounted for by tangible and intangible investment, plotted against an index of what the OECD calls "employment strictness," where a high value of the index, such as in countries like Italy, means that it is costly to hire and fire workers and a low value, for example, in the United States and the UK, means that it's relatively cheap.

The figure shows something interesting. Countries with more restrictive hiring and firing invest *more* in tangibles, but *less* in intangibles. The effect of labor market rules on tangible effect is intuitive: if hiring and managing staff is a real pain, then busi-

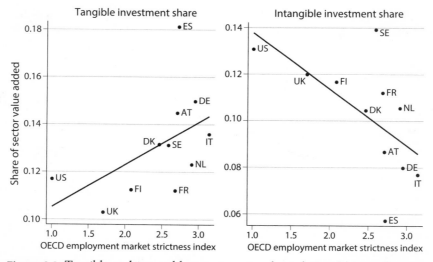

Figure 2.8. Tangible and intangible investment and regulation (shares of sector value added, average 1999–2013). Countries are Austria (AT), Denmark (DK), Finland (FI), France (FR), Germany (DE), Italy (IT), Netherlands (NL), Spain (ES), Sweden (SE), UK (UK), USA (US). Source: authors' calculations based on INTAN-Invest database (www.intan-invest.net) and OECD data.

nesses may invest in machines instead. But the effect on intangible investment is the opposite. Why? New intangibles often require workers to change the way they work: imagine a factory implementing a lean process—a type of organizational development investment—or changing the nature of its products. New intangibles might also be risky and entrepreneurs might reasonably forecast a high possibility of failure in the future. Less flexible workforces might deter such investment in the first place.[7]

This is not intended to be a blithe endorsement for undermining workers' rights. But it does provide a further possible explanation for the continued difference in investment in the last few decades, and a reminder that politics is not irrelevant to these changes.

Figure 2.9 shows there is a correlation between intangible spending, this time by the market sector, and R&D spending by the government. So countries like Finland and Sweden, for example, have very high government R&D spending and high market

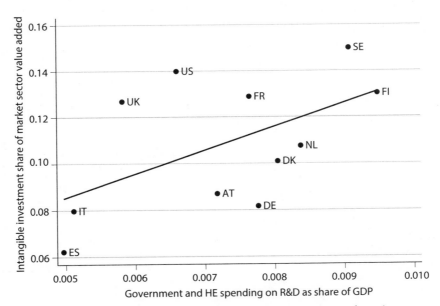

Figure 2.9. Intangible investment and government R&D spending (averages, 1999–2013). Countries are Austria (AT), Denmark (DK), Finland (FI), France (FR), Germany (DE), Italy (IT), Netherlands (NL), Spain (ES), Sweden (SE), UK (UK), USA (US). Source: authors' calculations based on INTAN-Invest database (www.intan-invest.net) and OECD data.

sector intangible spending, in contrast with Spain and Italy. Thus intangible investment can vary by country depending on the extent of public sector coinvestment.

Finally, it also seems that intangible investment is higher as a fraction of GDP in more developed countries. Corrado and Hao (2013), for example, document this for spending on brands, which is around 1 percent of GDP per capita in the United States but 0.1 percent for China (for their data, 1988–2011), and it is well known that most R&D is accounted for by a small fraction of developed countries (see, e.g., the data in van Ark et al. 2009). This might be due to low-income countries specializing in labor-intensive manufacturing or not having the financial and science base to make large-scale intangible investments.

Globalization and Growing Market Sizes

A final determinant is the size of the market. Many intangibles, such as Starbucks's brand or Facebook's software, can be scaled

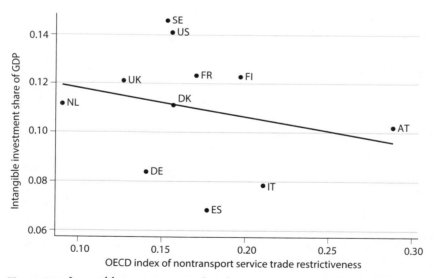

Figure 2.10. Intangible investment and trade restrictiveness, 2013. Countries are Austria (AT), Denmark (DK), Finland (FI), France (FR), Germany (DE), Italy (IT), Netherlands (NL), Spain (ES), Sweden (SE), UK (UK), USA (US). Source: authors' calculations based on INTAN-Invest database (www.intan-invest.net) and OECD data.

more or less infinitely (a point we shall return to in chapter 4). So, smaller markets (for example, countries surrounded by trade barriers) would be less attractive places to make intangible investment.

Figure 2.10 shows the share of GDP accounted for by intangible investment plotted against the OECD index of restrictiveness of trade in services (countries on the right of the graph have more restrictive trade in their services). This helps explain some of the spread in country investment patterns that we see: Austria, for example, hardly a basket case economy, spends relatively little on intangible investment but has quite restrictive trade opportunities, limiting, therefore, the possibility of scale.

The steady increase of international trade over the past fifty years would, therefore, provide a greater incentive for companies with exposure to it to invest in intangibles. And this means that if trade barriers rise, via either Brexit or trade policy, there will be lower incentive for intangible investment.

Conclusion: Capital's Vanishing Act

Intangible investment has become increasingly important. New methods of measurement show how it now exceeds tangible investment in some developed countries and has been growing for several decades, while tangible investment has steadily declined. There are a number of reasons for the growth of intangible investment, including the changing balance of services and manufacturing in the economy, globalization, the increased liberalization of markets, developments in IT and management technologies, and the changing input costs of services (which play a greater role in intangible investment). In the next chapter, we will look in more depth at how to measure intangible investment in the economy.

3

How to Measure Intangible Investment

This chapter explains how intangible investment can be measured, and how economists worked it out.

How Is Investment Measured and Why?

The story of how economists and statisticians came to measure intangible investment is a late episode in a much bigger story: the invention of GDP and systems of national accounts.[1] This story is engagingly told in Diane Coyle's *GDP: A Brief but Affectionate History* and Ehsan Masood's *The Great Invention: The Story of GDP*.

One of the biggest conceptual challenges involved in the creation of GDP was deciding what to count. This was an old problem. Adam Smith, in *The Wealth of Nations*, puzzled over whether England was producing more than it did at the fall of the Roman Empire. With no data to support this he simply asserted it was so, since there was more productive labor and less unproductive labor, the latter being occupations such as "servants . . . the sovereign . . . players, buffoons, musicians and opera-singers."[2]

By the time of the Great Depression, when economists were being pressed into service to understand what was going wrong with the economy, this problem had become urgent. Everyone knew that the economy was in a bad way. But they didn't know by how much production had fallen. Ford knew that sales of its main car, the Model A, declined by 50 percent from 1930 to the end of 1931. Steel producers knew that their production had collapsed: capacity utilization fell from 96 percent in September 1929 to 60 percent in December (CQ Researcher 2016). But how much had the *whole* economy declined? The problem was that the output of the steel makers was an input to the car producers, so it would be double counting to add up both their outputs. This is why calculating GDP is much harder than you would think: you can't just add up all the outputs in all the industries.

What about avoiding the double-counting by just counting the output of the car industry? This is fine if the carmaker only buys steel to transform into cars. But what if a carmaker bought steel machine tools and used those machines year after year? The steel in the machine tools would assuredly *not* be used up: as we saw above, they are *assets*. So, it looks like long-lasting goods should be treated differently from those used up. On this basis, the originators of GDP decided that spending on long-lasting goods, or investment, ought to be counted as part of the output of the economy.

You can see the importance of including investment in GDP from a quick thought experiment. Imagine we're back in the late 1940s, when the systems we use today to measure GDP were just becoming mainstream. Consider two very similar countries that both produce a thousand cars, all of which are bought by domestic consumers.

The only difference between them is that Country A is also making new machines for its car plants, while Country B isn't. The output of these machines wouldn't show up in our consumption spending statistics, since consumers don't buy lathes and conveyor belts and paint sprayers. But at the end of the year, Country A would clearly have produced more goods, since in addition to the shiny new cars its citizens enjoy, it has whizzy new equipment in its factories that will allow it to make better and cheaper cars in the years to come. We could measure that production directly by counting up the value of the car production and the value of the machine production and that would be GDP. We could get at it indirectly, which is to count up all the spending by consumers and also the spending on investment by companies. In this simple world, both these figures would be equal. In practice, counting up production turns out to be hard, so the first estimates of GDP are calculated using spending, which is a bit easier to measure. National statisticians do this by surveying consumers to find consumption spending and surveying firms to find investment spending. So investment is part of GDP.

When economists began measuring GDP in earnest in the 1940s, this sort of investment was very important to the world at large, which was rebuilding its industrial capacity after the destruction of the Second World War. So it should come as no surprise that measuring investment was taken very seriously.

In this framework, investment was strictly limited to *physical stuff.* The car factory's new machines were an investment; the time its designers spent planning a new model was not. That time spent was treated as a cost of doing business—an "intermediate input," like steel or the electricity bill—and not counted as part of output. Design was regarded as something entirely used up in the process of production, not something that lasts in the way that an investment does.[3]

It did not take long for economists to start questioning this. As early as the 1960s, economists began to wonder whether this type of knowledge spending might be long lasting. Fritz Machlup was an Austrian émigré who had moved to New York University during the Second World War (he was a student of the Austrian economist Ludwig von Mises, although Mises fell out with him when Machlup questioned whether the gold standard was a good idea—apparently the two did not speak for three years). In 1962 Machlup wrote a book entitled *The Production and Distribution of Knowledge in the United States,* in which he asked whether different types of knowledge were valuable things that could be produced, like lathes and paint shops. He started to measure spending on everything from research and development to advertising and branding to training (Machlup 1962).

Machlup's book was well received, not least by noneconomists. Economists, led in particular by Zvi Griliches at the National Bureau of Economic Research (NBER), America's applied economics brain trust, knew that R&D and knowledge production was a vital force in raising GDP. The NBER had convened a major conference in 1960 on *The Rate and Direction of Inventive Activity.* A working group of the OECD met in Frascati, Italy, to agree on a common framework for measuring R&D, codifying the approach in what became known as the *Frascati Manual*; these definitions (revised in several subsequent editions, the latest being OECD 2015) are still used to measure R&D today. The year 1966 saw the establishment of the University of Sussex's Science Policy Research Centre by Chris Freeman, a powerful proponent of the interdisciplinary study of innovation. But as far as the national accounts were concerned, tangible investment was still what mattered. Statisticians found better ways of measuring tangible capital stocks and made other developments, such as input/output tables and international trade estimates as economies globalized.

The thing that reignited economists' interest in the measurement of intangibles was ironically something tangible: computers. Over the course of the 1980s, economists had been wrestling with a puzzle. Since the mid-1970s productivity growth in developed countries had been disappointingly low. This was despite the advent of widely hyped new computer technologies that were supposedly going to transform business for the better. Robert Solow, who contributed more to the study of economic growth than most, famously pointed out in 1987 that the impact of the Computer Age could be seen everywhere but in the productivity statistics (Solow 1987).

Goaded by these criticisms, statistical agencies, led by the US Bureau of Economic Analysis (BEA), began to examine their treatment of information and information technology more closely. They introduced two types of innovation.

First, in the 1980s, in conjunction with IBM, the BEA started to produce indexes of computer prices that were quality adjusted. This turned out to make a very big difference to measuring how much investment businesses were making in computer hardware.

In most cases—food products, for example—prices for the same good tend to rise gently in line with overall inflation. But even if sticker prices for computers were rising, they were decidedly not the same good, since every dimension of their quality (speed, memory, and space) was improving incredibly. So their "quality-adjusted" prices were, in fact, falling and falling very fast, meaning that the quality you could buy per dollar spent on computers was in fact rising very fast.

As computers spread throughout the economy, the need to make this quality correction to official computer price data became more and more important, and a key paper by Steve Oliner and Dan Sichel (1994) showed that these quality adjustments were crucial in understanding US productivity. Meanwhile, OECD economists Alessandra Collecchia and Paul Schreyer (2002) documented that most non-US statistics agencies were *not* using this quality adjustment. When Collecchia and Schreyer used the US quality-adjustment figures in the non-US economies (after all, computers are pretty international) they found computers in the non-US economies were much more important contributors to growth than those national accounts had revealed.

This development dealt with computer hardware. But the second important development in the 1990s was around computer software. Some businesses, especially large ones, write a lot of their own software. Banks, in particular, are massive spenders: at one point, Citibank employed more programmers than Microsoft. The more that statisticians looked at this spending, the more they realized that the software that companies were writing was not a tangible good like the computers themselves, but an intangible good: knowledge written down in lines of code. And it looked like the code was long lasting. True, it needed to be periodically debugged, refreshed, and renewed, but it lasted at least a few years. Indeed, anyone who has worked in banking IT will confirm that big banks depend on large amounts of very old legacy code that is almost impossible to replace without literally breaking the bank.

Perhaps, economists concluded, software ought to be treated like an investment. The problem was that there was no place for software on the frequent investment surveys that statistical agencies asked firms to fill out. Those surveys asked for spending on computers, machinery, vehicles, and buildings—but not software. So the position echoed a fear voiced by Alan Greenspan, the then Chair of the US Federal Reserve, that there was a New Economy out there, and statistical agencies were not capturing it.

In 1999 the US BEA introduced software as an investment into the calculation of US GDP (Moulton, Parker, and Seskin 1999). They estimated investment by US firms in software by a mix of methods: information on their purchases of software, obtained from decennial surveys, and investment in-house, based on a multiple of wages of software workers. Supported by the OECD, other countries also introduced this method and started to bring software investment questions into investment surveys (the UK in 2001, for example, Chesson 2001). The UK took a while to incorporate these methods and in the meantime got the economist Nicholas Oulton to recommend a short-term fix. His advice was to multiply the current software spending by a factor of three—and indeed when the UK later incorporated the US method, spending went up by almost exactly a factor of three.

But the idea of a new economy also prompted economists to examine the role of knowledge investment more generally. Theorists like Robert Lucas, Paul Romer, Phillipe Aghion, and Peter Howitt had worked out economic models where knowledge played a key role in promoting growth, either via spillovers of knowledge from one producer to another, or via the competitive process of investment in continuous product improvement (see, for example, Lucas 1993; Aghion and Howitt 1992; Romer 1990).

Although the theorists had not quite articulated it this way, by the early 2000s there was a growing belief among business economists, in particular in the United States, that businesses were spending significant sums of money on things that had no physical presence, but that, nevertheless, were valuable and durable. But they were more than software and R&D: they included, for example, new organizational arrangements. Baruch Lev, a professor of accounting at New York University, wrote an influential book on how companies should manage and account for this new class of investment (Lev 2001). He set out some of the features of this intangible investment (which we shall discuss in the next chapter) and observed that firm balance sheets did not record such investment. In a similar vein, the US macroeconomist Robert Hall wondered whether these intangibles might help explain markets, his research neatly summarized by the title of his 2001 paper, "Struggling to Understand the US Stock Market" (R. E. Hall 2001).

Such thoughts started to make the transition from academia to the policy world. At the Philadelphia Federal Reserve, Leonard Nakamura made a first guesstimate at uncounted investment and thereby titled his 2000 paper "What Is the U.S. Gross Investment in Intangibles? (At Least) One Trillion Dollars a Year!" (Nakamura 2001; Nakamura 2010). And in Paris, the OECD was actively thinking about frameworks to incorporate these wider immaterial assets (Young 1998).

The excitement of the late 1990s dot-com bubble wasn't to last. It turned out that making money from the new economy was harder than the investors in Pets.com and Enron had assumed. But the broader idea of investment in ideas, knowledge, and networks, whether enabled by new information technologies or not, endured.

In the spring of 2002, with the high-tech NASDAQ index down 65 percent from its dot-com-bubble high, a group of economists began a project to think seriously and rigorously about measuring investment in the new economy. The Conference on Research in Income and Wealth, founded in the United States in 1936 to conduct research into measurement in economics, gathered in Washington under the leadership of Carol Corrado and Dan Sichel, then at the US Federal Reserve Board, and John Haltiwanger, a professor of economics at the University of Maryland. At this conference and afterwards, Corrado, Sichel, and Charles Hulten from the University of Maryland built a framework for recording different types of intangible investment and their contribution to GDP growth.

Then began a painstaking process of defining and measuring the different types of investment, first of all for the United States and gradually for other countries. In 2005 Corrado, Hulten, and Sichel produced the first set of estimates for the United States (2005). In 2006 Hulten gave a seminar at the UK Treasury on what the US team was doing. In what must be an example of one of the fastest reactions to an academic seminar ever, the UK Treasury immediately commissioned similar work to be done for the UK, and Tony Clayton, Mauro Giorgio Marrano, Jonathan Haskel, and Gavin Wallis produced estimates for the UK for 2004. Meanwhile work was going on in Japan by Kyoji Fukao, Tsutomu Miyagawa, Kentaro Mukai, Yukio Shinoda, and Konomi Tonogi, and in 2010 the *Review of Income and Wealth* published a special on intangibles, featuring the US, UK, and Japanese work (Corrado, Hulten, and Sichel 2009; Giorgio Marrano, Haskel, and Wallis 2009; Fukao et al. 2009).

At the same time, intangible investment also began to find its way into official statistics. The world's national statistical offices, the guardians of the GDP statistics that grace news bulletins and analyst reports, gradually began to take notice of the new sorts of investment that businesses were making and to include them in national accounts. In 1993 the System of National Accounts (the international rules for national accounting whose definition of investment we encountered in chapter 2) declared software admissible as investment, followed by the European System of Accounts in 1995 and the UK National Accounts in 1998 (Chesson 2001). The 2008 System of National Accounts recommended R&D as an investment, and this recommendation was introduced gradually by a number of countries (the UK in 2014). Much earlier, but rather unnoticed, the System of National Accounts had in 1993 proposed including investment in entertainment and literary and artistic originals as investment. Some countries had incorporated these measures, but many had not: only in 2013 did the United States do so fully. And these changes added up. In the United States, for example, the capitalization of software added about 1.1 percent to 1999 US GDP and R&D added 2.5 percent to 2012 GDP, with these numbers growing all the time (Corrado, Hulten, and Sichel 2005).

What Sorts of Intangibles Are There?

Let's now look at the framework that has been used to measure intangible investment. The first challenge of measuring anything in economics is one of definition: until you can describe what you're measuring, you can't begin to gather data. When Corrado, Hulten, and Sichel first began to measure intangible investment in 2005, they used and extended some of the same suggestions for the types of investment to be measured that had been originally advanced by Fritz Machlup in 1962, then developed around the turn of the millennium by a working group at the OECD (OECD Secretariat 1998), and elaborated on by Baruch Lev in his 2001 book and Leonard Nakamura (Nakamura 2001).

They divided intangible investment into three broad types: see table 3.1. There was "computerized information," "innovative property," and "economic competencies." As the table shows, each is a different type of investment, and each produces a different type of capital asset.

TABLE 3.1. CATEGORIES OF INTANGIBLE INVESTMENT

Broad category	Type of investment	Type of legal property that might be created	Treated as investment in National Accounts?
Computerized information	Software development	Patent, copyright, design IPR, trademark, other	Yes, since early 2000s
	Database development	Copyright, other	Recommended in SNA 1993, but OECD suggests uneven implementation
Innovative Property	R&D	Patents, design IPR	Yes, recommended in SNA 2008, introduced gradually since then
	Mineral exploration	Patents, other	Yes
	Creating entertainment and artistic originals	Copyright, design IPR	Yes in EU, in US since 2013
	Design and other product development costs	Copyright, design IPR, trademark	No
Economic Competencies	Training	Other	No
	Market research and branding	Copyright, trademark	No
	Business process re-engineering	Patent, copyright, other	No

Note: R&D should be thought of, in line with official definitions, as scientific-oriented spending as distinct from, say, artistic or design endeavors. "Other" in column 3 refers to things like trade secrets, contracts, etc. Column 3 refers to formal intellectual property: we would expect all intangible investment to produce tacit knowledge as well.

Source: Columns 1 and 2 from Corrado, Hulten, and Sichel 2005, column 3 based on Corrado 2010, column 4 from Corrado et al. 2013.

Computerized information is the clearest: it is any investment that involves putting information into computers to make them useful in the long run. The most obvious example is software, including both purchased software and software a company writes for itself. It includes databases as well; these were a relatively small proportion of this category of investment, but their inclusion was prescient given the subsequent explosion of big data and its importance to so many large businesses in the tech sector and beyond. (For more on the differences between data, information, knowledge, etc., see box 4.1).

Innovative property is a little harder to parse at first glance. It includes R&D, which economists and statisticians have long measured. It also includes other types of product and service development that don't rely directly on science and technology—for example, the design of a shop or an airline seat. This category also includes other forms of creation and discovery, from prospecting for oil to writing novels, and the rights that go along with them.[4]

Economic competencies cover other investments that don't directly involve innovation or computers. Corrado, Hulten, and Sichel's 2005 paper defined such investment as "the value of brand names and other knowledge embedded in firm-specific human and structural resources." In particular, such investment involves three main types: marketing and branding (investment in understanding customer needs and creating brands that appeal to them); organizational capital, such as creating distinctive business models or corporate cultures; and training that is specific to the company.

Table 3.1 also shows two other pieces of information. The third column looks at the kind of intellectual property rights (IPRs) that each type of investment might generate: patents for R&D, for example, or copyrights for entertainment investment. Some of these IPRs depend upon the country: business processes and software cannot be patented in some countries. (Note too that the table suggests that studying patenting, as many innovation metrics do, tells us only part of the innovation picture.) And the final column sets out whether statistical agencies treat such spending categories as investment: as can be seen, many of them are now so treated. However, this treatment is relatively recent and coverage can be uneven, so, for example, the counting of database investment is in practice inconsistent across countries (Corrado et al. 2013).

The section that follows will look at how to measure these investments; afterwards, we will consider some possible objections to classifying them as investments; finally, we will look at some future challenges for the measurement of intangibles.

Measuring Investment in Intangibles

As we set out in chapter 2, the purpose of investment is to create a valuable asset. Let's start by reviewing how we measure investment in these intangibles. Later we will set out how we measure the value of the asset this investment creates, since that raises an additional set of complications.

Measuring investment requires a number of steps. First, we need to find out how much firms are *spending* on the intangible. Second, in some cases, not all of that spending will be creating a long-lived asset: for example, a TV news flash does not create a long-lived asset, but a movie does. So we may have to adjust that spending to measure *investment*—that is, that part of spending creating a long-lived asset. Third, we need to *adjust that investment for inflation and quality change* so we can compare investment in different periods when prices and quality are changing.

Finding *spending* (that is, the pounds or euros or dollars or yen a firm spent in the last year, what economists call "nominal value") for most investment goods is easy. If national accountants want to know how much Heathrow is investing in snowplows, or Sainsbury in new delivery trucks, they just ask them. They send them a form asking them to list their spending on what the statistics office agrees are investment goods: for example, computers, plant, vehicles, buildings. The UK Office for National Statistics (ONS) calls this the *Quarterly Acquisitions and Disposals of Capital Assets Survey* and sends it to 27,000 firms every quarter.[5] In recent years, the ONS has added more investment goods to this survey, notably, spending on software, databases, artistic originals, and design (firms are also asked the value, if any, of investment goods they have sold).

There are two complications. First, what about investment not on the survey, like training or market research? For this, researchers have to look to other surveys or to the output of the market research industry.

Second, this only surveys *purchases* of investment assets. Now, for tangible goods this is fine, since very few firms make their own tangible investment goods: airports don't make their own snowplows or supermarkets their own trucks. But for intangibles, this generalization does not apply: many firms write their own software—banks, for example—or do their own R&D. So asking them how much they spend has to be done carefully to check that firms record *both* what they buy *and* spend on "in-house" or "own-account" investment assets.

To measure in-house spending, statisticians imagine there is a software or R&D or training "factory" inside the firm and try to measure how much spending it takes to run that "factory." How do they do this? Via labor force surveys. Statistical agencies throughout the world do pretty detailed labor force surveys and so can measure how many, say, designers work in retailing (designing shop fronts, for example) and what they are paid. Consultations with the industry will then tell you what extra costs are involved over and above the wages: overheads, capital costs, and so on; a figure for software is typically around 1.5. Thus an estimate of in-house spending on software would be 1.5 times the cost of wages paid to a range of software occupations.

This is only the first step, since this returns a figure for nominal spending. But that is not enough, for to measure investment, we need to know how much of that spending will last for more than a year. So that is step two and is done by consultation with industry. In software, for example, software programmers might spend 90 percent of their time creating long-lived software assets, whereas software managers might only spend 5 percent of their time, if they are mostly doing, say, administration. Similarly, evidence from time diaries indicates that junior designers typically spend much more time on design and less on marketing and administration, relative to senior designers, so their time has to be adjusted accordingly. Likewise, artistic original spending varies by, for example, whether TV production is for news (assumed short lived) or TV films (assumed long lived).

These two steps, then, give us nominal investment: spending times the fraction that is long lasting. Step three is to convert that nominal investment into "real" investment—that is, adjust that nominal investment for inflation and quality change, so we can compare £500 spent on software today with £500 spent five years ago (see box 5.1 for more on "real" and "nominal" measures).

Adjusting for inflation is harder than you might have thought. We know what the general level of inflation is since central banks target the price increases of a representative basket of goods. We know what specific inflation is for well-defined physical goods whose attributes have not changed very much: a ton of standard steel, a length of copper wire. But we don't know very much about the price of many services, like advice from a management or marketing consultant. Statisticians have tried to get at this. One method is to assume the price of such advice follows the general pattern of prices. Another is to try to break up "advice" into a basket of goods and measure their prices. Thus we might measure the price of legal services, for example, by looking at the prices of drawing up a will or transacting a house. A third method is "time-based," that is, to survey the number of hours and hourly cost of a basket of certain services (e.g., accounting services such as audit, payroll, and tax consulting).

Constructing a basket is much harder when quality is changing very fast, since a software package in one year might be much better than one in earlier years, and so one cannot be meaningfully compared with another. This means updating the basket very frequently. Another method is to try to agree on a series of quality attributes; for hardware it might be speed, memory, space, for example. Statisticians then correlate these changes in attributes with observed changes in prices for the entire computer, thereby establishing a "price" for each attribute. All in all, quality adjustment is one of the most difficult areas confronting national accountants. Hulten (2001) quotes Adam Smith, who said "quality . . . is so very disputable a matter, that I look upon all information of this kind as somewhat uncertain."

These steps are taken to estimate real investment. To measure the stock of the asset this investment creates, economists have to take another series of steps, starting with the question:

How quickly does the asset depreciate? Or to put it another way, roughly how much each year becomes obsolete or is scrapped? (This includes the case where intangibles are written down to no value at all—sometimes, as in the case of Enron due to fraud, other times due to, for example, changes in regulation or failing a clinical trial.) If we know the flow of investment into the economy year by year, and the rate of depreciation, we can work out the stock of intangible investment for any given year too. The appendix to this chapter discusses this.

Is Investment in Intangibles Really Investment?

Most people find the idea that software, R&D, and new product development are investments pretty intuitive. To go back to our definition of investment in the previous chapter, these are things that (a) cost money, (b) are expected to generate a longer-term return, and, what's more, (c) the company making the investment has a reasonable chance of enjoying a worthwhile portion of the return itself.

Are marketing, organizational capital, and training really investments? Some argue that marketing—especially that part of it concerned with advertising to build brands—is just a zero-sum game between companies: if my brand wins market share, yours loses. Some say that money spent on organizational development produces more bureaucracy and make-work. And some say that training should be excluded because it produces an asset for the person trained, not for the firm doing the training.

Each of these criticisms has a kernel of truth, but not so much as to disqualify these sorts of spending as investments.

Take the first objection, namely that *branding* is a zero-sum game and merely shifts sales from, say, Coke to Pepsi. This by itself is not an objection to it being an *investment*. An investment is something that produces a long-lived asset. Nobody would say that American Airlines is *not* investing when it buys a new plane that takes market share from British Airways. Rather, the question is whether the act of investment by company A results in a decline in the value of the asset of company B.[6] If the decline is 100 percent, then *net* effective investment in the economy is zero.

While it seems likely that at least some advertising spending has this "head to head" feature, it seems unlikely that all of it is firms exactly offsetting each other. What's more, at least some advertising would seem to benefit other firms, since it lets consumers know about the availability of all products, not just company A's product.

The economist Ferdinand Rauch took advantage of an unusual policy change to study this question (Rauch 2011). Up until 2000, Austria, which taxed advertising, had differential rates across regions. In 2000 a nationwide harmonization introduced a 5 percent tax rate in all regions. Thus the cost of advertising increased in some parts of the country while simultaneously decreasing in other parts. If advertising were simply a zero sum game, this tax change should have made no difference to company spending. After all, if they are simply in an arms race to outspend each other, they would be forced into doing this by competition, regardless of taxes. In fact, advertising did change, falling where it got more expensive and rising where cheaper. Overall, there was more advertising and product prices were lower, suggesting that consumers reacted to more advertising by buying more at a lower price. This is consistent with the idea that they had more information and the market was working better.

The objection to treating *organizational development* as an intangible investment tends to be that it is either not durable or not valuable. It is certainly true that some spending on managerial activities is wasted or valueless, especially in badly managed businesses—there's a rich tradition of literature from *Bartleby the Scrivener* to *The Office* about useless and counterproductive management. Equally, not all activities that superficially seem like organizational development are lasting—much management consulting, even when it works, is about helping make good short-term decisions rather than creating new organizational structures.

But it would be going too far to say that *no* organizational investment is lasting and valuable. It seems obvious that there are businesses with strong cultures of good management and high performance, that creating and maintaining these cultures takes investment (both of time and of money), and that these companies are more likely to succeed than ones with worse cultures: think, for example, of kaizen in Toyota, or Six Sigma in General Electric (GE). Further examples are discussed in chapter 8. We know that innovation often involves investing in organizational change, such as creating a new business unit to sell a new product line.

And it's also possible to think of examples of companies that have invested to create valuable organizational assets outside their own firms. The remarkable Apple supply chain that Tim Cook was responsible for developing is clearly a long-term source of value for Apple, allowing it to bring products to market extraordinarily quickly. A valuable asset of so-called sharing-economy businesses like Uber or AirBnB is typically their network of committed suppliers—Uber's drivers or AirBnB's hosts. This too is an asset of lasting value that both companies have invested heavily to develop (and which they invest to protect, for example, against legal actions requiring them to treat their suppliers as employees).

There's a more general point here as well. It's easy to identify examples of wasted spending by firms. But firms live under market pressure. Unless that pressure is absent, repeated spending on worthless projects will drive those firms out of the market. So at least for market sector firms, it's unlikely that their spending here is valueless.

So, while we have to be careful about how we define organizational development investment, it seems over the top to claim that successful organizational development should not be classified as an asset.

The objection to treating *training* as an intangible investment is not that it's not valuable or lasting, but that it is an asset of the employee, not of the firm. But it is important to remember the definition of investment from the System of National Accounts that we looked at in chapter 2. Ownership is not one of the criteria; what matters is who benefits. It is certainly true that training does generally produce value for the employee, and that the employer can only benefit while employing the trained worker. Paying for a member of staff to take a general accountancy qualification, for example, is investing in a skill that belongs to the employee, not to the firm.

But two factors mean that some training is more like an asset of the firm than of the employee. First of all, quite a lot of training is both useful to the firm doing the training and of fairly limited use elsewhere. Sometimes this is for technical reasons: our accountant may go on a training course run by the firm to learn processes that are used at the firm, but nowhere else, such as the use of a custom-made auditing software package. This kind of training is quite common because employees very often work in complex systems that are specific to their companies. (Making a cup of coffee with an espresso machine is in some ways a transferable skill. But many of the skills a Starbucks barista must learn are specific to the particular operating procedures of Starbucks.)

Second, employers can sign agreements with employees making it harder for them to take the fruits of their training elsewhere. Companies that pay for employees to take expensive courses often make them sign agreements to reimburse training costs if they leave within a certain period of time. Some employment contracts include noncompete clauses, making it harder—or impossible—for employees to take training and skills to a competitor.

So, although firms (thankfully) cannot own their employees, there are a number of situations where training could and should be seen as an asset of the firm, not of the employee receiving it.

Future Challenges of Measuring Intangibles

Despite these difficulties, the momentum is firmly to incorporate intangibles into official investment data. As we have seen, software, R&D, and artistic originals are all included. The UK official quarterly investment surveys now ask about design. The other assets in table 3.1—market research, training, branding, and organizational development—are not officially included, but experimental work is proceeding to simulate what would happen to investment and GDP if they were included. For example, the current UK ONS research forward plan intends to collect data on these assets. In the meantime, official agencies are using this experimental work to inform their thinking. The intangibles agenda is central to the OECD innovation strategy, for example, and intangible investment data has been included in the Economic Report of the President. As more intangibles are included, more conceptual questions will arise.

First, at least some knowledge comes into the firm by no investment at all. Some of that is simply taken from other firms, what we shall call spillovers and that are discussed below. Some is a by-product of the very act of production—learning by doing, for example. It seems that it is valuable knowledge for the firm, but it is not investment, since it doesn't involve costs incurred by the firm.

Second, when economists measure the value of a good, they usually look for a market price: a phone or ice cream or holiday. The method we have set out above looks instead at the costs incurred in creating the good. Economists are forced to do this when there are no market prices, as for an in-house design, since it's not on the market. But the cost-based method generates a string of difficult problems.

First, one might object that some very successful products yield firms a stream of returns massively out of proportion to the cost of creating them. So how can a cost-based method be accurate? The answer is that this logic might hold for a particular successful project. But in practice firms and economies do many, many projects. Each is uncertain. Some might succeed spectacularly and some fail miserably, ex post facto. On average, however, if the successes and failures balance out, the value of investment at the level of a large economy ought to equal the value of the spending.[7]

A second problem with the cost-based method is that one might object to the time adjustment as being hopelessly subjective and inaccurate. In fact, many professional services firms have charge sheets, billing rules, and logs, which their staff is expected to use. So, for example, junior consultants are expected to spend almost all their time on design and very little on management; for senior consultants the reverse holds. This time allocation problem is, however, particularly severe for trying to understand the building of organizational capital. We simply have very little information on what managers spend their time doing, other than some very early work by Henry Mintzberg (1990) and recent work by Rafaella Sadun (Bandiera et al. 2011). That work, however, does not tell us exactly about the building of organizational capital; rather it tends to document the large amounts of time that managers spend in meetings. So this is an area, at the moment, of substantial uncertainty.[8]

Returning to other conceptual issues: third, the public sector invests in intangibles too. It buys software, does training, invests in marketing (public information, for example, on crime prevention). Indeed, one might take the view that public sector knowledge investment is almost unbounded: schools, universities, libraries, and so on. What about the rule of law, public confidence in officials, the reputation of the central bank, or the cultural assets of museums, art galleries, and heritage?

To answer this, it is helpful to remember two rules of GDP. First, any spending must correspond to productive activity (in that past year) if it is to count in GDP. Building a new museum is part of GDP: it's production. Buying a Titian masterpiece to put into the museum is not included in GDP. The Titian painting was once "produced," but not in that year. Even if the purchase yielded a vast capital gain to the owner, that does not count as part of GDP. Capital gains do not arise from productive activity and so are not production. It is simply a redistribution of GDP from the seller to the buyer. (The same logic explains why the capital gains that homeowners make on their houses are also not included in GDP. Thus the GDP of, say, London or New York does not reflect the huge capital gains in those cities, but the value of production in the area.).

By this rule, large amounts of government spending *are* counted as GDP since they reflect productive activity: schools, hospitals, the police. But not all government spending is counted. Pensions and benefits ("transfer payments") are treated like capital gains: they do not have a counterpart in current productive activity, so they are not counted in GDP.

The second point to remember is that GDP excludes production activities by households. So washing your *own* car, clothes, or dishes is not production; paying a cleaner to do so is production. This can, of course, create anomalies—for example, Samuelson's famous observation that when a man marries his cook, GDP falls. But the difficulties around the valuation of domestic time are so significant it is omitted. For our purposes, education is one of the most important household investments. So while government spending on education is counted as GDP, the "human capital" created by households in all the time they spend in education is not counted as part of the nation's capital stock.

So, since most government spending is already counted as GDP, then the main issue with public sector intangibles is to isolate the knowledge investment. The public sector sponsors, for example, considerable R&D, so that is already counted. Jarboe, in a study for the United States, suggests counting spending on statistical agencies, the weather service, federal libraries, nonpartisan reporting, accounting offices, and the patent office. Blaug and Lekhi (2009), in a study for the UK, likewise suggest counting items including scientific and research data; mapping and weather data; national statistics; company information made available through Companies House; statutory registers such as those for birth, death, marriage, and land titles; and patent information held by the Intellectual Property Office. As an illustration, Jarboe's estimate for the United States for 2006 is $204bn, consisting of R&D funding of $122bn, $70bn for education and training, and another $12bn for statistical agencies, weather, product safety, and so on (Jarboe, quoted in Blaug and Lekhi 2009).[9]

Finally, what about the quality of life? GDP is about production. Insofar as some of the quality of life depends on consumption, GDP is surely related to it, since more production will enable, other things being equal, more consumption.[10] Similarly, a safe and tolerant society might be associated with a highly productive society, but these are not the proximate outputs of the country.

Conclusion: Measuring Intangibles

In this chapter we saw how, over time, economists have made increasing efforts to measure a growing range of investments. Starting in the 1980s, economists developed a way of measuring some intangible investments and incorporating them into the national accounts, giving rise in the 2000s to the approach we currently use for measuring intangibles, developed by Corrado, Hulten, and Sichel. We reviewed how these investments were measured, looked at some possible objections to treating them as investment, and highlighted some outstanding questions. While this area is not definitively settled, the overall trend of the rising tide of intangible investment is widely accepted. But does that rising tide matter? Surely the nature of investment changes all the time? We take this up in the next chapter.

Appendix: Measuring the Stock of Intangible Assets

If investment creates an asset, how do we work out the value of the asset? The way to think of this is that investment is a flow and the asset is a stock. More investment adds to the value of the stock. But if the stock depreciates in value, then its value declines. So we can at least measure *additions* to the stock as the investment, which we have measured above, minus the depreciation in value. And if we know the value of the stock at some previous point in time, we can add on the additions to get the values over time.

So the first question is how much does the value of an asset fall over a year? At first sight this looks like a depreciation question, familiar to accountants, who are used to working out the "wear and tear" or "decay" of vehicles, buildings, and machines. But to an economist this is only part of the answer. The question is how much does the asset *value* fall per year (called "economic depreciation"). Value can fall due to *decay*, the physical degradation of the asset, but it can also fall if, for example, a better asset comes along to replace it. Let us call this latter effect a *discard*. A *discard* arises if, for example, the commercial value of an idea falls due to competition from another one, or a worker leaves the firm with at least some of the firm's knowledge. So an idea might never decay, suggesting no decrease in value, but it might be quickly discarded, suggesting very quick value decline. In a remarkable paper, Charles Hulten and Frank Wyckoff (1981) showed that the interaction of these effects can give a smooth economic depreciation path over the lifetime of the asset, fast at first, but slower thereafter.

When it comes to tangibles, most of the work has sought evidence from engineers and firms on wear and tear/decay. For intangibles the question is mostly about discards. Direct estimates come from surveys. See, for example, those conducted by the Israeli Statistical Bureau (Peleg 2008a, 2008b) and by Awano and colleagues (2010) with the UK Office of National Statistics. These surveys ask about the "life length" of investments in R&D (by detailed industry in Israel) and intangible assets (R&D plus five other asset types in the UK). The Israeli survey supports the idea that R&D ideas are useful for around ten years, but this varies between industries, while the UK survey confirms other intangibles to have useful lives of around three years. In sum, the evidence seems to favor high economic depreciation (around 33 percent per year) for software, design, marketing, and training; medium rates for R&D (around 15 percent per year); and rather longer for entertainment and artistic originals and mineral exploration.

4

What's Different about Intangible Investment?

THE FOUR S'S OF INTANGIBLES

This chapter looks at the unusual economic characteristics of intangibles—the reasons why an intangible-rich economy exhibits different characteristics from a tangible-rich one. Those characteristics are summed up in four S's, namely that intangible assets, relative to tangible assets, are more likely to be scalable, *their costs are more likely to be* sunk, *and they are inclined to have* spillovers *and to exhibit* synergies *with each other.*

Investment changes all the time; from warehouses and wharves to mineshafts and mills; from machine tools and dynamos to cooling towers and cash registers, servers, and solar arrays. So why should we care about the move from tangible to intangible assets that we described in chapters 2 and 3?

As we will show, intangible assets are different from tangible assets in a number of important ways. This means that a business that is reliant on intangibles will behave differently from a business with mainly tangible assets. Managers and workers will face different incentives and rewards. And an economy made up of many such businesses will perform in distinctive ways. In this chapter we will look at the unusual characteristics of intangible investments from an economic perspective, and why they matter. We summarize these features under four S's: *scalability, sunkenness, spillovers,* and *synergies.*

A good way to think about these characteristics is with a story of intangible investments at work.

How EMI Got a Little Help from Their Friends

In the mid-1960s the Beatles were not just a cultural force, they were an economic one. At their peak, their records and ticket sales were generating $650 a second in today's money. The dollar receipts from their overseas tours are even credited with temporarily saving the British government from a currency crisis.

One of the beneficiaries of the rise of the Beatles to stardom was their record company, Parlophone, which since the 1930s had been owned by Electric & Musical Industries Limited, better known as EMI (and later to be the subject of a song themselves by the Sex Pistols). By 1967, 30 percent of EMI's profits were coming just from Beatles sales.

As their expanded name suggests, EMI wasn't only a record label. In the 1960s the company was as interesting for its electrical activities as for its musical ones. In 1959 it had launched a commercial computer called the EMIDEC 1100; it also made color TV cameras, recording equipment, guided missiles, and kettles.

The piles of cash brought in by Beatlemania helped create a culture of investment at EMI. One of the things they invested in was medical equipment research. Godfrey Hounsfield, the researcher behind the EMIDEC, began work on the first commercially viable medical scanner. As the project developed, he was significantly supported by the UK government, which provided over £600,000 of support or £7 million at 2016 prices (Maizlin and Vos 2012). Over four years, he and his team invented and built the first computed tomography scanner (CT or "CAT scanner"—the A stands for "axial").

This was a remarkable feat of science and engineering. For the first time, it allowed doctors to make accurate, 3D representations of patients' soft tissues. This was a real medical breakthrough, transforming everything from brain surgery to cancer treatment. Hounsfield was piled with honors: he received a Nobel prize and a knighthood and was made a Fellow of the Royal Society. But from a commercial point of view, it was something of a failure for EMI.

EMI took out patents on the underlying technologies and invested to build the business, creating partnerships with hospitals to work out how CT could help doctors and building a sales force to sell the scanners to American hospitals. But as the 1970s rolled on, it became clear that other companies were going to dominate the CT market. General Electric (GE) and then Siemens licensed some of the technologies from EMI and quickly built large CT scanning businesses. By 1976 EMI decided to get out of the CT scanning business entirely.

It may not be obvious to someone listening to a Beatles song or having a CT scan, but this story is all about intangible investments. And it neatly illustrates some of the things that make intangible investments of various sorts different from physical, tangible investments.

First of all, consider the Beatles catalogue, the vast profitability of which helped EMI back the CT scanner. Music rights are a type of intangible asset. Once you own them, you can press as many singles as you like at a pretty low cost (nowadays, in the age of digital music, that cost has fallen close to zero).

This isn't true of a physical asset like a factory or a shop or a telephone line: once these assets reach their capacity, you need to invest in new ones. But intangibles do not have to obey the same set of physical laws: they can generally be used again and again. Let's call this characteristic of intangibles *scalability*.

Next, consider what happened when EMI decided to get out of the CT scanner business. They'd made a lot of intangible investments: most obviously the R&D to design the scanner itself, but also the time they put into working with clinicians on how to use the scanners (in the framework we described in chapter 3, we would call this design, specifically service design); on building a business unit (organizational development); and establishing a market presence in the United States (branding and marketing).

On some of this EMI got a return—they received license fees from their patents from GE and Siemens. But a lot of it looks like it was written off. It's hard to recoup the money spent on setting up a sales force or on building an unsuccessful business unit or brand. Physical assets are often much easier to sell, even if they are quite specialized. Let's call this characteristic of intangibles *sunkenness*.

The role of GE and Siemens in developing the CT scanner illustrates another distinctive feature of intangibles: rather unfairly, the person or business making the investment in them doesn't always reap the rewards. The dazzling R&D that Godfrey Hounsfield carried out, the design work with hospitals, and the hard slog of making early sales yielded a small return to EMI, but a big new market for its competitors. This simply isn't the case with most tangible investments. GE obviously couldn't break into EMI's factories to produce their own CT scanners—there are locks and alarms and laws to stop that sort of thing. But they did manage to make use of EMI's intangible investments, at a relatively low cost. In the language of economics, you could say that it is sometimes hard for the original investor to appropriate the benefits of intangible investment, or, to put it another way, that intangibles often have *spillovers* beyond the company making the investment.

Finally, investments in intangibles become dramatically more valuable when you combine them. EMI's central R&D lab was a melting pot of research on computing, imaging, and electrical engineering; bringing these different types of knowledge together with the clinical expertise of the doctors at Atkinson Morley Hospital, where the first scanners were trialed, helped create a genuine breakthrough.

But it is not just ideas derived from R&D that can lead to these unexpected benefits when you combine them. The eventual success of GE's CT scanner relied on bringing together the technological investment in the device itself with GE's brand and customer relationships. And, of course, the success of the Beatles themselves relied on the bringing together of new musical ideas (from Elvis to Ravi Shankar) and Parlophone's own intangibles: their ability to promote and market the band. All of these are examples of the *synergies* between intangibles—synergies that are often large in size and hard to predict.[1]

The Four S's of Intangible Investment

It should come as no surprise that things that one can't touch, like ideas, commercial relationships, and know-how, are fundamentally different from physical things like machines and buildings.

This fact has not been lost on economists. Over the last century researchers in different subfields of economics have looked into various unusual properties of intangible assets.

David Warsh's fascinating book *Knowledge and the Wealth of Nations* tells the story of how the economist Paul Romer developed an improved theory of economic growth that included knowledge, in particular R&D, rather than treating it as an unpredictable exogenous variable. The work of Romer, Chad Jones, Philippe Aghion, and other pioneers of endogenous growth theory, as it's called, pointed out that knowledge is an unusual type of good because putting an idea into practice doesn't use it up. They used the term "non-rivalry" to contrast a "knowledge good," like an idea, that can be used by many, with a "rival good," like a sandwich, which can only be used by one person. This non-rivalry we express as scalability.

A parallel tradition looks at the way ideas spill over from one firm to another. Alfred Marshall first talked about these spillovers between different firms in the same industry in the late nineteenth century; Nobel laureate Ken Arrow expressed this mathematically in the 1960s, and twenty years later Paul Romer extended the theory (Arrow 1962; Romer 1990). The economist Edward Glaeser coined the term "Marshall-Arrow-Romer spillovers" to refer to these kinds of spillovers and in the same paper demonstrated the importance of spillovers across industries, work following that of Zvi Griliches (Glaeser 2011; Griliches 1992).

Similarly, researchers studying the financing of innovative firms, such as Bronwyn Hall and Josh Lerner, observed that investments in assets like R&D and product development are harder to finance with debt than physical investments (Hall and Lerner 2010). Scholars of the processes and nature of innovation, such as Brian Arthur (2009), have highlighted the importance of blending together different types of knowledge. And scholars of intangibles, like Baruch Lev, have remarked upon their spillovers (Lev 2001).

Let's now look in more detail at the ways in which intangible investment differs from tangible investment. In the section that follows, we'll look at each of the four characteristics of intangible assets—scalability, sunkenness, spillovers, and synergies—and discuss (a) why intangibles behave this way (especially in comparison with tangible investments) and (b) why each characteristic matters to the wider economy. Before we get there, since there are a lot of closely related concepts that are used variously in the literature, such as "ideas," "knowledge," "data," box 4.1 tries to clarify them. And after we discuss each of the four S's in detail, we shall look at how some emergent properties of intangibles, such as uncertainty and the creation of option values, arise from these S's. To be clear, we don't claim to have discovered these features ourselves. Rather, we think we can conveniently summarize the discoveries of others under these headings.

Box 4.1. Knowledge, Data, Information, and Ideas: Some Definitions

The words "data," "information," and "knowledge" seem interchangeable. As Goodridge and Haskel (2016) point out, the UK *Data* Protection Act "controls how your personal *information* is used," that the UK *Information* Commissioner "promotes data privacy for individuals," and the Freedom of *Information* Act allows citizens to request publicly held *data*sets (all our italics).* Romer (1991), when talking about intangibles, uses terms like "ideas," "blueprints," and "instructions." The OECD talks about the "knowledge economy," while economists typically refer to "knowledge" that is embodied or disembodied. Meanwhile, in his masterful work on the Industrial Revolution, the economic historian Joel Mokyr divides "knowledge" into propositional and prescriptive (Mokyr 2002). How does all this fit together?

Let's start with *data*. Define two kinds of data: raw records and transformed data. Raw records are raw data not yet cleaned up, formatted, or transformed—not ready for analysis. They can include, for instance, data scraped from the web, data generated by transactions between agents, data generated by sensors embedded in machines or equipment (the "Internet of Things"), or data generated as a by-product of some other business operation or process. Transformed data has been cleaned up, formatted, combined, and/or structured such that it is suitable for some form of data analytics.

Turning to *information*, we can think of information as synonymous with transformed data: for example, analyzable data on, say, sales of hurricane lamps and weather, constitutes information. Shapiro and Varian (1998) take information to mean anything that can be digitized, thereby implicitly defining information as digitized data.

We define *knowledge* as connections made between pieces of information, supported by evidence, to form a coherent understanding. Knowledge cannot exist without information, and knowledge is required to fully understand and interpret information. Knowledge can, therefore, include theories, hypotheses, correlations, or causal relationships observed from information constituted by analyzable data.

Joel Mokyr (2002) introduces a distinction between different types of knowledge, "propositional" and "prescriptive." Propositional knowledge includes science and discoveries: knowledge of nature and its properties. Prescriptive knowledge prescribes actions for the purposes of production, such as "recipes," "blueprints," or "techniques." So, for example, the invention by Appert in 1806 of the Appert jar, a method of preserving food by cooking it and sealing it in a jar, was simply a recipe that the inventors got to work, even though they knew nothing of Pasteur's work on food spoilage via microorganisms, which was to come in another fifty years. It was thus innovation founded on prescriptive not propositional knowledge. Mokyr's argument is that pre-industrial, stop-and-start growth was founded on chance discoveries. Postindustrial steady growth was only possible due to discoveries being founded on propositional knowledge.

Tangible assets, like airliners, consist of metal but also lots of knowledge, for example, from the production process. Why then isn't a tangible asset simply a collection of intangible assets? It's helpful to think of "embodied" and "disembodied" knowledge. To produce an airliner requires tangible inputs (like metal) and intangible inputs (like software or design). The resulting airliner is a tangible asset since the inputs and knowledge are "embodied" in it.

The software and design, insofar as they exist independent of the plane, for example, as code or as a blueprint, are intangible assets since they are "disembodied" from the airliner (and can likely be used again and again in other airliners)

Other classifications of knowledge are "tacit" as opposed to "codified," meaning whether the knowledge is experience-based or formally recorded, for example, in a blueprint; "applied" or "basic," meaning whether the knowledge is directed primarily toward a specific, practical objective or whether it is theoretical, with no particular application in mind (OECD *Frascati Manual* 2015). Finally, "commercialized" knowledge is knowledge applied to a particular business end.

* Quotes in this section are all taken from official UK government websites (.gov.uk): for Data Protection, see https://www.gov.uk/data-protection /the-data-protection-act; Information Commissioner: https://www.gov .uk/government/organisations/information-commissioner-s-office; on Freedom of Information, see https://ico.org.uk/media/for-organisations /documents/1151/datasets-foi-guidance.pdf.

Scalability

Why Are Intangibles Scalable?

Physical assets can only be in one place at one time. Intangible assets, by contrast, can usually be used over and over, in multiple places at the same time.

Once you've written the Starbucks operating manual in Chinese—an investment in organizational development—you can use it in each of the country's 1,200-plus stores. The costs of developing the app Angry Birds—and investment in software—can be spread over an arbitrarily large number of downloads (currently well over two billion). And an aircraft engine manufacturer only needs to design a particular type of jet engine—an investment in R&D and design—once, before it can then make an arbitrarily large number of engines.

This scalability applies to many sorts of intangible assets. Once a business has created or acquired an intangible asset, it can usually make use of it again and again at relatively little cost, compared to most physical assets.

The scalability of knowledge in general is something economists have known for decades. Paul Romer, one of the pioneers of how economists think about economic growth, used to give the example of oral rehydration therapy (ORT), a simple treatment that has saved countless lives in the developing world by stopping children's deaths from diarrhea. The insight of ORT is that just drinking water isn't a good solution to dehydration; you also need sodium, and sugar to help the body absorb the sodium.

Most of the physical things an aid organization might invest in to tackle death from dehydration don't scale. If you build a water pump, dig a well, or buy a water tanker, you can only meet the needs of so many people before you need to repeat the investment. But the idea of ORT can be used again and again, once you have discovered it.

The idea that knowledge is scalable sits at the heart of "New Growth Theory," the new approach to economic growth that Romer pioneered. Rather than treating technology as an exogenous force that manifests itself from time to time and makes the economy more productive, Romer and fellow theorists, such as Robert Lucas, treated it as an investment that yielded an economic return across the economy as a whole.

From an economic point of view, scalability derives from a key feature of ideas: what economists call "non-rivalry." If I drink a glass of water, you cannot drink the same glass: it is a "rival" good. But if I use an idea, you too can use the same idea: the idea is non-rival. While rivalry might then be the economic primitive behind scalability, we shall use scalability for mnemonic convenience.[2]

Scalability becomes supercharged with "network effects." A network effect exists when assets become more valuable the more of them exist. Network effects can be found among both tangible and intangible assets. So, for example, telephones or fax machines are much more valuable when almost everyone has them. Indeed, the current digital tech revolution has drawn people's attention to the potential network effects of physical assets, mobile phones and networked computers being prime examples. But if we look closer, it's really the intangible investments of the current wave of digital technologies where the big network effects are.

The network of Uber drivers and AirBnB hosts and Instagram users (all organizational development investments) or the power of HTML and the innumerable standards the Web is based on (variously, investments in software, design, and organizational development) are intangibles, not tangibles.

It's worth noting that real life intangibles are not usually infinitely scalable. The salt-sugar mixture for ORT, in fact, has to be tweaked for different levels of dehydration. The McDonald's menu and its recipes vary, sometimes quite significantly, by country. Software requires patches and updates. Most R&D-intensive companies are continually tweaking their designs. The scalability of training is limited by the number of hours the employee you have trained can work in a day.

But, nevertheless, we would expect intangible assets to be, on average, significantly more scalable than tangible ones.

Why Does Scalability Matter?

We might expect to see three unusual things happening in an economy where more investments are highly scalable.

First, there will be some very intangible-intensive businesses that have gotten very large. Starbucks has been able to leverage an effective brand, operating processes, and supply chains to allow it to spread across the world. Google, Microsoft, and Facebook need relatively few tangible assets compared to the manufacturing giants of yesteryear. They can scale their intangible-asset bundle or software and reputation and so get very big. This type of scalability is, of course, enhanced by network effects.[3]

Second, with the prospects of such large markets, more and more firms will be encouraged to try their luck in these markets. They face a hard choice, for although the prospective market might be large, encouraging them to have a go, competition might be very tough, thereby discouraging them. The net result of this was described by the economist John Sutton in the early 1990s: in markets where scalable investments (like R&D or branding) are important, you'd expect to see "industry concentration"—a relatively small number of dominant large companies.

Third, businesses looking to compete with the owners of scalable assets are in a tough position. On the one hand, the rewards are high. After all, Google started off as a competitor to a whole host of search engines that were once household names. But in markets with highly scalable assets, the rewards for runners-up are often meager. If Google's search algorithm is the best and is almost infinitely scalable, why use Yahoo's? Winner-takes-all scenarios are likely to be the norm.

Sunkenness

Why Are Intangibles Sunk Costs?

If a business makes an intangible investment and later on decides it wants to back out, it's often hard to reverse the decision and try to get back the investment's cost by selling the created asset—and, in general, it's harder than in the case of a tangible asset. Economists describe these kinds of irrecoverable costs as "sunk."

Consider a world in which some commercial disaster hits a hypothetical chain of coffee shops—let's call it Tarbucks—and the company goes bust. What assets could the liquidators sell to pay off its outstanding debts?

First to go would be the shops that the company owns or leases; there's an active and liquid market in commercial property, so finding a buyer at a reasonable price should be possible. Its coffee machines and shop fixtures and delivery vehicles and cash registers will also be salvageable: there are secondary markets where these sorts of things are bought and sold. (Indeed, as we saw in chapter 1, there are markets for all sorts of exotic plant and machinery, from oil tankers to tunnel-boring machines.)

But its intangible assets are harder to sell. Its brand may be valuable, but perhaps not—and even if it is, getting money for it may rely on a trade sale that has to be negotiated specifically for the purpose. Tarbucks's codified operating procedures and the processes it uses to serve customers quickly may have been very valuable to the company when it was in business, but they will prove difficult to sell to someone else, especially if they are specific to Tarbucks's layout or product offering. If Tarbucks has some valuable intellectual property, say, a patented roasting technique, the liquidators may be able to sell this. But if the knowledge isn't governed by formal intellectual property rights (say, the know-how involved in buying coffee beans effectively) or if it's distributed among the company's employees (for example, through training), it becomes, to all intents and purposes, impossible to sell.

Now, of course some tangible assets are also hard to sell if a company or a project fails. Very specialized machinery may be worthless to anyone but its original owner, implying a certain proportion of its cost is sunk. An isolated coal mine dug in a spot that can only sell to a local power station is worthless if the local power station does not want to buy its coal. The Channel Tunnel or Narita Airport can't be packaged up and moved should they no longer be required in their present location. But on the whole, the problem is worse when it comes to intangible assets.

In particular, there are two characteristics of tangible assets that make them easier to sell and less likely to be sunk investments.

The first are the phenomena of mass production and standardization. One of the wonders of mass production is that many tangible assets are copies of other tangible assets. The world's businesses own lots of Ford transit vans, lots of Windows servers, lots of ISO-668 shipping containers. This makes them easier to sell. (It also makes it easier to estimate their price, since there are often published market values for secondhand tangibles, a point we will return to.) Standards also help make tangible assets fungible between businesses. Common power sockets and voltages make it easier to move machine tools from one factory to another. Midsized vans are to some extent interchangeable. But there are far fewer standards among intangible assets, nor are most intangibles mass-produced.

The second reason tangible investments are easier to sell is that they are less likely to be uniquely linked to the firm that owns them and its business. Plenty of tangible assets, from buildings to land, are useful to many types of business. A patent, a clever set of operating procedures, or a brand are more likely to be mainly useful to the company that developed them in the first place. Even where markets for intangibles exists—such as for patents—many of the assets are much more useful to their original owner than to anyone else.

Why Does Sunkenness Matter?

Investments with high irrecoverable costs can be difficult to finance, especially with debt. One of the reasons banks love mortgage lending is that their loans are secured on a valuable, immobile asset that can, if the borrower defaults, be seized and sold.

Companies with lots of intangible assets are, on the other hand, a total pain in the neck for banks if it all goes wrong. First, can such assets be seized? In some cases they can simply walk out the door—such as knowledge and know-how in employees' heads. (This is a consequence of lack of property rights, which gives rise to spillovers that we discuss below.)

Second, can they be sold? A consequence of sunkenness is: likely not. Because the assets are often context-specific, it is hard for markets to emerge to trade them, unlike a house. With no market, you have to find another way to value the asset, which is hard to do. Do you value a patent at the cost it took to develop it (if so, you have to apportion the costs correctly), at a professional valuator's estimate (for which you have to pay, and they, in any case, might be wrong), or at a figure based on its future earnings potential (can you trust the borrower to tell you this)?

No wonder many small business loans, especially in the UK and the United States, demand a lien on directors' homes as security—it changes complex, messy intangible lending into something a lot more like a simple mortgage.

Sunkenness also contributes to the uncertainty around intangible assets. Part of the reason for sunkenness is that intangible assets are often very context-specific. It might be a supply chain relationship that is unique to the particular industry or suppliers. It might be a reputation for product quality in a very particular area. All this makes it harder and harder to value the worth of such an asset, for sunkenness stops the creation of markets for such assets. The lack of markets means that value is very hard to assign.

The sunkenness of intangible investment may also have an effect on the way businesses behave. Psychologists have long known that people have a tendency to become overattached to sunk costs and unwilling to write them off (Kahneman, Lovallo, and Sibony 2011). For example, as McKinsey[4] points out, promoters of the Vancouver Expo 86 kept refusing to cancel the project even as the costs ballooned by twenty times, from the original Can$78 million in 1978. This "sunk-cost fallacy" can be particularly fatal to good decision making when linked with other cognitive biases, such as confirmation bias, in this case massively overinflated forecasts of visitor numbers.

We might expect managers of businesses who have sunk lots of money into intangible investments like R&D or setting up new business units to overestimate their value and to be more reluctant to let them go. Indeed, a world in which this behavior was common would see an unsettling psychological shift. Because of the sunk-cost fallacy, we might expect to see more businesses sticking with bad investments that they were better off drawing a line under. What's more, the lack of markets for most intangible assets would make it harder for managers to obtain an external read-out on what their assets were really worth. In the short term, this could lead to overoptimistic overinvestment—and more frequent bubbles.

As well as helping inflate bubbles, the sunken nature of intangible investment could make it more painful when the bubbles finally burst. We're used to the idea that when a market crashes, businesses often have to sell their assets very cheaply, since almost everyone else also wants to sell. This is bad enough when the assets are somewhat fungible, like property or fiber-optic cable: the price plummets, but there is usually at least some residual value. But when a bubble based on sunk, firm-specific intangible assets bursts, there's the risk that the assets will be worth more or less nothing.

In light of this, you might well ask why firms ever make this kind of investment decision at all. First, some of the returns might be very high, high enough to reward all these risks. Second, although the cost might be harder to recover than in the market for secondhand tangible investments, there are other extra-market benefits. An investment in knowledge, even if it fails to create a marketable asset directly, might still be very valuable if it creates information that resolves uncertainty for the firm. Many firms perform simultaneous research projects: a failure of project A might not directly create a marketable asset (a patent, say), but may very well contribute to the success of project B by revealing what not to do. Thus intangible investment might give a very high payoff via giving very valuable information to the firm about the opportunities that it faces, what is called an "option value" (Dixit and Pindyck 1995). We treat this value as an emergent property arising from the irreversibility/sunkenness of an asset. See the section on emerging characteristics below.[5]

Spillovers

Why Do Intangibles Generate Spillovers?

Some intangible investments have unusually high spillovers: that is to say, it is relatively easy for other businesses to take advantage of intangible investments they don't themselves make.

The classic example is R&D: copying other people's ideas is relatively easy, unless the law prevents it by means of patents or copyrights. In the language of economists, the ideas created by R&D are non-rival—my using a piece of knowledge doesn't prevent you from also using it. In Thomas Jefferson's words, "He who receives an idea from me, receives instruction himself without lessening mine; as he who lights his taper at mine, receives light without darkening me."[6]

Ideas are also to some extent "nonexcludable": that is, it is relatively hard to prevent you from using an idea that I came up with, unless I keep it secret, or unless I can use legal means, like a patent, to stop you. The benefits of non-rival, nonexcludable investments are likely to spill over beyond the companies that make them, and ideas, such as those from R&D, are a prime example. Oral Rehydration Therapy is a perfect example.

But spillovers don't just arise from R&D. After Apple released the iPhone, almost all smartphones started looking just like it. Apple's investments in software, design, and supply chains (for example, creating the software supply chain we call the App Store) were adopted or imitated by its competitors as they sought to create phones like Apple's. By creating what marketing experts would call the smartphone "category" (or more precisely, growing it significantly), Apple benefited not just themselves but other smartphone manufacturers.

The iPhone also provides an example of marketing spillovers. Part of the iPhone's success was a result of Apple's willingness to throw its brand behind the new product. Earlier smartphones had been rather clunky, but Apple had a reputation for making stylish, user-friendly devices. By creating the category, as marketers would say, Apple not only made a lot of profits for themselves (the iPhone is now around 66 percent of Apple's total revenues [Miglani 2016]), but they also helped Samsung, HTC, Google, and other competitors create profitable smartphone businesses.

Perhaps less obviously, we can also see examples of spillovers in organizational design, training, and branding and marketing. In the 1950s and 1960s the consulting firm McKinsey & Company pioneered a new way of providing business advice that was in essence an organizational innovation.

Rather than hiring industry veterans to tell businesses how to improve, which was what most early management consulting consisted of, McKinsey hired graduates from elite business schools and put them to work together in small, focused consulting teams. These teams disaggregated problems into parts using a set of replicable methodologies, allowing bright and hardworking, but relatively inexpert, consultants to work collectively to solve relatively complex business problems. An aggressive culture of performance management and promotion attracted suitably high-flying youngsters and kept them hungry and mean enough to ensure a high work rate.

This set of organizational innovations is now the norm in the management consulting industry. It got that way by being copied; indeed, McKinsey copied aspects of it from the legal profession (McKinsey's managing partner at the time was a former lawyer).

Finally, training spillovers occur every time a trained employee leaves a company and goes to work for another firm where their training is useful.

Now, it must be said that tangible assets might have spillovers: if you own a port and I build a freight railway leading to it, my investment probably benefits you, to the extent that a well-connected port is more useful and profitable than a poorly connected one. If a popular department store opens a branch in a mall, it may benefit other shops by attracting more passing trade.

But the physical nature of tangible assets makes solving the excludability problem much easier: if I run a bus company that owns a fleet of buses, my competitors can't simply sneak into my depot and use them—the buses have ignition keys and locks, my depot has an alarm, and I have hundreds of years of property law to enforce my rights.

You might just take the view that spillovers would disappear if property rights can be sensibly established. But it seems very hard in practice to do this, despite centuries of trying.

To explain the contested nature of intangibles, let's return to the bus company. We used the bus company as an example of how relatively straightforward it is for a firm to appropriate the benefits of tangible assets. But we slyly failed to specify the country the bus company was based in. While bus companies in developed countries can be fairly sure their buses can't simply be borrowed by others, in some parts of the world this isn't the case.

In 2014 news emerged of a horrific incident in which dozens of students were abducted and, it seems, murdered by some combination of police and organized criminals in the Mexican state of Guerrero. One of the incidental details of the crime was that the students were, at the time they were kidnapped, riding in one of a number of buses they had commandeered to take them to a protest in Mexico City. It turns out that commandeering buses was "routine" and generally tolerated, so much so that the bus companies and their drivers had established protocols for what to do when it happened.

In developed countries, we are not used to people being able to take valuable things like buses and to use them against their owners' wishes. Social norms and law enforcement conspire to make it transgressive and rare. The background to the Guerrero kidnapping is a reminder of how dependent this is on our social context.

But when it comes to intangible assets, the rules around ownership and control are much more contested, even in developed countries. Patents and copyrights are, on the whole, less secure and more subject to challenge than the title deeds to farmland or the ownership of a shipping container or a computer.

One important reason for this is history. About four thousand years ago, a scribe in the south of what is now Iraq wrote a list on a clay tablet. People in ancient Mesopotamia had been using clay tablets for centuries to write down everything from lists to legends.

But this clay tablet was something different: it was a list of laws, the laws of the King of Ur, Sumer, and Akkad, who was called Ur-Nammu. It is the earliest code of laws that survives today. What's interesting about it for our purposes is that alongside the standard fare of ancient legal codes—dealing with murder, mutilation, fornication—it contains plenty of mentions of property. The code describes people owning land, silver, grain, unspecified other goods, and slaves.

To put it another way, people have been making rules about the ownership of tangible things for as long as they have been making rules at all. The four thousand years that have passed since Ur-Nammu has given human societies a lot of time to think about what ownership of physical things means and how to resolve difficult issues.

This process is not just difficult from an intellectual point of view. It is political and gets resolved not just by brain work but by social and societal conflict, which takes time. The better part of a million people died when the United States fought a civil war over the question of whether it was right to own other human beings. The world reached the brink of nuclear annihilation in a cold war between countries who disagreed on the question of whether owning property was in fact theft. But over time, people's understanding of what it meant to own things grew and became clearer, especially in developed countries with stable legal systems.

Now consider intangible assets. It's a matter of debate when the first law on the ownership of intangible assets was made. People tend to mention late medieval Venetian laws on glass-making techniques and French and English grants of monopolies for protoindustrial techniques in the sixteenth century. But in any case, it was millennia after the Code of Ur-Nammu.

Intangible property laws then went through a process of slow evolution, as the economic historian Zorina Khan has pointed out (2008). Some early modern English monopolies enjoyed the right to operate what we would call new technologies, but others covered the right to trade (to sell salt or whatever). Gradually, monopolies become restricted to new ideas, and legislators started thinking more programmatically about what a good patent or copyright law should look like.

By the eighteenth century, English patents were becoming more detailed. Rather than a patent to run steam-powered machinery, government granted patents for specific processes that had to be described and published. At the same time, the 1709 Statute of Anne represented the beginning of English copyright law.

The newly formed United States took intellectual property very seriously. Indeed, America's Constitution includes a clause on patents and copyright.[7] The US system was from the start simpler, more rational, and radically cheaper than that of contemporary Britain or France.

This development process continued. Countries started to tweak their patent and copyright systems to encourage more invention. Trademarks acquired legal recognition in various countries in the nineteenth century, creating a legal basis for the idea of branding and marketing assets.

In the 1920s Edgar Rice Burroughs acquired a trademark for Tarzan, one of his fictional creations, in addition to his copyright. This fusion of creative and commercial intangible property is what we have to thank for the media franchises of today, from Star Wars lunchboxes to Princess Elsa costumes. And, of course, today issues of intangible property continue to be contested. Global trade negotiations founder on disputes between the United States and China over piracy and fair use. Patent trolls pursue their controversial calling in the courts of the Eastern District of Texas or of Moscow. Controversies arise when companies try to push the limits of the intellectual property rights in new ways, such as when, in 2015, tractor maker John Deere argued that, under the US Digital Millennium Copyright Act, customers who had bought its tractors did not have the right to repair them themselves.

In the long process of agreeing on norms and rules, tangible property has a three-and-a-half-millennium head start on intangible property. If the same holds true for intangibles, this means 3,500 more years for the technicalities and ethics of ownership to be worked through, debated, and fought over, and more uncertainty.

So the tendency of intangible investments to spill over to other firms works on two levels. On the one hand, it is an inherent characteristic of assets that consist of knowledge, because knowledge is non-rival. At the same time, the difference between the spillovers of tangible and intangible investment are exacerbated by history. The fact that developed countries have better institutions for deciding who owns tangible assets than intangible ones is partly the result of history and the way institutions have evolved.

Why Do Spillovers Matter?

Spillovers matter for three reasons: first of all, in a world where companies can't be sure they will obtain the benefits of their investments, we would expect them to invest less. Second, there is a premium on the ability to manage spillovers: companies that can make the most of their own investments in intangibles, or that are especially good at exploiting the spillovers from others' investments, will do particularly well. Third, spillovers affect the geography of modern economies.

The classic answer to the problem of spillovers is government funding. If businesses can't make the most of their intangible investments, especially in R&D, the government should step in and either fund the research directly (for example, in university or government labs) or support businesses to do it. And indeed, this happens a lot. The US government funds 30 percent of R&D that goes on in the country (Appelt et al. 2016). Public R&D is especially important in areas of basic research and in new fields (like the US military's development of the semiconductor sector in the 1950s.)

Spillovers also affect the behavior of individual companies, as businesses strive to maximize the value of the intangibles they do make. Indeed, a significant part of the strategy of intangible-rich companies is combining and managing their intangibles in such a way as to minimize the spillovers and maximize the benefits they get from them.

Someone who is unusually honest about the lengths businesses go to in order to stop others benefiting from their lovingly created intangibles is venture capitalist and entrepreneur Peter Thiel, the so-called don of Silicon Valley's PayPal Mafia. Thiel's refreshingly candid book on entrepreneurship *Zero to One* makes it clear that the way to create very valuable start-ups is to create businesses that, as far as possible, have monopoly positions in big markets.

In Thiel's management philosophy, you create these defensible opportunities by investing in the right sorts of software, marketing, and networks of customers and suppliers (three classic intangibles) and by bringing them together in ways that competitors find hard to copy.

What's more, the ability to attract the spillovers of other firms' intangible investment is perhaps just as important as the ability to maximize the gain from one's own. Being well networked, knowing about important developments in one's field, and having the standing to bring together collaborations, ask for favors, and coordinate partnerships becomes more important in a business where investments have greater spillovers. After all, exploiting the spillovers from another firm's investment is in some ways a free lunch.

The crudest way companies can keep their knowledge to themselves is through the law. James Watt and the Wright brothers riled their contemporaries with their willingness to enforce patents to stop other people's research on steam and flight, respectively. Patent trolling can be thought of as a pure-play form of this strategy. The patent troll buys up patents, often from defunct companies, and goes around seeking to enforce legal rights against anyone who might otherwise benefit from the spillovers of the original investment. There are good reasons to deplore patent trolling—but it is a pretty straightforward consequence of the spillover characteristic of intangible assets.

If the law isn't strong enough, companies can lobby to have it changed. Copyright lawyers sometimes talk about the Mickey Mouse Curve—the steadily increasing length of copyright in US law that grows just fast enough to stop Disney's iconic mouse from entering the public domain. When Disney first created Mickey, his copyright was due to expire in 1984. Extensions in 1976 and 1998 mean that this won't happen until 2023. And who knows what new laws might be made between now and then.

Patent trolls and copyright lawsuits catch our attention because they are newsworthy, but other ways of capturing the spillovers of intangible investment are more common—in fact, they're part of the invisible fabric of everyday business life. They often involve reciprocity rather than compulsion or legal threats. Software developers use online repositories like GitHub to share code; being an active contributor and an effective user of GitHub is a badge of honor for some developers. Firms sometimes pool their patents; then they realize that the spillovers from each company's technologies are valuable, and that enforcing everyone's individual legal rights is not worth it. (Indeed, the US government helped end the patent war between the Wright brothers and Curtiss Aeroplane and Motor Company that was holding back the US aircraft industry in the 1910s by getting everyone to set up a patent pool, the Manufacturers Aircraft Association.)

Finally, to reap the benefits of spillovers people can organize themselves in various ways. One of the most obvious of these is into cities. As Edward Glaeser, one of the leading economists working on cities, has put it, one of the puzzles of urbanization is the increased willingness of people to pay very high rents to live next door to other people paying very high rents (Glaeser 2011). This seems a particular puzzle in our connected world, where the importance of proximity would surely have declined. One answer is that the spillover benefits of living in cities have increased. Indeed, given the undoubted increase in the *disbenefits*—congestion, prices, and air pollution—there must be some offsetting benefits, and those might very well be around the chances of more interactions and collaborations.

All this means that in an intangible-intensive economy, the ability to make good the problem of spillovers becomes very important. This calls for a particular range of skills: technical skills to understand the intangibles themselves, such as scientific or engineering knowledge; in some cases, legal expertise or a talent for deal-making; in others, softer skills like leadership and networking. And it calls for more living together in cities. We will explore the implications of these skills for inequality in chapter 6.

Synergies
Why Do Intangibles Exhibit Synergies?

Ideas and other ideas go well together. This is especially true in the field of technology.

Take the microwave oven. Toward the end of the Second World War, the US defense contractor Raytheon was busy mass-producing cavity magnetrons, a sort of vacuum tube that was an important part of the radar defenses the British had pioneered earlier in the war. Percy Spenser, an engineer working for Raytheon, realized that microwaves from the magnetrons could heat food by creating electromagnetic fields in a metal box.

Within a few years, the technology was sufficiently advanced that you could buy a "Speedy Weeny" microwaved hot dog at a novelty stand in New York's Grand Central Station. A few companies tried to sell domestic microwave ovens, but none were very successful. Then, in the 1960s, Raytheon bought Amana, a white goods manufacturer, and combined their microwave expertise with Amana's kitchen appliance knowledge to build a more successful product. At the same time, Litton, another defense contractor, invented the modern microwave oven shape and tweaked the magnetron to make it safer.

In 1970 forty thousand microwaves were sold. By 1975 it was a million. What made this possible was the gradual accumulation of ideas and innovations. The magnetron on its own wasn't very useful to a customer, but combined with other incremental bits of R&D and the design and marketing ideas of Litton and Amana, it became a defining innovation of the late twentieth century.

The story of microwave ovens is entirely typical of how new technologies evolve. Brian Arthur of the Santa Fe Institute wrote a memorable book, *The Nature of Technology* (2009), which made the point that technological innovation was "combinatorial." That is to say, any given technology depends on the bringing together of already-existing ideas. In Arthur's words: "Every novel technology is created from existing ones, and therefore . . . every technology stands upon a pyramid of others that made it possible in a succession that goes back to the earliest phenomena that humans captured."

Science writer Matt Ridley took the idea a step further, stressing the evolutionary nature of ideas. "Exchange is to cultural evolution as sex is to biological evolution"; Ridley described innovation as what happens "when ideas have sex" (Ridley 2010, 453).

Another way of looking at this is to say that intangible assets—ideas, like the outputs of R&D, new designs, or new ways of structuring a business or marketing a product—have synergies with one another; they are worth more when you combine them. Now, tangible assets have synergies too. A bus and a bus stop; a supply of electricity and a Marshall stack; a PC and a printer. But the scope of different ideas to interact, and the fact that ideas are not expended when they are combined, makes the potential synergies much higher.

The microwave oven story also reflects another aspect of the synergies between different ideas—that they are often unpredictable and jump across domains. In this case, military information technology gave rise to a kitchen appliance. This kind of exaptation seems to happen again and again in the world of ideas, making it relatively hard to predict where synergies between intangibles will arise.

Intangible investments also show synergies with tangible assets, in particular information technologies, especially networked computers and smartphones. A striking example of this is the role of Walmart in saving the US economy in the 1990s. In the 1980s the US economy had been experiencing sluggish real productivity growth. People worried this was becoming a "new normal" and that growth might never recover. But as the 1990s went on, productivity went up. In 2000 the McKinsey Global Institute analyzed the sources of this productivity increase. Counterintuitively, they found that the bulk of it came from the way big chains retailers, in particular Walmart, were using computers and software to reorganize their supply chains, improve efficiency, and lower prices. In a sense, it was a technological revolution. But the gains were realized through organizational and business practice changes in a low-tech sector. Or, to put it another way, there were big synergies between Walmart's investment in computers and its investment in processes and supply chain development to make the most of the computers.

It's a relationship that has been documented in detail by Erik Brynjolfsson, an economist at MIT and a guru of the digital economy. Brynjolfsson's research showed that organizational investment and tech investment were highly complementary; that is to say, the businesses that got the most out of their whizzy software were the ones that invested in organizational change too (Brynjolfsson, Hitt, and Yang 2002). Nicholas Bloom, Raffaella Sadun, and John Van Reenen (2012) compared the productivity of American businesses that invested in IT to European ones and found that European ones didn't get the same level of benefits from computers because they weren't willing or able to change organizational and management practices as much.

The synergies between IT and intangibles work on a couple of levels. First of all, computer hardware has a direct, and in a sense trivial, synergy with one type of intangible: software. That's the point of software. To put it another way, computers are physical devices that become useful and valuable when you fill them with useful, *intangible* information.

Because computers and networks of computers deal in information, they also help make other intangible investment easier or more effective. Consider the network of big sharing-economy companies like Uber or AirBnB. There is nothing about their business models that absolutely requires computers and the Internet. Before everyone had a smartphone, there were networked cab companies, some of which, like London's ComCab or Radio Taxis, used independent drivers. Before AirBnB, there were house-share clubs with brochures and telephone booking systems. Both the house-share clubs and the taxi networks made investments of time and money to develop their networks of suppliers.

But in both cases, the Internet and smartphones made it possible to build very big networks, to do it more cheaply, and to strengthen the value of being a member of the network (through ratings and searchability, for example). Here again, there is a strong synergy between IT—technologies that deal with information and networking—and intangible investment, which to a great extent is investment in information and connections.

So it seems that intangible investments have synergies with one another, whether they relate to ideas (which have a tendency to create new ideas when you bring them together) or new structures (which seem to be complementary to new technologies). What's more, it's often difficult to predict how these combinations will happen or to plan them: serendipity and chance seem to play an important role.

Why Do the Synergies of Intangible Assets Matter?

If the spillovers of intangibles encourage companies to keep their investments to themselves, or at best to share in a self-interested way, then the synergies of intangibles have the opposite effect.

If your ideas are worth more when combined with other ideas, there's a strong incentive to get access to as many ideas as possible. One manifestation of this is the increasing prominence of open innovation.

In its simplest form, open innovation happens when a firm deliberately connects with and benefits from new ideas that arise outside the firm itself. Cooking up ideas in a big corporate R&D lab is not open innovation; getting ideas by buying start-ups, partnering with academic researchers, or undertaking joint ventures with other companies is.

Open innovation became a management buzzword in the 2000s, after it was popularized in a best-selling management book (of the same title) by Henry Chesbrough, though other researchers had been observing it since at least the 1970s, and companies had been doing it long before that.

Consider nineteenth-century blast furnaces, an example famously analyzed, using very detailed contemporary records, by Robert Allen from Oxford (1983). Key determinants of the efficiency of blast furnaces were height and temperature. But the physics of the time were inadequate to allow an engineer to deduce the optimal design for the blast furnace. So how did they design it? There was a host of experimentation with different heights and temperatures by local entrepreneurs. Regional and national societies, like the Institution of Cleveland Engineers, the South Wales Institution of Engineers, the Institution of Mechanical Engineers, and the 1869 Iron and Steel Institute swapped information. What was the outcome? As Allen described, this "open" innovation transformed the industry:

Between 1850 and 1875 several important changes in blast furnace practice were developed in England's Cleveland district. The most dramatic were the increase in the height of the furnace from fifty feet—the previous norm—to eighty feet or more, and the increase in the temperature of the blast from 600°F to 1400°F. Together, these improvements reduced the fuel requirement for making pig iron enough to justify scrapping the original short, low temperature furnaces and replacing them with the new designs. (Allen 1983, 3)

Much of the rhetoric around open innovation today takes an almost moral tone: it's about sharing knowledge; it is about working together; it is even about humility. This moral aspect of open innovation derives from the synergies of intangible investment—which can make sharing ideas mutually beneficial. (There's also a sense in which open innovation is more self-interestedly about exploiting the spillovers of other firms' investments, but that tends to be less talked about.)

What's particularly interesting is that the existence of synergies between ideas creates a tension with the spillovers we discussed above—a dilemma for intangible-rich businesses. Closing itself off to the world and relying on strong intellectual property law can help keep a firm's intangibles from spilling over, but it's a fatal sort of isolation because it reduces the opportunities for synergies with other people's ideas—and most ideas are other people's ideas. In Bill Joy's words, "no matter who you are, most of the smartest people work for someone else" (Lakhani and Panetta 2007).

The effect of the synergies of intangibles also matters at the level of national and local economies. If my business's research or process innovations become more valuable if your business and a dozen other businesses are also coming up with great, synergistic ideas, an economy can end up in either a virtuous or a vicious cycle. If everyone else is doing research or developing new processes, and if that makes my investment more valuable, it is in my interests to invest in R&D too. If no one else is, it may not be worthwhile for me either.

This idea of complementary know-how sits at the heart of the idea of the "industrial commons," developed by economists Gary

Pisano and Willy Shih (2009). Pisano and Shih argued that America's manufacturing sector was suffering because there was no longer enough expertise and research in basic industrial processes needed to create a shared knowledge base.

The synergies between ideas also create a tension between serendipity and coordination. On the one hand, the vast number of ways that ideas can combine usefully makes it hard to plan centrally. The accidental discovery of new properties of technologies—like how the magnetron became the microwave—seems to be a common phenomenon.

Based on this logic, if we want to increase productive investment in ideas, we should encourage "interdisciplinarity," casual exchanges between people working in different fields and diverse places. Where these exchanges will happen a lot is in large, walkable cities with plenty of public spaces and opportunities for social interaction.

On the other hand, sustained research in a particular area matters too. At least some of the synergies between different ideas work best in a particular field. The microwave oven was a success not just because of the radical leap from military communications to cooking, but also because lots of researchers from Amana, Litton, and their Japanese competitors worked on the design and improved the technology of the magnetron.

Sometimes this coordination happens spontaneously. But we can also think of things that help it along. Prizes, like the eighteenth-century Longitude Prize or the twenty-first-century Ansari-X Prize for private spaceflight, can help crowd investment into a neglected area. No doubt, part of the reason the technology press hypes new technologies, like the Internet of Things or solar energy, is not only because it makes for more exciting stories, but because it also has a functional role of drawing attention to up-and-coming areas and encouraging coordinated investment. Perhaps the hype is misplaced; but the role of encouraging coordination is important nevertheless.

Finally, the synergies between intangibles can be a valuable competitive tactic for individual companies. Consider the epipen—or rather the EpiPen®. EpiPens are the pen-like devices that can give epinephedrine (hence the name) injections, thereby saving the lives of people suffering from anaphylactic shock. EpiPen is by far the market-leading epinephedrine device. But this isn't because it has patented epinephedrine, which is in the public domain. Nor does it have an uncopiable design: several competitors have come up with alternative designs for injectors, some of them arguably better than the EpiPen. But a combination of intangibles has kept it as the market leader: the name and brand, its design, the widespread understanding among first aiders of how to use the device all act to make it hard for competitors to succeed (we discuss the EpiPen some more in chapter 5).

These synergies not only give companies an advantage over competitors: they also affect the dynamics between companies and their talented employees. Consider an expert designer at Apple, a company famed for, and to some extent reliant on, its good design. What stops that designer, from an economic point of view, demanding more and more money in return for not leaving for the competition or setting up a new, design-led start-up?

One answer to the question is synergies. Apple's design is especially valuable in the context of a whole set of intangible assets Apple owns: its technologies, its customer service, and the power of its brand and marketing channels. All of these things make an Apple designer more valuable to Apple than to an alternative employer, and they reduce the incentives to leave.

So, synergies matter because they create strong incentives for companies and governments to bring together different intangibles, especially new ideas. To this extent they work in the opposite direction of spillovers, encouraging openness and sharing rather than appropriating. They also matter because they create an alternative way for firms to protect their intangible investments against competition: by building synergistic clusters of intangible investments, rather than by protecting individual assets.

Some Emergent Characteristics of Intangibles Due to the Four S's

So we have seen that intangible investments differ from tangible investments in a number of ways: they are more likely to be scalable, to have costs that are sunk, to generate spillovers, and to exhibit synergies with one another.

Let's conclude this chapter by noting that these properties combine to produce two other, more general characteristics of intangibles: *uncertainty* and *contestedness*.

Any investment, tangible or intangible, is a step into the unknown. No business can know for sure what the return will be. But it seems that because of the four S's we have discussed, intangible investment has a tendency to be more uncertain. First of all, owing to its *sunkenness*, intangible investments tend to be worth less if they go wrong. It's harder to recover their value by simply selling them. Second, the upside of an intangible investment is potentially much higher, since it is more likely to benefit from *scale* (so a modest investment can reap a big return) or *synergies* (increasing its value directly). So when things go wrong, intangibles tend to be worth less, and when they go well, they tend to be worth much more.

But this is not just a case of replacing a narrow distribution of possible outcomes with a wider one. The tendency of intangible investments to generate *spillovers* makes it radically harder to estimate the future returns to the company making the investments. And the absence of markets for many intangibles (which contributes to their *sunkenness*) makes it harder to form a realistic estimate of their value.

All other things being equal, then, we would expect firms in an intangible-rich economy to exhibit more uncertainty. And part of this uncertainty shows up in giving intangible firms *option values* to their investment. Consider an intangible investment that is sunk and proceeds in stages. At each stage, the firm might learn something, say, about the feasibility of the investment. That information is valuable to it, especially if the spending is sunk. So intangible investment tends to have an option value associated with it (see the discussion above).

Intangibles also tend to be *contested*. People and businesses will often vie to see who can control them, own them, or benefit from them. This is partly a function of *spillovers*. As we have seen, businesses often seek to get the benefit of intangible investments made by other firms. Sometimes this happens by mutual consent (for example, when businesses undertake open innovation); sometimes not (for example, Google's development of the Android operating system, which enraged Apple's Steve Jobs).

Synergies between intangibles also increase their contestedness. When particular combinations of intangibles are unusually valuable, the power of people who are sufficiently networked or knowledgeable to broker these connections increases, a theme we will return to in chapter 6.

Contestedness is exacerbated by the ambiguity of rules over who owns intangible investments: firms dispute patents so often because the ownership of intangible property is less well established and less clear-cut than the ownership of tangible property.

Conclusion: The Four S's of Intangibles

Intangibles have four unusual economic properties. These properties can exist with tangible investments, but on the whole intangible assets exhibit them to a greater degree. These characteristics are:

- Scalability
- Sunkenness
- Spillovers
- Synergies

Three further characteristics emerge from these four, namely, uncertainty, option value, and contestedness. The rest of the book discusses the consequences of an increasingly intangible-rich economy that emerge from these characteristics.

PART II

The Consequences of the Rise of the Intangible Economy

5

Intangibles, Investment, Productivity, and Secular Stagnation

This chapter looks at the role of intangibles in secular stagnation, the puzzling fall in investment and productivity growth seen in major economies in recent years. We argue that the increasing importance of intangible investment may have an important role to play in this troubling phenomenon.

One of the most troubling and widely talked about trends in economics at the moment is secular stagnation: the fact that business investment is stubbornly low despite every indication that it shouldn't be. There have been a variety of explanations put forward for what is wrong with business investment, from the failings of monetary policy to a slowdown in technological progress.

This chapter is the first of our chapters discussing the consequences of the rise in intangible investment. We will argue that at least part of the reason for the secular stagnation puzzle is the shift in the balance of business investment toward intangibles. Furthermore, we shall make that argument on the basis of the four characteristics of intangibles we pointed out in chapter 4. Because (a) intangibles can be scaled, leading firms break away from laggards, and because (b) they are unmeasured, measured productivity and profitability look high. And because they spillover when the pace of intangible investment slows, as it did after the Great Recession, productivity slows down as reduced intangible growth throws off fewer spillovers.

Secular Stagnation: The Symptoms

Before we look at the link between secular stagnation and intangible investment, it is worth reviewing what secular stagnation actually consists of. Secular stagnation is characterized by a number of symptoms.

The first is low investment. As figure 5.1 shows, for the United States and the UK, investment fell in the 1970s, recovered somewhat in the mid-1980s, and then fell precipitously in the financial crisis. Since then it has not recovered.

Now, this would not be so surprising were it not for the second symptom: low interest rates. As figure 5.2 shows, long-run real interest rates have been declining since the mid-1980s and have been particularly low since the financial crisis. But there has been no recovery in investment since then, even though the costs of making such investments are very low.

The coincidence of low investment and low interest rates is a puzzle for economists. Once upon a time, central bankers thought they understood what to do about low investment. When businesses got nervous about the future, as they did from time to time, and reduced investment, central banks would respond by

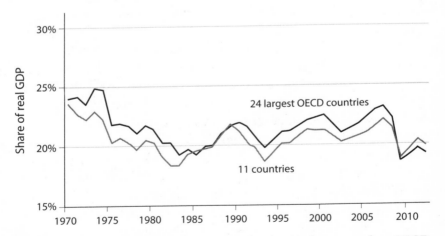

Figure 5.1. Real investment as a percentage of real GDP for twenty-four OECD countries and a restricted sample of eleven countries (Australia, Austria, Denmark, Finland, Germany, Italy, Japan, Netherlands, Sweden, the UK, and the United States). Source: Thwaites 2015.

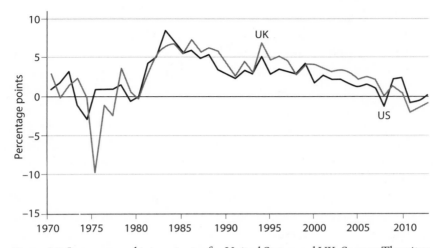

Figure 5.2. Long-run real interest rates for United States and UK. Source: Thwaites 2015.

lowering their base interest rate, making money cheaper. Cheap money made it less costly for businesses to raise financing and for consumers to borrow. So businesses and consumers borrowed and investment and consumption went back up.

But this tactic seems to have stopped working. For central bankers this is the equivalent of being a captain headed for a rocky shoal and finding that your wheel will no longer turn the ship. This coincidence of very cheap borrowing and the apparent unwillingness of businesses to invest was what Larry Summers was talking about when he popularized the term "secular stagnation" in a 2013 lecture to the IMF.[1]

One immediate explanation for this weird mix of cheap money and low investment is simply that the demand for investment has fallen. In his 2011 bestseller *The Great Stagnation*, economist Tyler Cowen suggested that developed countries might have exhausted easy sources of good investments, such as settling new land or getting children to spend more years in education. Most memorably, he argued that technological progress might have slowed down, or, more specifically, that the economic benefit of new discoveries was less than had been the case in the past. The economist and economic historian Robert Gordon developed this theme in his influential 2016 book *The Rise and Fall of American Growth*, in which he argued that the inventions over the twentieth century, such as electricity, indoor plumbing, and the like, were part of "one big wave of innovation" that will not be repeated.

This explanation for secular stagnation has proved controversial, not least because it turns out to be very difficult to measure whether technological progress has slowed down. A totally out-of-the-blue technological slowdown that is not easy to confirm using data has seemed to some too much of a deus ex machina, and many of those interested in secular stagnation have looked around for other causes.

And then there are three further symptoms associated with current-day secular stagnation, all of which demand explanation.

The first is the fact that corporate profits in the United States and elsewhere are, on average, higher than they have been for decades and seem to be steadily increasing. Far from being under pressure, firms' profits have never looked better. Some measures of these are shown in figure 5.3.[2] The most directly comparable measure is average return on capital (figure 5.3B), which has grown sharply since the 1990s; it certainly does not suggest an Age of Lead, where investment has fallen because there is nothing worth investing in.

At first glance, this does not seem to be compatible with the idea that there are few good investment opportunities out there; on the contrary, if profits are high, one would expect businesses to be tempted to invest more to take advantage of cheap money to invest in all the attractive business opportunities that are driving high returns.

The second curious fact is that when it comes to profitability, businesses are not equal—and more to the point, they are becoming increasingly unequal. As figure 5.3C shows, profits for firms at the top are booming. It doesn't look like investment opportunities have fallen away for firms at the top. This has led to a lively debate around whether competition—which we would normally expect to level the playing field between leading firms and laggards as the leaders' profit margins regress to the mean and the laggards go out of business—has fallen.

The picture for profits looks similar to that for productivity. Figure 5.4 shows the results of an influential research project by

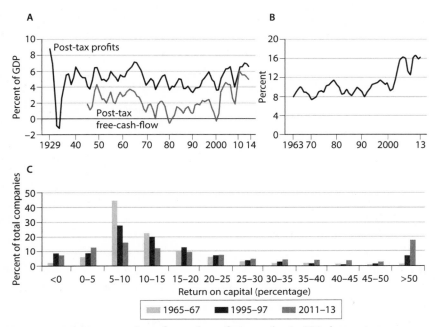

Figure 5.3. Measures of profits and profit spreads. A: US domestic corporate profits. B: US companies' global return on capital (excluding goodwill). C: Distribution of profits among US companies. Source: *Economist*, March 2016, https://www.economist.com/news/briefing/21695385-profits-are-too-high -america-needs-giant-dose-competition-too-much-good-thing.

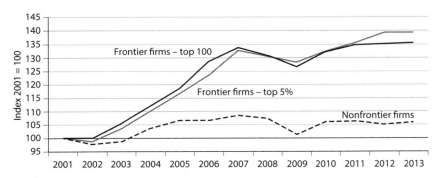

Figure 5.4. Labor productivity spreads. Data are value added per worker. "Frontier" are 100 or 5 percent globally most productive firms in each two-digit manufacturing or business services industry for a twenty-four-country sample from Orbis database. Source: Andrews, Criscuolo and Gal (2016), quoted in OECD, Economic Outlook, 2016, http://www.oecd.org/eco/outlook/OECD-Economic -Outlook-June-2016-promoting-productivity-and-equality.pdf.

Dan Andrews, Chiara Criscuolo, and Peter Gal of the OECD, who looked at how the productivity gap between the top firms in different industries and their competitors was developing, using accounting data from the OECD-ORBIS database. Of course, there has always been a gap—some firms have always done better than others—but that gap seems to have widened considerably, starting before the financial crisis.

The final fact surrounding secular stagnation is that the sustained decrease in productivity growth that we have seen in developed countries does not seem to be driven solely by lower investment. Labor productivity growth (see box 5.1 for a fuller explanation of labor productivity, profitability, and total factor productivity) can fall for two broad reasons. It can fall because investment falls, thus giving workers less capital to work with. Or it can fall because workers are working less effectively with whatever capital they have; this is called a fall in "multi-factor" or "total factor" productivity (TFP). Now, since the financial crisis, investment has fallen, but not by enough to account for all the loss in labor productivity. In fact, the bulk of the slowdown in productivity growth has been a decline in total factor productivity. Figure 5.5 shows, since about the mid-2000s, a fall in OECD multi-factor productivity growth.

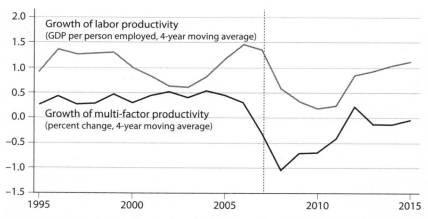

Figure 5.5. Growth of labor and multi-factor productivity (OECD, 1995–2016, four-year moving average). Source: The Conference Board Total Economy Database™, May 2017.

Box 5.1. Productivity and Profitability Explained

Productivity is "real" output per unit of input. Behind this seemingly innocuous definition lies a host of productivity measures and difficult conceptual issues, so it's worth reviewing some of them.

Let's start with explaining what we mean by "real" output. Take the UK railways. In 2010 there were 1.35 billion passenger journeys, with an average distance of 40 kilometers per journey. Thus UK rail companies provided 54.1 billion passenger kilometers (that is, the number of passengers times the average distance each passenger travelled). In 2015 that figure was 64.1 billion passenger kilometers. (If you were wondering why UK railways are so crowded, the 1986 figure was 30 billion, less than half that.)

How much did passengers pay? In 2010 they paid, on average, 12.2 pence per kilometer, rising to 14.4 pence per kilometer in 2015. So passenger revenues (passenger kilometers multiplied by price paid per passenger kilometer) went up by 6.8 percent per annum (from a revenue of £6.62bn in 2010 to £9.2bn in 2015).

It is clear, however, that the revenues went up for two reasons: (a) rail companies carried more passengers more kilometers, and (b) they charged passengers more. If you use the data above, you find out that the 6.8 percent rise in revenue was accounted for by a rise of 3.5 percent in passenger kilometers and 3.3 percent in fares.

So what's the right output measure for productivity purposes: passenger kilometers or revenues? *Productivity* analysts prefer to strip out the rise in prices, to get the change in volumes of output rather than its price. They do this since they are interested in the "productive efficiency" of the firm, that is, how readily it can convert input into output. The extent to which a firm can charge high or low prices is interesting, but it's the domain of *profitability* analysts, not productivity ones. See below.

This is where the notion of "real" output comes in. Statisticians call the revenue from output "nominal" output (that is, price times volume), but stripping out price changes (so you have only volume) is called "real" output. In this case then, the rise in "nominal" output was 6.8 percent, due to a rise in "real" output of 3.5 percent and a rise in prices of 3.3 percent.

This highlights a difference between productivity and profitability. Productivity compares output to input, and uses real output. Profitability compares output to costs, both being nominal measures. So if a firm raises its prices but does nothing else, its *profitability* has risen, but its *productivity* has remained the same. That's why productivity is often linked to efficiency: in this example, the efficiency of the firm has not changed at all. Indeed, it is perfectly possible for a firm to have very low productivity (or be very inefficient), but be highly profitable, as long as it has sufficient pricing power. And consumers know this; this is after all their complaint against most monopolies. Even though profitability is a perfectly interesting subject, it is a combination of both productivity and pricing power. Most productivity analysts confine themselves to productivity, especially since it's perfectly possible that productivity and profitability are negatively correlated.

Returning to our main theme, let's look at the measure of input. The rail network requires a host of inputs to produce the output: the trains, the track, the staff, the fuel, etc. So let's define two productivity measures. *Single-factor productivity* is real output per single unit. *Multi-factor productivity* (MFP) (confusingly, sometimes called "*total factor productivity*" [TFP]) is real output per multiple inputs. An example might help.

Consider agriculture (Pardey, Alston, and Chan-Kang 2013). Between 1961 and 2009, world population rose from 3 billion to 6.8 billion, a rise of 127 percent. How was everyone fed? In 1961 the world produced US$746bn worth of agricultural output and, controlling for inflation, that had risen to US$2,260bn in 2009, a rise in real output of 203 percent, far outpacing the rise in population. Now, it's easy to increase food output: you just bring more land under cultivation. Did that happen? No. In 1961 the world had 4.46 billion hectares under cultivation and in 2009 that had only slightly risen to 4.89 billion hectares, a rise of 10 percent. Thus world agricultural single-factor productivity—that is, real output per hectare—rose, remarkably, by 176 percent. Other measures of single-factor productivity rose too. Agricultural labor rose by 70 percent, as more people worked on the land (from 1.5 billion to 2.6 billion), but real output rose even faster, so real output per agricultural worker rose by 78 percent.

What about multi-factor productivity growth? Here analysts tend to choose the number of inputs they enter (the "multi" bit) depending somewhat on the industry and the output they are comparing. Consider then agriculture, where the real output is tons of produce. The typical inputs to a farm would be (a) land, (b) labor: the number of people working on the farm, (c) capital: machines used on the farm, and (d) intermediates: inputs used up in production, for example, seed, fertilizer, feed for animals, etc. Now, it's perfectly possible that agricultural output went up because of more land, more labor, farmers using more tractors, or maybe better fertilizer. Thus multi-factor productivity in this case is real output per unit of land, labor, capital, and intermediates (we'll explain how to combine these inputs in a moment). If then there is growth in farm output over and above that accounted for by all these inputs, then the inputs themselves are being better utilized. Thus multi-factor productivity growth measures not how many more inputs the farm is using, but rather how well the farm is combining the inputs.

Multi-factor productivity growth is then a very useful indicator for (at least) two reasons. First, it helps better understand single-factor productivity growth. If output per worker or per hectare has risen, then we naturally want to understand whether this is because those workers had more tractors (capital) and/or more fertilizer (intermediates) to work with.

Second, multi-factor productivity growth helps us understand where growth is coming from. Suppose the economy consists of farms and tractor manufacturers. Suppose a farmer claims productivity (output per laborer) on the farm has doubled. If the farmer has only brought in more tractors (not changing other inputs), then multi-factor productivity growth will have stayed the same and any productivity growth in the economy as a whole will be due to improvements in the tractor industry. If the farmer has improved the efficiency of operations, maybe innovated in crop rotation or improved work practices on the farm, then multi-factor productivity growth in farming will have risen. As a matter of fact, researchers have found that world agricultural multi-factor productivity growth is about 45 percent of productivity growth over this long period. That is, improved machines and fertilizer account for about 55 percent of productivity growth and better farming practices 45 percent of it. Those improved farming practices are particularly concentrated in the re-organization of collective farms in the ex–Soviet Union and China.

A few final points. First, in most industries or services, land is not typically a varying input, so analysis of single-factor productivity tends to be real output per worker. Second, the input of workers can vary by person and the hours they work, so single-factor productivity analysts looking at labor productivity often work with output per worker, or output per worker-hour. Third, in calculating multi-factor productivity growth, inputs are combined using their payment shares in total costs, so a very labor-intensive process would give labor a high weight and capital a low weight (the economic ratio-nale for this is set out in Solow 1957). These payment-share combined inputs are called input services, so for example, capital services are combined inputs of capital assets like ICT, buildings, and vehicles, weighted by their payments.

Finally, many statistical agencies calculate real output in two ways, including intermediates, called real gross output (number of tons of wheat, say), and excluding intermediates, called real value added (wheat output excluding the intermediates). Thus gross output MFP is typically real gross output per input of labor, capital, and intermediates, and value added MFP is real value added per input of labor and capital. (The former turns out to be a [complicated] weighted average of the latter, the weights called Domar-Hulten weighting, after two brilliant papers that derived them by Evesy Domar and Charles Hulten [Domar 1961; Hulten 1978].)

An Intangible Explanation

A good explanation for secular stagnation should ideally explain the following four facts:

1. A fall in measured investment at the same time as a fall in interest rates
2. Strong profits
3. Increasingly unequal productivity and profits
4. Weak total factor productivity growth

Can intangibles explain any of this? The rest of this chapter suggests it might have some part to play, for the following reasons.

First, in the earlier chapters of this book we presented evidence that the nature of investments that businesses are making is shifting from tangibles to intangibles, that in several developed countries intangible investments now dominate, and that these intangible investments are poorly measured in national accounts. Maybe then, at least in part, investment seems low because we are not measuring all the investment that is being made.

Second, in chapter 4 we also saw that intangibles had particular economic properties. One was the ability of firms to scale intangibles over their operations. Maybe then firms are investing in intangibles and scaling up their sales: think Uber, Google, and

Microsoft. They can achieve this giant scale with relatively little employment. So their productivity (revenue per employee) rises, perhaps massively. And since they have relatively little tangible capital, which is what is measured, their revenue per unit of capital employed also rises massively. The successful firms that achieve great scale, therefore, become leaders, breaking away from the laggards in the industry that haven't managed to scale up as much (at least not at the moment).

Third, another property of intangibles is spillovers. A firm cannot use its rivals' factories but can potentially use its rivals' designs, organization structure, or ideas. This has two implications. On the one hand, if firms reduce their investment in intangibles, we might expect fewer spillovers to be generated. Since spillovers are picked up in TFP growth, we would expect TFP to fall. The second issue is that, in a world where it is harder for a given firm to be sure it will appropriate the benefits of its investments, it may choose to invest less.

We'll go through these possibilities one by one.

Mismeasurement: Intangibles and Apparently Low Investment

As we saw in chapter 2, intangible investment in countries like the United States and the UK now exceeds tangible investment. Much of it is not included in national accounts—and, therefore, is not included in the figures used to demonstrate secular stagnation. So does investment seem low because we are simply not counting it right? Or to put it another way, could the world's economy be growing much faster than we thought because we've been failing to include the value of investment in intangibles?

The effect of counting these investments on the investment/GDP ratio depends on a number of things. First, it depends on the extent to which national statistical offices are counting intangibles. As we saw in chapter 3, statistical offices are increasingly counting the intangible assets set out in table 3.1. Second, when we include new investment in national accounts we also raise GDP, so the effect on the investment/GDP ratio is potentially ambiguous.

As figure 5.6 shows, it turns out that the effect of including previously unmeasured intangibles is to raise the investment/GDP ratio, but not to greatly affect its trend, partly because of the effects above and the relatively short time period. So the undercount does not appear to greatly affect the trend, at least not since the Great Recession. (The undercount in investment also affects growth of GDP and might potentially mean GDP appears to be growing more slowly. In the appendix we show this is not, in fact, a big effect.)

Profits and Productivity Differences: Scale, Spillovers, and the Incentives to Invest

The effect of intangibles on investment goes beyond issues of measurement. As we saw in chapter 4, intangible investments are unusual in a number of ways. It seems plausible that these unusual characteristics could have an effect on businesses' incentives to invest. Of particular relevance here is the fact that intangibles are *scalable* and exhibit *spillovers*. (A *scalable* asset, like Uber's software or Starbucks's brand, can be scaled across a very large number of locations. Firms that are good at exploiting *spillovers*—for example, because they are good at open innovation—can benefit not only from their own intangible investments but also from

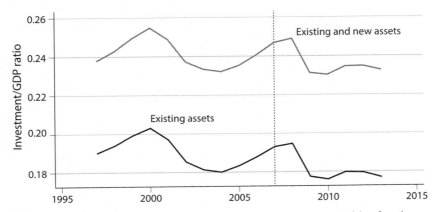

Figure 5.6. Investment/GDP ratios with and without new intangibles for eleven European Union countries and the United States. Data are whole-economy; GDP is adjusted to include or exclude new assets investment. Source: authors' calculations based on the INTAN-Invest database (www.intan-invest.net).

those of other firms. Think of how Apple learned to develop the iPhone from the failures of early smartphone makers like Nokia and Ericsson and from decades of government research.)

Scalability increases the appeal of intangible investment. If a firm has confidence it can scale an investment across a large volume of business, the incentive to invest increases. If a firm genuinely believes its latest project could be the next Google PageRank or the next blockbuster drug, it would be justified in betting the farm on it because the returns on these sorts of scalable intangible investments are so high.

We would expect the presence of spillovers to reduce the willingness of the average firm to invest. Consider the case study of EMI and the CT scanner we discussed in chapter 4. Most firms would be very wary of following in the footsteps of EMI, investing millions in a radical new product only to see competitors walk away with the gains (and indeed EMI themselves might not have made the decision to invest in the CT scanner had they not received considerable government R&D subsidies to do so).

Spillovers may discourage the average firm from investing in intangibles, but of course, not all firms are average. As we discussed in chapter 4, the benefits of intangibles do not spill over entirely at random. Indeed, management gurus have studied the art of appropriating the spillovers of other firms' investments and have even given it a name: open innovation. Like any art, some are better at open innovation than others. A glance at the business news reveals that some companies have a reputation for being especially good at absorbing and exploiting good ideas from elsewhere. (An extreme example is Rocket Internet, a German incubator of e-commerce businesses, which systematically identifies good online ideas and executes them faster and better than their originators.)

These characteristics affect firm performance: firms that can create and manipulate intangibles can reap outsize benefits. In a world where intangible investment is very important, we would expect to see the "best" firms—that is, those firms that (a) own valuable scalable intangibles and (b) are good at exacting the spillovers from other businesses—being highly productive and profitable, and their competitors losing out.

Now, as we saw in figure 5.4, the gap between the most and least productive firms is widening. One popular explanation for this is that perhaps competition policy is becoming weaker, allowing powerful incumbents to protect their market position. But it's not clear that there has been any sort of worldwide weakening of competition policy; indeed, most governments seem to take competition policy quite seriously. So might it be that scalability and spillovers have created the possibility for leading firms to pull away from their competition and entrench their advantages?

The idea that intangible-rich firms are scaling up dramatically seems plausible on an anecdotal basis: Uber, Google, Microsoft, and so on. To really nail it down, we would need to collect intangible investment data for each firm and see how that data correlates with inequality of profitability. But accounting conventions don't let us do this yet (see chapter 10). In the meantime, we can look at the industry level, where we do have data. Now, if firms are taking advantage of intangibles, then they will be best placed to do so in industries where intangibles are important. For example, public water and sewerage utilities could potentially scale up using intangibles, but there's probably much less scope for doing so than in intangible-intensive industries like pharmaceuticals or financial services. Thus we would expect larger rises in the productivity spread in industries and countries that are more intangible-intensive. Figure 5.7 tests this out.

Figure 5.7 shows the relationship between the change in the productivity spread (the gap in productivity between the best and worst firms), averaged from 2001–7 (we stopped before the financial crisis years) and intangible intensity in 2001. The panels show manufacturing and marketing services, respectively. So, for example, in manufacturing, Italy and Austria don't invest very much in intangibles and have had only a small rise in the manufacturing productivity spread. By contrast, the UK, Sweden, and France do invest a lot in intangibles and have had a much larger rise in the productivity spread. The same goes for services.

What about profits? We do not have direct data on profits, but if we are willing to use R&D and/or patents as a proxy for intangibles, there is more evidence that supports this view of productivity spread. The economists Bronwyn Hall, Adam Jaffe, and

Manuel Trajtenberg (2005) collected financial and R&D data on a panel of US firms and linked this data with their patents and how heavily cited the patents were. They found strong correlations, controlling for a range of other factors, between the stock market value of a firm and its R&D spending and its well-cited patents. Stock market values may not be the best measure of company prospects, but this does suggest a link between company performance and (one dimension of) intangibles, which is consistent with the idea that an intangible-heavy firm can outperform its rivals.[3]

So, productivity spreads rose a lot in countries where industries invest a lot in intangibles. Clearly more work on this question is needed but if the story holds up under more research, then the rise in intangible investment might be part of the explanation for the rise in the performance/productivity spread. This, in turn, could account for a divergence in investment behavior: leading firms, which are confident of their ability to create scalable assets

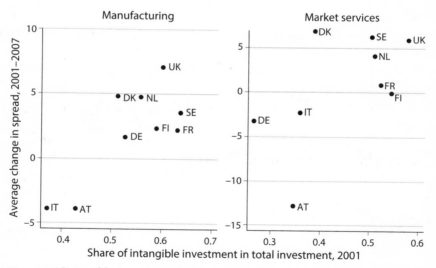

Figure 5.7. Intangible intensity and change in productivity spread. Change in productivity spread is change in top less bottom quartile of sector labor productivity between 2001 and 2007. Countries are Austria (AT), Denmark (DK), Finland (FI), France (FR), Germany (DE), Italy (IT), Netherlands (NL), Sweden (SE), UK (UK). Source: authors' calculations based on productivity spread data from ESSLait (https://ec.europa.eu/eurostat/cros/content/impact-analysis_en) and the INTAN-Invest database (www.intan-invest.net).

and to appropriate most of their benefits, will continue to invest (and enjoy a high rate of return on those investments); but laggard firms, expecting low private returns from their investments, will not. In a world where there are a few leaders and many laggards, the net effect of this could be lower aggregate rates of investment, combined with high returns on those investments that do get made.

Spillovers: Intangibles and Slowing TFP Growth
A Lower Pace of Intangible Growth?

While the mismeasurement of intangible investment does not explain most of the investment problem, it may help account for one aspect of the secular stagnation puzzle: poor TFP performance in recent years.

As figure 2.4 showed, intangible investment has grown steadily over the past decades in most countries. Further, both intangible and tangible investment slowed after 2007. Now, while it has recovered, the growth rate is not as fast. Figure 5.8 shows that, as a result, the growth rate of the capital services of intangibles and also of R&D has slowed since 2007. (The capital services accounts for both investment and depreciation and so is a better measure of the flow of intangible services than just investment; see the appendix to chapter 3 and box 5.1.)

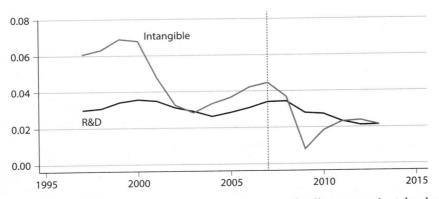

Figure 5.8. Intangibles and R&D capital services growth: all countries (weighted using GDP at PPP). Source: authors' calculations from INTAN-Invest (www.intan-invest.net) and SPINTAN (www.spintan.net) databases.

Consider then two of the economic features of intangibles: spillovers and scalability. Suppose a firm invests in some tangibles and some intangibles. It should reap the benefits of both, but from intangibles it should get higher productivity, since it may be able to *scale* up those intangibles. In addition to that, if the benefits of intangibles spill over, other firms should be able to raise their productivity. We would expect these additional effects to show up in total factor productivity.[4] The flip side of this is that if intangible capital growth falls, as we have seen in figure 5.8, then total factor productivity growth should fall as well.

Figure 5.9 takes a look at this, plotting TFP growth and intangible capital growth for ten countries before and after the Great Recession. Before the Great Recession, most of the countries were to the top right of the figure, indicating positive growth in intangibles and positive TFP. After 2008, all the countries except Spain moved down to the bottom left as their intangible growth and their TFP both fell. The upward-sloping line of best fit summarizes this: there

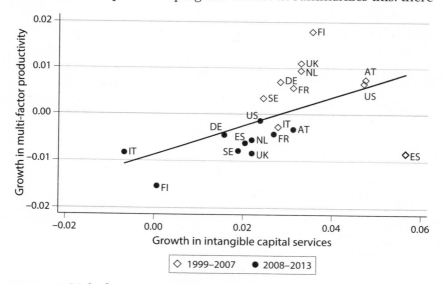

Figure 5.9. Multi-factor productivity and intangible capital services growth. The figure shows average annual growth rates between 1999 and 2007 (open diamonds) and 2008 and 2013 (closed circles). Data are whole-economy. Countries are Austria (AT), Finland (FI), France (FR), Germany (DE), Italy (IT), Netherlands (NL), Spain (ES), Sweden (SE), UK (UK), USA (US). Source: authors' calculations from the INTAN-invest (www.intan-invest.net) and SPINTAN (www.spintan.net) databases.

does seem to be an association between the slowdown in intangible capital growth and the slowdown in TFP growth. A more sophisticated investigation involving more years confirms this, and Figure 5.10 confirms a similar pattern for R&D capital growth.

Granted, both pictures are noisy and other things might be going on, which future research will have to explore. But the figure suggests that the TFP slowdown might be in part accounted for by the intangible slowdown.

Are Intangibles Generating Fewer Spillovers?

Another reason why there might be slower TFP growth is that intangibles are somehow generating fewer spillovers. This is inevitably rather speculative, but let us consider why it might be.

One possibility is that lagging firms have become less effective at absorbing spillovers. If the benefits of intangible spillovers accrued to firms at random, this would have no obvious effect on firm profitability. Any firm would have as good a chance of ser-

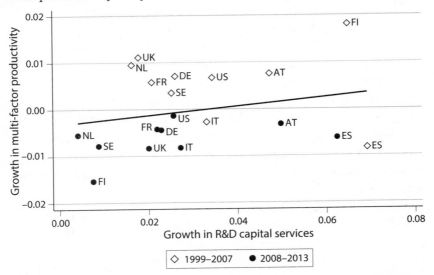

Figure 5.10. Multi-factor productivity and R&D capital services growth. The figure shows average annual growth rates between 1999 and 2007 (open diamonds) and 2008 and 2013 (closed circles). Data are whole-economy. Countries are Austria (AT), Finland (FI), France (FR), Germany (DE), Italy (IT), Netherlands (NL), Spain (ES), Sweden (SE), UK (UK), USA (US). Source: authors' calculations from the INTAN-Invest (www.intan-invest.net) and SPINTAN (www.spintan.net) databases.

endipitously gaining from another firm's intangible investments as it would have of losing the returns of its own investments to a rival. But even a casual acquaintance with the business press or with management studies research suggests that the world does not work like that.

Certain businesses are thought to be unusually good at benefiting from other firms' ideas. Google's ability to purchase, grow, and promote the Android operating system, which Steve Jobs believed was a rip-off of Apple's iOS, is a famous example of this. But it is a trend we see throughout the economy: management gurus offer advice on "open innovation" and "fast followership." People often observe that while the early bird catches the worm, it is the second mouse that gets the cheese. (Economist and blogger Chris Dillow made the point that the incentive to be a "fast follower" might be higher in a sector experiencing a lot of technological progress: waiting not only allows a firm to benefit from the spillovers of the first firm to invest, but it might also benefit from falling prices for investments like software.)[5]

The scalability and synergies of intangible investments also play a role in making leading firms more willing to invest. Leaders are more likely to be larger and to grow faster and, therefore, to be able to take advantage of the scalability of intangibles. (Consider how Starbucks can deploy its brand and operating procedures in every new café it opens without more intangible investment.) They are more likely to possess other valuable intangibles that are synergistic with new investments they make. (Consider how Apple's preexisting reputation for attractive, intuitive products made consumers willing to try the iPhone, even though previous smartphones had been hard to use.)

Even if lagging firms are investing less, an overall fall in investment depends on the composition of the industry. If only a few leading firms were able to internalize the benefits of intangible investment, those firms could, in theory, increase their levels of investment so much that they would be taking up the slack for all the laggards—only a few firms would invest, but those that did would invest massively. For overall investment and growth to be reduced, the level of investment by the leading firms that are still happy to invest in intangibles would have to be insufficient to fully make up for the putative shortfall in investment by the laggards.

There are a couple of reasons why this shortfall may occur. The first comes back to our earlier discussion about the fundamental characteristics of intangibles as investments generally. Even a big firm with many complementary assets that is good at open innovation is likely to struggle to capture the benefits of some intangible investments. A firm like Tesla Motors that makes many large long-term R&D and design investments (as well as big tangible investments) is considered to be unusual by media and stock market analysts alike.

The second possibility is that perhaps even when a leading firm is theoretically willing to make big intangible investments, management attention and the difficulty of delivery act as a bottleneck. Consider Amazon, a market leader with overwhelming scale and lots of valuable intangibles. It has a reputation for being very good at execution and for adopting the ideas of challenger firms and beating them at their own game, and it is willing to invest and defer profitability for the long term. Amazon has certainly invested heavily to develop new businesses, expanding from its original bookselling business to general retail, computer hardware, and cloud computing and is now moving into groceries. But these investments have taken time. Perhaps the need to focus management attention on so many priorities limits the speed with which individual firms, even if they are market leaders, can make big strategic investments. Certainly the idea of managerial focus, and of not biting off more than a company can chew, is popular in management books and business journalism. If this is true, the perceived need to focus could limit total investment in sectors where only a few companies felt confident of reaping the rewards of investment.

Finally, we should consider the possibility that the true nature of intangible investment has changed. Maybe it conceals rent-seeking activities that superficially look like they increase productivity but actually do nothing of the sort.

Common sense tells us that, tangible or intangible, some investments that firms make are good and some are bad: that's the nature of business. Over time, and at the level of the economy as a whole, the good investments and the bad investments balance out, and the marginal investment of an average company delivers a market rate of return.

Of course, the private returns to the firm making an investment will not always be the same as the wider returns to the economy as a whole. When an intangible investment has beneficial spillovers, as we discussed above, the social rate of return exceeds the private rate, and other firms benefit too, just as Samsung and HTC benefited when Apple invested enough to convert mobile phone users to smartphones.

But it is also possible to imagine investments, intangible and tangible, that produce little or no social return; the private return they generate for the firm that makes them is the result of shifting value that had already been created somewhere else.

Consider two businesses that have been in the news recently: Mylan, a drug company that sells the EpiPen, and Uber, the global ride-sharing business. As we mentioned in chapter 4, the success of the EpiPen depends on a set of interlocking intangible investments: its design has been approved by drug regulators; its name (which is protected) is recognizable; first aiders are trained in how to use it; and it has sales and marketing channels into important customers, like schools (some of which are supported by laws, like the US Schools Access to Emergency Epinephrine Act of 2013). There is also a darker side to the EpiPen's success: EpiPen's makers have sued the makers of competing products, delaying or preventing their access to the market. Some of the things that make the EpiPen profitable create a social benefit as well as a private one: the fact that first aiders know how to use an EpiPen, or that many anaphylaxis sufferers know the EpiPen brand, is good both for consumers and for Mylan. But it is less clear whether lawsuits against competing products, or the difficulty of the process for approving new autoinjectors, are in anyone's interest but Mylan's.

Uber raises similar questions. One of the valuable intangibles that Uber profits from, alongside its software and its brand, is its large network of driver-partners. (A sign of the value of these networks to Uber is the fact that when Uber opens in a new city, it sometimes offers generous deals and premia to new drivers to sign up with the service.) Now, in some respects, this intangible asset provides a public as well as a private benefit: building a network of quality-assured, networked drivers is a valuable service for Uber's customers. But critics have argued that at least in some respects, Uber's "investment" in its driver network is a zero-sum game: the purpose of maintaining a network of drivers, they argue, is to allow Uber to get the benefits of hiring a lot of staff without having to comply with employment laws or minimum wages. To this extent, Uber's investment in a network of drivers is valuable to Uber at least in part not because it creates new value but because it takes value away from drivers (who would otherwise benefit from minimum wages, etc.).

The allegations against Mylan and Uber are that some of their intangible investments do no good for the economy as a whole, but instead are about slicing the existing economic pie to the exclusive benefit of the intangible investor.

We can think of other examples of this. Consider two companies, GoodCo and BadCo, both of which spend money on legal fees and business restructuring costs to set up a new subsidiary—an example of an organizational development investment. The purpose of GoodCo's subsidiary is to deliver a new, profitable service to customers; it will be a positive private return to the firm and also a positive social return (that is to say, GDP will go up).

But suppose that the sole purpose of BadCo's subsidiary is to help the company avoid tax. In this case, there would be a private return to BadCo in the form of a lower tax bill, but no social return, and no increase in GDP; the firm's private return is just the appropriation of money that would have otherwise gone to the government.

When this sort of rent-seeking spending is made, and if it is counted as investment, then investment would increase. Perhaps the position of the leader will also rise, but total output would not increase at all. This would manifest itself as a decline in TFP, the residual between the contribution of labor and investment to growth and the observed rate of growth itself. To the extent that there are spillovers, the spillovers are negative.

We can think of other sorts of spending like this: so-called blocking patents developed solely to keep rivals out of a particular field of research; or advertising campaigns that are only about stealing market share from other firms (although, as we saw in chapter 4, the evidence is that most advertising does not do this). Intangible investment might have other negative externalities that are harder to measure: it is a long-standing criticism of capitalism that following bureaucratic rules is dehumanizing and depressing for workers—it is plausible that some types of organizational development investment might make workers less happy by removing their autonomy. Although the opposite case could also be made: some organizational development investment, like lean processes, are predicated on giving workers greater agency rather than less. Some tangible investment may also generate limited social returns: consider the fiber-optic cables installed by high-frequency trading firms for the sole purpose of shaving fractions of microseconds off trading times (described vividly by John Kay 2016). And not all money spent on rent-seeking generates an intangible investment, at least not in the main methodologies used to measure intangibles. But it does seem that rent-seeking or zero-sum investments are more common among intangible investments than among tangibles.

This could have a bearing on investment and productivity figures. It is possible that the increase in intangible investment is concealing a rise in rent-seeking investments that do not increase GDP. This would not explain the fall-off in investment that has been observed in the economy, but it would help explain the fall-off in productivity and in TFP. It is conceivable that in a poorly governed economy, the amount of intangibles whose purpose is to attract rents goes up. So for any given level of intangible investment, output would be lower, and TFP would fall. This risk provides a good reason for policymakers to guard against rent-seeking in an increasingly intangible economy.

There is also the possibility that the rise of intangible investment may be encouraging more rent-seeking, which may be increasing the gap between leaders and laggards that we discussed earlier.

A paper by James Bessen specifically asks whether the gap between leaders and laggards among US nonfinancial businesses has been caused by increasing intangible investment or by greater rent-seeking by leading firms. Bessen looks at the relationship between regulation in industries (measured by an index of regulation and by political lobbying expenditures) and the valuations of public companies. He concludes that while a significant portion of the increase in stock prices since 1980 has been caused by intangibles (measured by R&D), spending on regulation and lobbying has an even stronger effect on valuations (Bessen 2016).

Now, perhaps the *contestedness* of intangible assets that we discussed in chapter 4 encourages firms to spend money asserting or protecting their claims to them. In recent years, an increasing proportion of lobbying in the United States has been carried out by technology firms; typically, these firms are lobbying in relation to valuable intangible assets they own, such as Google's right to use its valuable data and software in particular ways, or Uber's and AirBnB's rights in respect of their valuable networks of drivers and hosts. The rewards for successful lobbying are very high: all these intangible assets are highly scalable and are intrinsic to their owners' business models. They are also what make their owners leaders rather than laggards—which in itself may discourage laggard competitors from investing in the future.

So, it is not that intangible spending is mismeasured and is really lobbying spending. It is, perhaps, that we have entered a phase where the transition to an intangible economy is requiring a new set of institutions to resolve the inherent contestedness of intangible assets.

An optimistic interpretation of this is that the legal and institutional structures behind a transformation to an intangible-intensive economy are being worked out and that until they are, there will be a disproportionate incentive for firms to spend more on rent-seeking relating to intangible investment. For example, as spillovers and scale effects become more important, existing tax and competition and IP rules get tested to destruction, requiring lobbying, legal arguments, and institutional reboots. This adjustment to a new type of economy will need a lot of spending by firms and governments that is not immediately productive. Thus a given dollar of business intangible spending has less productivity-raising effect. A more troubling interpretation is that these types of rent-seeking are linked to the inherent characteristics of intangibles, in particular their contestedness: this would imply that TFP growth will continue to be low until governments learn to do a much better job of preventing rent-seeking and designing the institutions an intangible economy needs.

Conclusion: An Intangible Role in Secular Stagnation

Secular stagnation is clearly a complex phenomenon, with a wide range of possible causes. We have identified four possible ways that the long-term shift from tangible to intangible investment could be causing or exacerbating it.

First, mismeasurement helps explain a little of the puzzle. The inclusion of intangible investment, which has been rising, shows that the investment drought is not as bad as it seems. It also marginally improves GDP growth. But the bulk of the secular stagnation problem remains.

Second, it looks like the scalability of intangibles is allowing very large and very profitable firms to emerge. These firms may also be better placed to appropriate the spillovers of other firms' intangible investments. That raises the productivity and profits gap between the leaders and the laggards and simultaneously decreases the incentives to invest for laggard firms. This could help explain how low levels of investment coexist with high rates of return on the investments that do get made.

Third, after the Great Recession, the pace of intangible capital building has slowed. This might throw off fewer spillovers, thus causing firms to scale up by less than beforehand and slowing total factor productivity. There is some evidence to support this: roughly the largest TFP growth slowdowns are in the countries with the largest R&D and intangible capital growth slowdowns.

Last, and more speculatively, lagging firms may be less able to absorb spillovers from leaders, perhaps because leading firms are much more able to exploit the synergies between different intangible types than the laggards. Or perhaps the economy is in a phase where the transition to an intangible economy, which requires a new set of institutions to resolve the inherent contestedness of intangible assets, has skewed investment toward lobbying, legal arguments, and institutional reboots, none of which are immediately productive.

Appendix: Effect of Unmeasured Intangibles on GDP Growth

The effect of unmeasured intangibles on GDP growth is a bit complicated. Since measured GDP levels include measured investment, then GDP growth includes measured investment growth (multiplied by the share of investment in GDP). So mismeasurement only occurs if the omitted investment is growing faster or slower than GDP growth: if they are growing at exactly the same rate, we get the level of GDP wrong, but the growth rate is right. Thus if the omitted intangible investment grows faster than measured GDP growth, measured GDP growth is too low, which can look just like secular stagnation (in the sense of low growth). Figure 5.11 sets out the net effect on growth, for all eleven EU countries and the United States, which turns out to be rather small: GDP growth since 2008 is very slightly higher, but only by fractions of a percentage point per year.

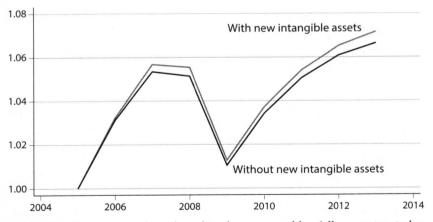

Figure 5.11. Output growth with and without intangibles (all countries; index to 2005 = 1). Source: authors' calculations from the SPINTAN database (www .spintan.net).

6

Intangibles and the Rise of Inequality

This chapter suggests a relationship between the increasing importance of intangible investment and the widely documented rise in the many types of inequality seen in recent decades in many developed countries. We argue that the rise of intangibles might be expected to increase inequality both of wealth and income. Increasingly intangible-intensive firms will need better staff to create synergy with their other intangible assets: better managers, better movie stars, better sports heroes. Firms will screen them more thoroughly and pay them more handsomely. As for wealth inequality, the spillovers from intangibles make living in cities even more attractive, forcing up housing prices and wealth for those fortunate enough to own. More speculatively, we suggest that the cultural characteristics required to succeed in an intangible economy may help explain the socio-economic tensions that underlie populist politics in many developed countries.

One of the most debated economic issues of the 2010s is inequality. According to the painstaking work of Thomas Piketty, Anthony Atkinson, and others, the rich (in terms of earnings and wealth) have over the past few decades been getting richer, and the poor poorer. And other dimensions of inequality have become more salient: inequalities between generations, between different places, and between elites and those who feel alienated and disrespected by modern society. Perhaps this multidimensional element to inequality is why it has such huge public resonance. The news provides a steady stream of stories about billionaires buying £150-million apartments in London and Manhattan, juxtaposed with reports of people in "left-behind" communities falling prey to opiate addiction, embracing political extremism, and dying young.

Many reasons have been proposed for why inequality is increasing, from new technologies to neoliberal politics to globalization. But as we've seen in the past few chapters, there is a deep and long-term shift going on in the nature of developed economies because of the rise of intangibles. Might this also have contributed to levels and different dimensions of inequality that we see in today's societies?

In this chapter, we'll argue that the growth of the new intangible economy does indeed help explain the types of inequality we're currently seeing.

Inequality: A Field Guide

Economic inequality is a hydra-headed beast. It's helpful to differentiate between a few different sorts of inequality that crop up in the public debate, and these are set out in box 6.1.

Box 6.1. Measures of Inequality

To clarify the types of inequality it's helpful to distinguish between two economic concepts: *income* and *wealth*. *Incomes* are earned by labor and by capital (an asset) and are a "flow." The incomes of labor consist mostly of earnings. Incomes of capital are rental payments and dividends, both being flows of payments received over a time period. *Wealth* is the value of assets/capital owned, which is a "stock." For households, wealth is typically a house; for businesses, the tangible and intangible assets owned and used in production. The flow is computed from the stock by means of a rate of return: your capital income is your wealth times the rate of return you are earning on wealth. You can think of your labor income flow in terms of rates of return as well: it's the rate of return on your stock of "human capital." Wealth capital is typically the result of saving and inheritance, human capital of education and talent. Data show that in developed economies labor income is typically about 65–75 percent of total national income (also called GDP), the rest being capital income. The annual return on wealth is around 6–8 percent, so total wealth is about 400 percent of GDP/total income. How can wealth be so much larger than GDP? Wealth is a stock and is accumulated over potentially many years of building assets. GDP/income is an annual flow. Finally, as the Institute for Fiscal Studies notes, wealth inequality is much higher than income inequality. The wealthiest 10 percent of households hold 50 percent of the wealth. The least wealthy 25 percent of households hold almost no wealth at all. The Gini coefficient, which is a summary measure for how unequal a distribution is, ranges from 0 to 1, where a measure of 0 is equality and 1 is where only one person accounts for the entire measure. The Gini coefficient is 0.64 for wealth and 0.34 for net income (Crawford, Innes, and O'Dea 2016).

The first and most obvious type is *inequality of earnings*. In the UK and the United States, there was a big rise in earnings inequality in the 1980s and 1990s; inequality has remained at this higher level since. Developed countries have also seen a rise in the income gap between educated and poorly educated workers since the 1980s. Figure 6.1, showing data for the United States, is representative of many, but not all, countries: in 1979, college-educated men earned around $17,000 more than those with only high school educations; by 2012 that gap was almost $35,000 (adjusted for inflation).

But this is not just a case of graduates doing well. The power of the Occupy Wall Street movement's slogan "the One Per Cent" was that it crystallized in people's minds that income inequality today seems to be fractal. The incomes of the richest 1 percent, the richest 0.1 percent, and the richest 0.01 percent have risen by even more dizzying levels (see below). And as development economist Branko Milanović pointed out, this is part of a global phenomenon: over the past two decades, incomes have risen sharply for most people in the world, in particular people in big, once-

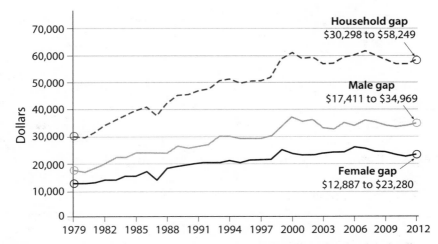

Figure 6.1. Inequality in median annual earnings between high school and college graduates, United States (in constant 2012 dollars). Source: Autor (2014).

poor countries like China (Milanović 2005). The world's richest people have done well too. But one big group has not done as well: people between the seventy-fifth and ninety-fifth percentiles of world income—which represents a lot of the traditional working class in developed countries.

Thomas Piketty's blockbuster book added another flavor of inequality to the mix: *inequality of wealth.* One of the many dazzling features of Piketty's *Capital in the Twenty-First Century* (2014) and the research that underpins it was the light it cast on the wealth of the very rich, which is often hard to measure. It will not come as a huge surprise that this showed that the wealth of the richest in countries like the United States, the UK, and France has increased dramatically in the past few decades.

Three other sorts of inequality seem to matter to people too, even if they have received less attention in the mainstream economics debate on inequality.

First, there has been a rise in *inequality between the generations.* In the UK the picture is particularly stark and well documented in the David Willetts's influential book *The Pinch* (2010). For example, as figure 6.2 shows, in the 1950s the poor were overwhelmingly pensioners (along with relatively small numbers of unemployed and low-wage earners). Now the situation is completely changed. Pensioners, particularly in wealth terms, are some of the richest people in the country, while the ranks of the poor are dominated by low-paid workers.

Another dimension is rising *inequality of place*, even within developed countries. There is nothing new about industrial decline making once rich places poorer, least of all in Britain, where it was a problem for most of the twentieth century. Nor is there anything new about certain places being hotbeds of economic activity. But events like the 2016 Brexit referendum in the UK, where thriving cities voted one way and the rest of England another, and the election of Donald Trump on the back of a surge of votes from so-called left-behind communities away from America's prosperous coastal cities, make this divide more salient.

The divides revealed by the UK's Brexit referendum and the election of Donald Trump also point to a different form of inequality, one that economists typically focus on little, if at all. That is *inequality of esteem*. The reasons for the rise of populist political movements around the world, from the supporters of Donald Trump in the United States, to Britain's United Kingdom Independence Party, to the Five Star Movement in Italy are many and varied. But one

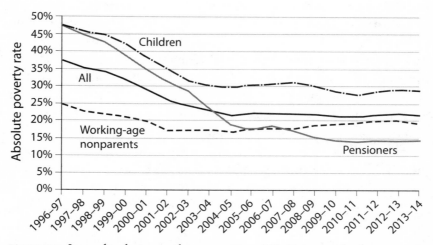

Figure 6.2. Inequality between the generations, UK. Data are absolute poverty rates after housing costs (share of group below 60 percent of real median income in 2010–11). Source: Data from Institute for Fiscal Studies, Belfield et al. 2014, https://www.ifs.org.uk/uploads/publications/comms/R107.pdf.

thing many of their supporters repeatedly invoke is their anger at being patronized and disrespected by what they perceive as an out-of-touch, technocratic, even degenerate Establishment. Some of the supporters of these movements are undoubtedly also poor in income or wealth terms—but not all. The inequality that fuels their anger seems to be as much about regard as about money.

The Standard Explanations

Economists have developed a number of explanations for the rise in inequality. Three of the most prominent are the rise of modern technology, the rise of globalization, and the basic tendency for wealth to accumulate.

The first story holds that inequality is the result of *improvements in technology*. New technologies replace workers, which means wages fall and profits rise. Modern versions of this story focus on the big technological trend of our age: computers and information technology. In the workplace, so the story runs, computers are particularly good at replacing routine tasks: switchboards in telephone exchanges, repetitive tasks on production lines, giving out money at a bank. And in the last years computers have gotten even smarter: issuing boarding passes, checking you out at supermarkets, and answering routine questions over the phone. As these computers have gotten cheaper and cheaper, it's become more and more worthwhile for firms to replace low-skilled workers with computers. Demand for those workers has fallen and so, therefore, have their wages.

More recently, Erik Brynjolfsson and Andrew McAfee (2014) have warned that, because of the speed with which information technology improves, computers may start replacing humans much faster than we are used to. This "race against the machine" or "rise of the robots" could be expected to make poorer workers redundant, to the benefit of rich capitalists.

It's a story as old as the industrial revolution itself, and back then it gave rise to the mythical figures of Ned Ludd and Captain Swing. Modern economists, displaying an admirable flair for taking something exciting and giving it a boring name, called this trend "skills-biased technical change." Labor market economists, particularly Martin Goos, Alan Manning, and David Autor, have suggested a twist on this story that computers are especially good at replacing routine tasks. The twist is that computers don't replace high-paid knowledge workers, but they are not necessarily replacing the low-paid either. The reason is that many currently low-paid tasks are distinctly nonroutine: waiting on a table, cleaning a bath, or looking after the elderly. Rather, the routine tasks that computers are good at tend to be middle-income jobs, and so they "hollow out" the labor market by replacing middle-income workers (Goos and Manning 2007; Autor 2013).

The second explanation for modern-day inequality focuses on *trade*. It was vividly described by the economist Richard Freeman as "The Great Doubling" (2007). As he points out, in the 1980s, before the collapse of Soviet communism and before China and India moved to market reforms, the global trading economy consisted of around 1.46 billion workers in the developed countries and some parts of Latin America, Asia, and Africa.

Then, more or less all at once in the 1990s, came The Great Doubling. China, India, and the ex-Soviet bloc joined the global economy. This change increased the size of the global labor pool to around 2.93 billion workers, almost exactly doubling it. When the supply of something increases, all other things being equal, economists expect the price to fall.

And so it came to pass: these new entrants to the global labor market were employed producing goods that require relatively little skill (textiles and bulk steel, for example, rather than aircraft engines and semiconductors). This put pressure on lower-skilled workers making the same kinds of goods in developed countries, and many lost their jobs or saw their pay stagnate. This is a staggeringly good outcome for people in poorer countries, as Milanović's (2005) research shows: the last two decades have seen a huge and long-overdue rise in prosperity of the developing world. But the working classes in the developed world have, it is argued, borne most of the costs. Immigration can play a similar role, increasing competition for low-skilled jobs (especially between new and recent immigrants).

The third explanation for today's inequality, focused on wealth inequality, is more basic: it is the idea that *capital tends to accumulate* unless some countervailing force prevents it. Piketty's now famous $r > g$ inequality (explained in box 6.2) implies that if returns on capital (r) exceed the growth of the economy as a whole (g), then the slice of the economic pie owned by the rich will generally grow. Piketty argues that in the postwar period, political choices reduced r: in particular, high taxes on the rich and government policies that encouraged full employment and union rights. The reversal of those policies and the fall of economic growth have shifted economies to where r now exceeds g and will continue to do so.

Box 6.2. An Outline of Piketty's $r > g$ Condition

A sketch of Piketty's argument, from a brilliant review by the economist Robert Solow (2014), is this. We want to find out whether the slice of the economic pie going to capital, the capital/income ratio, is rising or falling. Suppose national income is 100 and growing at, say, 2 percent. So income is growing from 100 to 102. At the same time saving and, therefore, investing grows capital as well: suppose saving is 10 percent of income this year. Thus capital is growing by 10 (10 percent of 100). The only level of capital that keeps the capital/income ratio constant is if capital is 500 (so the capital/income ratio is 500/100 = 5 in the first year and 510/102 = 5 in the second year). It follows that if the savings rate "s" equals the economic growth rate "g," $s = g$, the capital/income ratio stays constant. It further follows that if g falls, perhaps because scientists run out of ideas, and s remains the same, then $s > g$, in which case the capital/income ratio rises. Piketty argues this will happen over the next century. The link with $r > g$ is that, as we discussed in box 6.1, the earnings of capital holders equals the rate of return (denoted "r" by Piketty) times the capital they own. So if the capital/income ratio rises, and the rate of return does not fall, then the owners of capital will get an increasingly large share of the economic pie: this dimension of inequality, therefore, rises. Piketty's critics have mostly argued that capital returns would likely fall if there was more capital around.

Four Problematic Stories

Technology, trade, and the tendency of wealth to accumulate: while all three of these explanations for modern levels of inequality seem plausible, there are aspects of today's distribution that the simple versions, at least, don't seem to explain.

Let's consider four phenomena that are hard to square with the standard explanation of inequality: the unpredictable relationship between technology and wages; the continuing rise of the one percent; the disproportionate role of housing prices in inequality of wealth; and the importance of differences in wages between firms.

Consider *technology* first. We saw earlier that the idea that technology would replace jobs and impoverish workers is far from new. The other thing history shows us is that this idea is not always correct.

In mid-nineteenth-century Britain, economists worried not about robots and computers but about mules. Mules are machines for spinning cotton fiber into yarn, an important job in the textile industry, which sat at the heart of the Industrial Revolution.[1] At first, working a mule involved a variety of complex tasks. You needed to control the speed of the spindle, ensure the yarn was wound into the right shape, and periodically unwind the yarn properly; this made mule-spinning a relatively skilled job—at least at first.

In 1824 a Welshman named Richard Roberts invented the so-called self-acting mule. Far easier to use than existing mules, this set Roberts on a path to becoming one of the most celebrated engineers of the nineteenth century. Mill owners liked it too. In the words of Andrew Ure, a sort of nineteenth-century management theorist, "the effect of substituting the self-acting mule for the common mule is to discharge the greater part of the men spinners, and to retain adolescents and children" (Lazonick 1979). From Ure, this observation made it into Karl Marx's *Capital*: "the instrument of labour," Marx proclaimed, "strikes down the labourer." The mule was a symbol of the dangers of technological progress: new technologies would make jobs fewer and worse and only the rich would benefit.

But this story didn't turn out quite the way Marx expected. Far from being replaced by unskilled kids, adult mule-spinners prospered. The economic historian William Lazonick pointed out in 1979 that mule-spinners evolved into "minders," taking on training, managerial, and supervisory roles in the mills. And the British textile trade expanded, creating more rather than fewer of these skilled jobs. Minders in Lancashire cotton mills enjoyed relatively high wages well into the twentieth century.

The moral of the tale of the mule-spinners is that more technology doesn't necessarily equal fewer jobs or lower wages. The same lesson is suggested by the introduction of automated teller machines in banks. As James Bessen (2015) pointed out, the introduction of machines to dispense money actually saw a *rise* in the number of bank tellers in the United States. The reduction in branch costs and the increase in employees' time available to talk to customers and sell financial products (having been freed from handing out cash) meant that banks opened more branches.

Indeed, stories that technology would spell the end of employment and lead to social crisis have been a mainstay of economic punditry for over a century. Louis Anslow, an enterprising journalist, collected an archive of news stories to this effect, with examples dating back as early as the 1920s, including a speech by Albert Einstein in 1931 blaming the Great Depression on machines, and the British Prime Minister James Callaghan asking Downing Street civil servants to review the threat to jobs from automation shortly before he was ousted by Margaret Thatcher.[2]

All this suggests that while technology has the potential to displace jobs and create inequality, it ain't necessarily so.

The second challenge to the mainstream explanations of inequality comes from Piketty's observation that *the rise in wage inequality is very concentrated* at the very top. In the United States, the gap in income between skilled and unskilled workers, which initially gave rise to explanations based on skills-biased technical change, stopped diverging in about 2000. Since then, the big rises have accrued mostly to the top 1 percent. See figure 6.3.

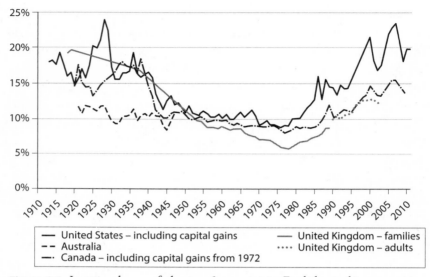

Figure 6.3. Income shares of the top 1 percent in English-speaking countries. Source: Alvaredo et al. 2013.

It's easy to imagine how low-skilled workers in developed countries might lose out if they don't have the skills to work with computers, or if their jobs are threatened by lower-paid workers in other countries. But the way these changes would benefit only the very rich is less clear.

Some of the very rich have gotten richer because of technology or because they employ cheap foreign labor. But certainly not all. For every Silicon Valley mogul or quantitative hedge fund owner, there are a lot of senior managers of what we'd think of as normal businesses among the new elite. Piketty, for example, estimates that between 60 and 70 percent of the top 0.1 percent are chief executives and other senior corporate managers.

A third confounding fact is the *role of housing* in wealth inequality. Not long after the publication of Piketty's *Capital in the Twenty-First Century*, the French economists Odran Bonnet, Pierre-Henri Bono, Guillaume Chapelle, and Etienne Wasmer noted that a big chunk of the growth in wealth inequality in both the United States and France was caused by the increase in value of residential property; Matthew Rognlie, an MIT graduate student who became known for his critique of Piketty, found the same (Bonnet et al. 2014; Rognlie 2015).

This suggests that to understand why wealth inequality is rising, we need to understand why housing wealth has risen so dramatically. This trend seems to have little to do with the rise of technology, of globalization, nor is it a feature of pure accumulation.

The last of the four phenomena, the differences in wages between firms, is a surprising source of income inequality. Economists have only recently begun to explore new and rich data sets combining both employer and employee data, and a recent study by Jae Song, Nicholas Bloom, David Price, Fatih Guvenen, and Till von Wachter (2015) looked at how earnings of workers in US firms changed between 1981 and 2013. Now, if the gap between managers and cleaners is rising, you might think that you would see a rising gap at *all* firms: the gap at an international legal firm rises and the gap at your local law firm rises. But it turns out this is not quite the case. Rather, leading firms are paying *both* their managers *and* their cleaners more relative to other firms: the gap between the occupations is still rising, but in addition the gap between these and the other firms is rising. Indeed, the authors found that "over two-thirds of the increase in earnings inequality from 1981 to 2013 can be accounted for by the rising variance of earnings between firms and only one-third by the rising variance within firms." (They noted one exception to this: the fact that among the very largest firms, chief executives and other senior managers are being paid a lot more, in ways that seem correlated with their firms' stock prices—a familiar finding.)

How Intangibles Affect Income, Wealth, and Esteem Inequality

So it seems that neither new technology nor globalization nor simple accumulation fully explains the current levels and types of inequality we see in developed countries. Could the rise of intangible investment provide part of the answer? Let's look at the possible ways in which an intangible economy might result in more of the kinds of inequality that people have been observing.

Intangibles, Firms, and Income Inequality

First of all, let's consider the ways in which the rise of intangible investment could have driven the increase in income inequality that has arisen from differences between firms. As we have seen in chapter 4, some of the key characteristics of intangibles are scalability and spillovers. So in a world where intangible investment is very important, we would expect to see the best firms, firms that own valuable, scalable intangibles and that are good at exacting the spillovers from other businesses, being highly productive and profitable, and their competitors losing out.

As we saw in chapter 5, this is indeed the case. The rise in the spread between the top and bottom firms seems to be in industries with lots of intangibles. On the face of it this looks like a prime candidate for a rise in inequality. However, one has to be a bit careful. Just because a firm is profitable doesn't mean it pays its cleaners more. After all, if they ask for a pay raise, the firm can potentially hire somebody else. So for a rising firm performance gap and rising wage inequality to be related, something in addition must be happening.

Who Is Benefiting from Intangible-Based Firm Inequality?

To get at this, let us ask: What sort of people are benefiting from the growing gap in firm performance?

One group is what we might call the "superstars": people who are personally associated with very valuable intangibles that scale massively. This line of analysis was developed by the economist Sherwin Rosen (1981). In many cases the job of one person can be done by others, or a combination of others (so a fast hamburger-server's job can be done by two slower ones). But in so-called superstar markets this is not true: the best opera singer or football player cannot be replaced by two not-quite-so-good ones. When technology, say broadcasting, raises the reach of such workers, their earnings can potentially rise very sharply. The intangible version of this story is that many superstars have privileged access to very valuable scalable intangibles that reap vast rewards: in some cases this is by outright ownership—for example, the tech billionaires who own significant equity stakes in companies they founded; in others, the superstar has special privileges to create more of a certain type of intangible—only J. K. Rowling can write new Harry Potter books, for example.

But, of course, most rich people are not stars or tech entrepreneurs; a significant proportion of the very rich are simply senior managers. What could account for this aspect of the rise in inequality?

It turns out the literature on interfirm inequality has some clues. The paper by Song and others that we discussed above used a clever technique to understand why the world seemed to be dividing into low-paying firms and high-paying ones. They looked at what happened to employee pay levels when they moved to firms that tended to be either high-payers or low-payers.

They were looking for evidence that low-paid people would tend to get significant pay rises when they joined high-paying firms. If true, this would suggest that what was really important was the firms themselves—that they were sitting on a money machine and were sharing out the proceeds among anyone lucky enough to land a job there (a phenomenon that will be familiar to anyone who has dealt with state-owned oil and gas companies in emerging countries). It turned out they didn't find this. Instead, they found that the people joining high-paying companies tended to be highly paid already (a phenomenon they call "sorting"), and vice versa, and that this tendency got stronger between 1980 and 2008.

The Song study doesn't tell us anything about the types of workers being hired by high-paying firms. But there is some evidence from a similar study by Christina Håkanson, Erik Lindqvist, and Jonas Vlachos (2015) looking at workers in Sweden. As (researcher) luck would have it, young Swedish men take standardized tests as part of their military service. These tests profile conscripts' cognitive and noncognitive skills. Combined with the high-quality employee and employer data that Scandinavian governments produce, they are a gold mine for labor economists. Håkanson's study showed that the workers moving to the high-paying firms were those who did well on their tests for cognitive and noncognitive skills.

What does this mean for inequality? It looks like those high-paying firms are possibly being more careful to sort and screen their workers. It seems to us that this sorting of workers is related to intangibles in two ways. First, it is a response to the importance of intangibles. Second, it is enabled by the rise of intangibles—or at least intangibles of a particular type. Let's look at each of these in turn.

Sorting Workers: The Return of the Symbolic Analysts

You'll recall from chapter 4 that one of the characteristics of intangibles is their *contestedness*. The right to use them and the ability to make the most of synergies between them are often up for grabs in a way that physical assets aren't. This characteristic makes particular kinds of employees especially valuable to a firm that wants to make the most of its valuable intangibles.

To illustrate this, let's take a step back in time to the turn of the twentieth century. Around 1900, it turns out that about a quarter of late-Victorian British companies hired a lord or a member of parliament (MP) to sit on their board of directors. Now, because British company archives are thorough, historians have been able to look in some detail at who these elite directors were and what good they did for the companies that hired them. The economic historians Fabio Braggion and Lyndon Moore (2013) looked at the records of 467 listed companies in the decade around 1900 to understand the benefits of having a politically and socially connected director. It turns out that for most companies, there was no measurable advantage to elite board members—companies that had them did about as well, on average, as companies that didn't, in terms of share price growth, financing, fundraising, and other measures of performance.

But there was one group of companies for which having MPs or lords on the board brought a measurable advantage: companies working in the emerging technology sectors of their day: synthetic chemicals, car and bike manufacturing, electricity generation and distribution, and so forth. Braggion and Moore showed that new tech companies with grand directors saw increases in their share price, including specific jumps if an existing director was elected to Parliament. They also found it easier to raise financing.

It seems that in industries with lots of uncertainty, involving new technologies, new markets, and unclear ownership rights, these well-connected directors helped smooth over some of the problems we've seen that affect intangible investments: uncertainty of ownership, difficulty of valuation, and the need for good relations with a wide range of potential partners.

An MP could help make sure the company got the benefits of its investments (for example, using influence to make sure a patent was honored), and their presence acted as a signal to investors that the company was well positioned to enforce its rights.

The MPs who secured board positions on new tech companies were useful not because they were tech experts, but because new technology businesses often depend on intangibles (from R&D to the organizational and branding investments needed to bring new products to market). These intangibles generate contestable uncertainty (Can the patent be defended? Will our distribution rights be honored?), and having big shots on the board both helped manage these uncertainties and gave investors confidence that they would be managed.

Braggion and Moore's Victorian grandees have their modern equivalents. Back in the early nineties, when intangible investment was growing but before it had come to dominate tangible investment, economists were beginning to notice changes in the economy.

Future US Treasury Secretary Robert Reich predicted that power in the workforce of the future would be in the hands of what he called "symbolic analysts": product managers, lawyers, business development people, design engineers, marketers, headhunters, and so forth. Like the Swedish workers who benefited from higher salaries in Håkanson's study, symbolic analysts are educated, smart people with a combination of noncognitive skills (because managing spillovers often involves social interaction) and cognitive skills (because intangibles are usually knowledge assets).

It also seems to reflect what we see when we survey companies in particular sectors. A qualitative study by the innovation foundation Nesta of companies that made intensive use of data and analytics showed that these companies are particularly eager to hire people who combine decent data analytical skills with the soft skills needed to broker relationships inside and outside their own company (Bakhshi, Mateos-Garcia, and Whitby 2014).

This provides a striking link between the rise of intangibles and increasing income inequality. Intangible investment increases. Because of its scalability and the benefits to companies that can appropriate intangible spillovers, leading companies pull ahead of laggards in terms of productivity, especially in the more intangible-intensive industries. The employees of these highly productive companies benefit from higher wages. Because intangibles are contestable, companies are especially eager to hire people who are good at contesting them—appropriating spillovers from other firms or identifying and maximizing synergies. These are Reich's symbolic analysts, Braggion and Moore's influential elites, or Håkanson's talented conscripts: people who are already doing well and, in a world of increasingly important, scalable intangibles, are likely to do even better.

Sorting Workers: Intangibles and Worker Screening

The second way that intangibles encourage income inequality is by helping hierarchies emerge both between and within firms.

Research by the economists Luis Garicano and Thomas Hubbard (2007) looked at the pay of American lawyers between 1977 and 1992. They found that the pay of the highest-earning lawyers increased dramatically over the period (a trend that seems to have continued in the two decades since). What was particularly interesting was the reason their pay had increased. They were being paid more because they were working with greater numbers of associates (junior lawyers), or, in the paper's words, because the "coordination cost of hierarchical production" decreased. The best lawyers invested in new ways of dividing up work so that they could improve what they call their "leverage"—their ability to focus on the most complex and remunerative tasks.

This kind of trend is a result of investment in intangibles, in particular organizational development, software, and to some extent service design. It involves designing new ways of working, developing hierarchies within firms, and putting in place software and systems to manage them.

We can see something similar going on in the field of management consulting. We saw in chapter 4 how consulting firms in the 1950s and 60s came up with organizational innovation that allowed them to staff projects with a junior staff, leavened with a small number of high-paid partners. Later in the twentieth century, further organizational innovations caused the business of management consulting to segment further. In the 1980s it would be typical for a McKinsey project to begin with a few weeks of data gathering—understanding market sizes and shares, learning about customers, and so forth—before the strategic advice began. As a result, projects were longer. By the 2000s much of this market-sizing work had been outsourced to specialized market-intelligence firms, which would prepare detailed reports and projections on dozens of industries and sectors, which would be sold to consultants and bankers for a fixed fee. Consulting firms invested in knowledge management departments to order and curate these reports. The market for these market-intelligence reports was pretty competitive, and quickly they became far cheaper than the customized market sizings carried out by consulting staff (Bower 1979).

In the management consulting industry, the kind of institutional innovation described by Garicano and Hubbard led to inequality among firms, with the industry separating into companies providing higher- and lower-cost services and employing different types of staff—exactly the kind of division that Song and others observed in the United States.

Intangible Myths

The effects of growing intangible investment on income inequality that we have looked at so far have been in a sense rational. They show particular workers being paid more either because they are intrinsically worth more to their employers in an intangible-intensive economy, or because an intangible economy encourages a division of labor that has made them more useful to their employers than others.

But there may also be irrational factors at play. As Song and others pointed out, along with the rise in inequality between firms, there has been a big increase in inequality at the largest firms between the highest-paid employees, especially CEOs, and everyone else. The correlation between high CEO compensation and company performance seems weak. So what is going on?

One possibility is that in a world in which abundant intangibles are increasing uncertainty, and where talented employees are able to some extent to help firms make the best of this uncertainty, it becomes easier to create a cult of talent that can be exploited by people at the top of firms to demand higher pay.

As the economic journalist Chris Dillow[3] likes to point out, humans are particularly prone to what psychologists call "fundamental attribution error"—the mistaken assumption that outcomes (such as how well a company does) are related to salient inputs (such as the skill of the CEO) rather than dumb luck or complex, hard-to-observe factors. A world in which increased intangible investment makes skilled managers a bit more important could easily lend fuel to the fire of fundamental attribution error, providing a rationale for powerful people like CEOs to increase their pay by more than the economic fundamentals of the change would justify.

A final possibility is that shareholders are being insufficiently attentive to the pay of CEOs, thereby allowing it to rise. Brian Bell and John Van Reenen (2013) have some interesting evidence here, showing that CEO pay is more correlated with performance the more share ownership is concentrated (in their sample, in institutional investors). Perhaps dispersed shareholders have less incentive to monitor CEO pay, a matter we return to in chapter 8.

Housing Prices, Cities, Intangibles, and Wealth Inequality

One of the many achievements of Piketty's *Capital in the Twenty-First Century* was to remind pundits and policymakers that inequality was not just about income, but also about wealth.

It seems to us that the rise of the intangible economy can help explain the long-term rise of inequality of wealth as well as inequality of income. There are two main ways this is happening. First of all, intangibles have helped drive the increase in property prices, which explains a significant chunk of the increase in wealth of the world's richest people. Second, the fact that intangible capital tends to be geographically mobile has made it harder to redistribute wealth via taxation in the way that governments of the 1950s, 60s, and 70s did.

Let's consider property prices, first of all. Of course, a house or an apartment is quintessentially tangible. Real estate originally got its name because it is immobile; it's real-ly there. But in fact, the value of property, especially the kinds of property that have risen most dramatically in value over the last thirty years, derives to a great extent from intangibles.

As we discussed earlier, a number of commentators on Piketty's work have pointed out that a significant proportion of the increase in wealth of the richest people in the United States (and almost all of the extra wealth of France's richest) stems from the rising value of their property. As Rognlie (2015) pointed out, this does not seem to be because they are buying more properties; it is because the houses and apartments they own have steadily and powerfully risen in value over the last three decades.

Now, house price inflation is not evenly distributed. As figure 6.4 for some US cities and figure 6.5 for UK regions show, the price of housing has more than doubled in real terms in some places and stayed more or less the same in others.

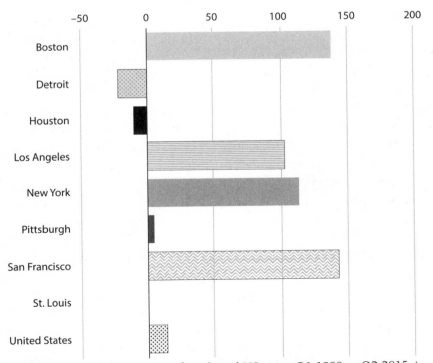

Figure 6.4. Rises in house prices for selected US cities, Q1 1980 to Q2 2015, in real terms. Sources: Zillow, the Bureau of Labor Statistics, and *Economist*.

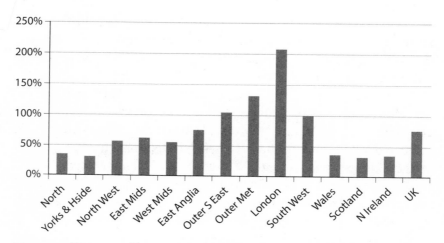

Figure 6.5. Rises in real house prices for UK regions, 1973–2016. Source: ONS.

The cities where housing prices have risen dramatically tend to be the ones with thriving economies, where it is hard to build new dwellings. But this explanation only raises a further question: Why are the economies of some of these cities thriving?

Here we can turn to the work of the economist Edward Glaeser, whose influential research has focused on how economic growth happens in cities (see, for example, Glaeser 2011). It had long been known that cities are rich in spillovers. Dense populations mean people exchange, observe, and copy ideas from one another. Initially, economists had focused on spillovers within industries; the Marshall-Arrow-Romer spillovers we referred to in chapter 4. Glaeser's research highlighted the importance of a different effect: positive spillovers between industries. Indeed, he argued that for thriving US cities like New York these types of spillovers, where ideas or opportunities from one sector are exacted into another, were more important. Glaeser's example was the invention of the bra, which was developed not by lingerie makers but by dressmakers (Glaeser 2011; Glaeser et al. 1992).

Indeed, cities that relied on single industries, like Youngstown, Ohio, which made steel, or Akron, which made tires, or most famously Detroit, the motor city, tended to do less well in the modern age than cities with a range of industries. Glaeser called these "Jacobs spillovers," in honor of Jane Jacobs, the urbanist and defender of messy, unplanned cities.

It seems that this effect is still going strong. A recent paper by Chris Forman, Avi Goldfarb, and Shane Greenstein (2016) showed not only that the San Francisco Bay Area has become an increasingly important location of invention in the last few decades, but also that it has become a source of inventions in many diverse areas, not just software and semiconductors. In fact, it is an important originator of patents not mentioning IT at all.

Glaeser's model of urban spillovers fits neatly with the characteristics of intangibles we described in chapter 4. Cities provide an opportunity to profit both from spillovers (that is to say, benefiting from intangible investments made by other firms) and synergies (combining different intangibles to produce unexpectedly large benefits). Viewed in this light, the link between the so-called creative class and cities is not surprising.

In a world where intangibles are becoming more abundant and a more important part of the way businesses create value, the benefits to exploiting spillovers and synergies increase. And as these benefits increase, we would expect businesses and their employees to want to locate in diverse, growing cities where synergies and spillovers abound. One possible result of this would be to encourage people to build more houses and offices in big cities. But, of course, in most cities there are big regulatory barriers to building, from zoning rules to legal action by NIMBYs. So instead, the price of housing rises, and the wealthy, who are more likely to own this kind of prime real estate, get wealthier, as Piketty described.

Taxes, Mobile Intangibles, and Wealth Inequality

It also seems that the growing importance of intangibles is contributing to another element of Piketty's story of rising wealth inequality, specifically, the apparent unwillingness of governments to tax capital in the way they once did. Piketty argues that redistributive taxation (together with higher inflation rates) helped erode the accumulated wealth of the rich in the postwar decades, but that governments have lost the nerve for this kind of taxation since 1980.

It is certainly true that there have been major ideological shifts in how willing governments are to redistribute wealth through taxation. But perhaps the rise of intangibles has also played a role.

In countries like the United States and the UK, capital gains have since the 1990s been taxed at a lower rate than income. This is a political sticking point, not least because it is mainly rich people who have capital gains because they are much more likely to own capital. The reason for this lower rate of taxation is that capital is mobile, and so taxing it will, according to a large body of economic research, encourage its owners to shift their capital to a lower tax jurisdiction. The same can't be said, or at least not to the same extent, for income from employment, since most people's jobs take place in a particular location and are much harder to move. So, although it might seem fairer, from the point of view of redistribution, to tax capital income more than employment income (as governments in the 1950s and 1960s did, with their separate tax rates for "unearned income" and the like), most governments have concluded it is not possible: capital is just too flighty.[4]

Now consider the effect of the rise of intangibles. Nowadays, the average firm invests far more in intangibles than its equivalent back in the 1990s. And intangible assets are, on the whole, more geographically mobile than tangible assets. For an oil company to move its physical refining operations from the UK to the Netherlands would be a massive undertaking, a decade-long project of the kind most firms would undertake only if absolutely necessary. But if Starbucks wants to move the ownership of their brand or the IP behind their UK store operations to the Netherlands or Ireland or Luxembourg, it can be done with some modest legal work.

This intensifies what policymakers call "tax competition": the idea that businesses and owners of capital will shop around for the most favorable tax policies. This makes it harder for governments to increase taxes and exacerbates the problem that led to lower taxes on capital in the first place.

Let's summarize. The rise of intangible investment helps explain wealth inequality in two ways. Because businesses flock to cities to exploit the spillovers and synergies associated with intangibles, it is a major cause of the rise in the value of prime urban property, which accounts for much of the new wealth of the very rich. And because it is unusually internationally mobile, intangibles increase tax competition, which makes it harder for governments to reduce inequality by taxing capital more.

Openness, the Left-Behind, Intangibles, and Esteem Inequality

At the beginning of this chapter, we mentioned a type of inequality that is as much social and attitudinal as it is economic. This is the inequality of esteem that is increasingly prevalent in society in the United States, the UK, and elsewhere in Europe—that is, the growing sense that the population is dividing into two halves: one more cosmopolitan, more educated, and more liberal and the other more traditionalist, and more skeptical of elite opinion and of metropolitan values.

It's a divide that has made itself felt dramatically in politics. Supporters of Donald Trump, of Brexit, and of many of Europe's growing populist parties share a sense of being alienated from and patronized by the dominant elites in their country who do not share their values.

One might expect that these groups are alienated because they are poor. But the evidence of the UK's referendum on leaving the EU suggests there may be more to it than this.

Political scientist Eric Kaufmann pointed out that it's not class and wealth that predict whether someone will vote to leave the EU, but rather social conservatism and attitudes toward authoritarianism. In Kaufmann's words, "culture and personality, not material circumstances, separate Leave and Remain voters. This is not a class conflict so much as a values divide that cuts across lines of age, income, education and even party." Kaufmann suggested that Leave voters tended not only to want to leave but also to hold other socially conservative views, for example, to be in favor of corporal punishment: polling conducted by Lord Ashcroft supported this conclusion (Kaufman 2016a; Kaufman 2016b).

The psychologist Bastian Jaeger[5] explored this by looking at the correlation between areas that voted to Remain in the EU and psychological traits. Psychologists have settled on five psychological traits that they believe capture dimensions of human personality. Jaeger looked at the trait of "Openness to Experience," which is associated with cosmopolitanism and an interest in the new. As figure 6.6 shows, people who are open to new experiences seemed to vote Remain, and those who are more traditionalist tended to vote Leave, regardless of income or class.

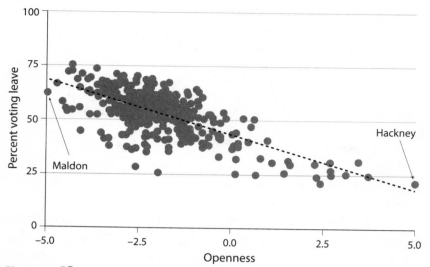

Figure 6.6. "Openness to Experience" and voting to leave the EU. Source: Krueger 2016 after Bastian Jaeger.

Now, let's consider the kinds of people who might benefit from an economy in which intangibles are more abundant and important. We know that in an intangible economy, the ability to appropriate spillovers and make the most of synergies is prized. Research by psychologists suggests that people who are more open to experience are better at this. Perhaps this is because they are better at making the kind of connections between different ideas and people that, as Edward Glaeser and Jane Jacobs pointed out, are so important to the economic magic that goes on in cities. Perhaps creativity and innovation require openness to ideas (there is evidence that openness to experience helps in innovative and creative jobs).

This suggests a new explanation for why the divide between supporters of Trump, Brexit, and similar movements and their respective nonsupporters is growing. The supporters tend to share certain underlying attitudes such as traditionalism and low openness to experience. But they find themselves in an economy that, because of the growing importance of intangibles, is increasingly favoring people with different psychological traits and value systems. The cultural causes of Brexit and Trump are exacerbated by the economic causes—causes that arise from the emergence of an intangible economy.

Conclusion: The Implications of an Intangible Economy for Inequality

We've argued that the rise of intangibles explains several aspects of the long-run rise in inequality.

First, inequality of income. The synergies and spillovers that intangibles create increase inequality between competing companies, and this inequality leads to increasing differences in employee pay (recent research suggests these interfirm differences account for a large proportion of the rise of income inequality). In addition, managing intangibles requires particular skills and education, and people with these skills (such as Reich's symbolic analysts) are clustering in high-paid jobs in intangible-intensive firms. Finally, the growing economic importance of the kind of people who manage intangibles helps foster myths that can be used to justify excessive pay, especially for top managers

Second, inequality of wealth. Thriving cities are places where spillovers and synergies abound. The rise of intangibles makes cities increasingly attractive places to be, driving up the prices of prime property. This type of inflation has been shown to be one of the major causes of the increase in the wealth of the richest. In addition, intangibles are often mobile; they can be shifted across firms and borders. This makes capital more mobile, which makes it harder to tax. Since capital is disproportionately owned by the rich, this makes redistributive taxation to reduce wealth inequality harder.

Finally, inequality of esteem. There is some evidence that supporters of populist movements (Brexit in the UK, Trump in the United States) are more likely to hold traditionalist views and to score low on tests for the psychological trait of openness to experience. Openness to experience seems to be important for the kind of symbolic-analysis jobs that proliferate as intangibles become more common. So the increasing importance of intangibles leads to economic pressures that underscore the political divides driving today's populist movements.

7

Infrastructure for Intangibles, and Intangible Infrastructure

The idea that inadequate infrastructure investment is holding back economic growth is widespread, particularly in the United States and the UK. This chapter looks at how the economy's greater reliance on intangible investment changes the infrastructure debate. An intangible-rich economy needs different sorts of physical infrastructure; it also has a greater need for intangible infrastructure: the standards, rules, and norms that underpin businesses' intangible investment.

It is hard to think of anything *less* intangible than infrastructure. Bridges, highways, power stations, and dams are huge and heavy; they are physically present in an unmissable way. The modern economy depends on billions of tons of physical infrastructure that encrusts the world in steel, concrete, copper, and optical fiber. It's no surprise that infrastructure is a subject of passionate concern for many economists and politicians: the idea that we might not have enough infrastructure, or that what we have is not modern enough, is a common theme in public debate, especially in the Anglo-Saxon world.

This chapter will ask what types of infrastructure are particularly useful for an intangible-intensive economy. It will look at both physical infrastructure and the infrastructure that is itself intangible—the rules, norms, and processes that help the economy function.

Defining Infrastructure

Infrastructure is intimately connected to the modes of production that dominate the economy at any given time. Since "infra" means "below," infrastructure consists of those structures that underpin the way society works. One way of thinking about infrastructure is the set of durable assets that are complementary to the capital employed by firms and households. So, for example, the electricity grid is important because businesses and consumers use lots of electrical devices. Gas stations and highways are useful because so much transport happens by car and truck. Some infrastructure may be publicly owned (for example, a public highway); some may be owned by firms (for example, a private airport or a telephone cable)—but whoever owns it, infrastructure has a public character in that it enables economic activity on the part of a large number of other people or firms.

Because of this *enabling* character of infrastructure, we would expect that when the modes of production in the economy and its capital stock change, its requirements for infrastructure might change too. An economy of canal boats and horse-drawn wagons needs canals and staging posts; an economy of electrical machines and cars needs electricity grids and gas stations.[1]

Thinking about intangible investment also leads us to a different aspect of the infrastructure story. For all that bridges, roads, and airports dominate the political debate on infrastructure, there is another sense of the word infrastructure that refers to things that are themselves intangible: rules, norms, common knowledge, and institutions. Like physical infrastructure, they are costly to produce, are durable, tend to have a public and social character, and tend to make the economy as a whole more productive.

Hype and False Promises

The idea that the growth of intangible investment would radically change the kind of infrastructure the economy needs will be familiar to anyone who has dipped into the more utopian end of the literature on the so-called knowledge economy, especially in the run-up to the dot-com bubble of 1998–2000. Commentators predicted the "death of distance": that knowledge combined with digital technology would render unimportant the constraints of space and place that much of our infrastructure is an attempt to resolve. Investment in telecommunications infrastructure was seen as vitally important, leading to a bidding frenzy for 3G mobile spectrum licenses and to the US telecoms bubble and crash of 2001.

In fact, traditional physical infrastructure has not become obsolete. Historian of science David Edgerton (2011) has demonstrated the importance of old-fashioned infrastructure from irrigation ditches to corrugated iron roofs in a supposedly modern world. Environmental scientist Vaclav Smil points out the importance of infrastructure based on early twentieth-century technology for everything from our food system to our energy system (Smil 2005). However the rise of intangible investment plays out, it seems likely that investment in energy, passenger transportation, and logistics will continue to be important.[2] Jess Gaspar and Edward Glaeser (1998) showed that the death of distance idea was more complicated than it first appeared: better information technologies might replace some face-to-face meetings, but they might create the need for other meetings—and, therefore, increase the value of living in cities, where it is easier to meet people. By way of analogy, the steam locomotive was described as an "iron horse" from the early nineteenth century, but did not replace horses or even reduce demand for them. Indeed, the railway era saw an increase in the demand for horses—"peak horse" in the United States occurred in 1910, eighty years after the opening of the first steam railway.

But the fact that some of the early claims made for the intangible economy and the knowledge economy turned out to be hype does not mean that society's infrastructural needs are not changing. Innovation scholar Carlota Perez made the provocative claim that major epochal changes in how the economy uses technology happen periodically and involve first of all an interval of hype and speculation (both intellectual and financial), followed by a crisis, and then a long period of deployment and bedding-in (Perez 2002). To continue the railway analogy, the steam locomotive did not make horses obsolete, but its descendant, the car, eventually did. The corollary of this idea is that the debunking of the death-of-distance rhetoric around the year 2000 does not necessarily mean it was entirely wrong, but rather that it marked the shift from a phase of early exuberance to a more workmanlike period in which the new technologies get applied, scrutinized, and rolled out, often alongside rather than instead of more familiar infrastructure.

In an age of increased intangible investment, we would expect that certain types of infrastructure will become more important: in particular, infrastructure that helps make the most of the unusual characteristics of intangibles that we set out in chapter 4: scalability, sunkenness, spillovers, and synergies.

In the rest of this chapter, we will look at the different types of infrastructure that help make an intangible-rich economy work well—first of all, at physical infrastructure; then at infrastructure that takes the form of public investment in the kinds of intangibles that firms also invest in; and then at infrastructure in its least proximate sense: standards, norms, and frameworks.

Physical Infrastructure, Synergies, and Spillovers

As we have seen, intangible investments generate spillovers, and bringing the right intangible investments together can create surprisingly valuable synergies. Individuals and organizations that can make the most of these trends—by exploiting the spillovers of other people's investments and by spotting and taking advantage of synergies between new ideas—will prosper. Infrastructure can help them to do this, in particular, by increasing the number and quality of connections that take place. Indeed, to give a traditional infrastructure example, hub airport operators have known about spillovers for a long time in that demand for access to an airport rises the more routes the airport operator can connect you to.

One way of doing this is to try to build or nurture dynamic clusters—places where innovative businesses and people are more likely to come together and share ideas. As we saw in chapter 4, clusters have played an important but occasional role in the history of economic thought, not least in the work of Alfred Marshall, Kenneth Arrow, Paul Romer, and Edward Glaeser.

But clusters are absolute catnip for policymakers and pundits. It is rare to see a modern government that does not have some sort of strategy for supporting or building local clusters, especially in high-innovation sectors. (Witness the dozens of Silicon-soundalike names that have been coined around the world in homage to northern California's tech cluster—from Silicon Roundabout in London and Silicon Wadi in Israel, to any number of more aspirational variants elsewhere.) Cluster policy is appealing in part because of the glamorous and well-publicized success of places like Silicon Valley and Israel's tech sector—what politician wouldn't want their country to be at the forefront of a technological revolution? Cluster policy can also be politically convenient: governments that for ideological reasons are anxious about seeming too interventionist can point out that they are only helping out clusters that are already there, not trying to create clusters from scratch; governments unable or unwilling to spend much money will find that when it comes to cluster policy, moral suasion and cost-effective networking events go a long way. It is no surprise that the writings of commentators like Michael Porter and Richard Florida, both of whom have stressed the importance of aspects of clusters in economic growth, have been very popular with policymakers over the last thirty years. The flipside of cheap, light-touch cluster policies is that it is difficult to show whether they have been effective. There are relatively rigorous ways of evaluating the economic effect of grants, tax breaks, or infrastructure investments. But when it comes to ongoing, subtle policies meant to accelerate clusters that are already forming, it is hard to test whether the policy itself has changed anything. (For some policymakers, that a policy is difficult to evaluate may—as they say in the world's most famous tech cluster—be a feature, not a bug.)[3]

At the risk of traducing decades of cluster policy, we would suggest that there are two types of infrastructure that really matter in an age where clusters are becoming more important.

The first is affordable housing and working space in existing clusters. In August 2016 Kate Downing resigned from the Planning and Transportation Commission in Palo Alto, the low-rise city at the heart of Silicon Valley, saying she and her partner could no longer afford to live there. They are by no means minimum-wage workers: rather they are an attorney and software engineer.[4] Now, as we saw in chapter 6, the price of real estate in thriving cities seems to have risen inexorably over the last forty years. One of the reasons for this is that it is costly and time-consuming to build new houses and offices in many of the world's most prosperous cities. Some of these costs reflect the need to build safely or to minimize disruption—that is to say, they force builders to bear some of the costs that new buildings entail, which seems reasonable.

But some costs represent the ability of existing property owners to maintain or increase the value of their own properties. Palo Alto's homeowners, for example, use planning laws to preserve their town's character as a suburban city of one-and-two-story houses with gardens (which accordingly command very high prices), even though the town sits at the heart of the world's most famous tech cluster, and many people would like to buy new houses there if any were built. Rules and regulations that allow more building to happen faster and more cheaply would provide more of the basic infrastructure—homes and offices—that cities need to make the most of intangible investments.

But a city of nothing but apartments and offices would be a dull thing indeed—and in an intangible age this matters economically. The second type of urban infrastructure that is important for intangible investment are places where people can come together to interact. Not long ago, one of the authors appeared on a radio program looking at political attitudes in the UK's EU referendum. The program's host had been interviewing voters in Lambeth, a diverse district not far from the center of London; in passing, he noted how odd it was that almost every single business he visited seemed to double as a café. In fact, it is less odd than it seems. Since the days of London's coffeehouses in the seventeenth century, places where people meet and socialize seem to have been important to the coming together of new ideas. Cultural and artistic venues seem to play a special role in the ferment of intangible investments. Research by the innovation foundation Nesta suggests that places with high concentrations of creative organizations and institutions show higher levels of innovation more generally (Higgs, Cunningham, and Bakhshi 2008). Neutral spaces, perhaps especially ones with an artistic or creative leaning, create opportunities for combinatorial innovation.

This creates something of a dilemma for policymakers. Loosening regulations on building helps get more houses and offices built, which, all other things being equal, helps city clusters thrive and grow. But liberal building rules can have unintended consequences. Anyone who has lived in a big city in the developed world in the last decade will be familiar with stories like that of the Black Cap pub in Camden in London. The Black Cap was for many years a center of gay culture in London and a not unimportant artistic venue—it played a significant role in the development of modern cabaret. If we set aside its cultural and historical importance and look at it solely through a reductionist economic lens, it was exactly the kind of place we would expect to magnify the synergies and spillovers of city life. But in 2015 it was closed and scheduled for conversion into apartments. In a busy, congested city, people were willing to pay more for luxury apartments than for drinks and admission to a cabaret pub. Perhaps this is the right decision for the economy as a whole—after all, it is very hard to measure the future productivity gain that might result from a single cultural venue in the future—but it is easy to believe that the vibrancy and interactions provided by places like the Black Cap might be underprovided by the market. Which brings us back to the dilemma facing urban planners: how do you cut regulations that prevent NIMBYs blocking the new buildings that an intangible economy needs to thrive, while not inadvertently hastening the closure of venues and institutions without which the city would not be such an effective cluster in the first place?

There is a further challenge facing policymakers looking to encourage intangible investment by supporting clusters in cities: that is, the question of when to put the needs of a growing cluster over an established one, and the kinds of biases that affect that decision. This is compounded in countries, like the UK, where political decision making is highly centralized in prosperous regions. If the capital of a country also happens to be an economically successful, bustling place, it is very easy to underestimate the economic potential of the rest of the country. Some research suggests that this happens in the UK, where there is a widespread attitude among London-based policymakers that only London has the economic potential to thrive and, therefore, that investing public funds anywhere else is the equivalent of King Cnut seeking to turn back the tide (Forth 2015). This leads to an exaggerated unwillingness to invest outside of London, such that the ratio of public R&D funding to private R&D funding is higher in London than elsewhere, and transport investments with high estimated benefit-to-cost ratios go unbuilt outside of London, while ones with low benefit-to-cost ratios that happen to be in London get funded.

Technological Infrastructure and Spillovers

A technologically minded reader might at this point ask why, in an era where software and semiconductors are changing the way people communicate, this section on building networks to exchange ideas has focused mainly on the infrastructure of face-to-face interaction. The premise of the 2001 telecoms bubble was that people would soon be relying on fiber optics and mobile data to interact and forsaking "meatspace" for "cyberspace."

It is certainly true that telecoms infrastructure is and will continue to be important for the economy in general and for enabling the kind of social interactions that help make the most of intangible investments. The continued rollout of fiber-optic cables, 4G and 5G cell phone towers, and connected chips in more and more devices will in time increase our ability to interact.

There are two complicating factors that disrupt the relationship between investment in telecoms infrastructure and connectivity and productivity. The first is the speed of technological change in the infrastructure itself. The decision to invest in cell phone towers or optical routers today is not just a choice between investing or not investing; it is also a decision whether to delay the investment until tomorrow or next year, by which time the cost of the infrastructure may be much cheaper, or a new and better technology might be available.

The second challenge is perhaps trickier for the would-be infrastructure investor: new technological infrastructure is most useful in conjunction with new ways of working and without these new ways of working may not be very useful at all.

In 1990 the economist Paul David (1990) came to this conclusion while studying the introduction of electrical power in the United States. David pointed out that for a factory to make the most of electrical power, it needed to restructure radically the way it worked. Whereas in a steam-powered factory, all machine tools had to be powered by a belt connected to a single rotating shaft, electricity allowed every tool to have its own motor; this, in turn, made possible the twentieth-century production line. David also observed that nearly forty years after the development of the first central electrical power plant, still only slightly more than 50 percent of factory mechanical-drive capacity had been electrified. Until then, the remarkable innovation of electrical power delivered remarkably little in the way of increased productivity for factory owners.

It is possible that the high-bandwidth, universally connected telecommunications systems of the twenty-first century are analogous to David's electrical power stations. It will take time, experimentation, and (intangible) investment to devise really effective and economically transformational ways of using these new technologies to communicate. As is often the case with new technologies, the future may already be here among us. Software developers have been using online tools like Slack and GitHub to collaborate for years now. There are any number of firms experimenting with new ways of Internet-enabled collaboration, in fields from healthcare research (such as Patientslikeme or 23andMe) to brokering intellectual property among companies (such as Nathan Myhrvold's Intellectual Ventures) to data analytics (such as Kaggle, recently acquired by Google). It is easy to laugh when technology advocates make predictions that don't come to pass. Where is the paperless office? Where is the Internet of Things? But the fact that widespread effective teleworking has not seriously reduced the importance of face-to-face communication may be a sign not that it will never happen, but rather that it is a complicated type of change and takes time.

So telecoms infrastructure will matter more in an intangible economy as a way to build connections and make the most of spillovers. But the fiber, routers, processors, and base stations may not be the most important aspect of this infrastructure—what will really make them valuable is the development of new tools and habits of using them to connect and work together.

These trends increase the importance of communications and connections between people and between businesses, and of the infrastructure that enables this.

Standards, Frameworks, and Norms

Economists have long known that effective rules, institutions, and norms can encourage investment. Conversely, Hernando de Soto memorably showed how bad institutions—specifically, weak property rights—discouraged poor people in the developing world from investing in their own houses, developing businesses, and thereby escaping poverty (Soto 2001). The invention of the limited liability corporation encouraged business investment by safeguarding business owners' assets from repossession if the company failed.

Intangible investment is also affected by institutional infrastructure, both formal and informal.

The most straightforward aspect of this is property rights. As generations of rights-owners have pointed out, strong intellectual property law encourages businesses to invest in the kinds of intangibles that can be protected by patents, copyright, or trademarks because they reduce the problem of spillovers that affects intangibles. On the other hand, intellectual property rights that are overly broad, overly strong, or overly vague can discourage innovation in the longer run because they discourage competition and make it harder for firms to exploit synergies between intangibles. For example, the very broad patent granted to the Wright brothers for flight control in 1906 is thought to have held back the aviation sector in the United States until the patent was placed in an industry-wide pool at the government's request in 1917. There is a lively debate about how strong intellectual property rights should be and what types of knowledge they should cover—but there is general agreement that making them work well is important for investment.

But the institutions that affect intangible investment go beyond formal rights over intellectual property. As we have seen, because intangible investments often generate synergies when they are combined, big intangible projects often involve large numbers of investors and firms, investing across long time frames. Coordinating the investments and managing the handoffs between different firms and organizations is complex; institutions and norms can help investors to navigate and simplify this complexity.

Consider the development and launch of a new medicine. It typically involves an underpinning of basic science, a process of drug discovery, and several rounds of testing to see if the drug is both safe and more effective than existing drugs; the drug must then be marketed and sold—a process that involves a complex dance between payers (a mixture of health insurers and governments), clinicians, regulators, and patients. As well as being very capital intensive, this is an undertaking of dizzying complexity.

One thing that reduces the complexity of the drug discovery process is a set of widely agreed norms and rules about what happens when. So, for example, drug trials come in phases, the purpose and duration of which are specified by regulators like the US Food and Drug Administration. There are rules about which kinds of research are funded by public bodies and medical charities, and which are not. The academic research upon which many drugs depend is governed by a host of time-honored norms about rigor, peer review, and publication practices.

The market has rules too, which help simplify complex decisions about pricing and sales. Many governments and insurers have rules about what sort of drugs they will fund and what they will not—such as those of the UK's National Institute for Health and Clinical Excellence, which will only approve drugs that can give patients what health economists call a quality-adjusted life-year at less than a stated price. And there are unwritten rules too: biotech start-ups typically work in the expectation that if they can get through the first round or rounds of clinical trials, they will be acquired by a deep-pocketed pharmaceutical company rather than having to raise ever larger amounts of money to bring their product all the way to market. Drug testing is frequently carried out under contract by university labs, under arrangements that are well defined and understood by anyone looking to set up a life sciences company. And the business of raising money for life sciences ventures has its own rules, specialist investors, and professional services firms with shared norms and understandings.

Now it is true that many of these rules have a narrowly economic function: rules capping how much governments will pay for drugs protect taxpayers' interests; the various rounds of venture capital (VC) funding allow investors to manage their risk, and so on. But the rules of the pharmaceutical innovation system also play a more subtle role: they make the vast complexity of developing a drug, an undertaking of great uncertainty and expense, manageable and understandable for the various parties (researchers, entrepreneurs, regulators, financiers, corporate managers, and others) that have to come together to achieve it. Innovation scholar Paul Nightingale described norms and rules as "invisible infrastructure" that creates "local predictability" in otherwise unpredictable and complex undertakings (Nightingale 2004).

Similar institutions exist in other fields that make it easier for different businesses to make complementary investments. Some of these are formal information technology protocols, such as the Internet Protocol Suite and the Hypertext Transfer Protocol that form the basis of the Internet and the World Wide Web, respectively. Others are social norms, such as the phasing and structure of venture capital rounds for tech start-ups, or are rules designed or enforced by public bodies, such as regulatory regimes or international standards.

Of course, rules and standards also apply to tangible investments: railways have gauges; plug sockets have standardized shapes and voltages; automobiles have somewhat standardized controls. But because intangible investments are unusually likely to give rise to synergies and to reward effective collaboration, we would expect invisible infrastructure to be more important in an intangible economy. It helps make the most of synergies by creating clear interfaces between different firms with synergistic assets (for example, a biotech start-up with a promising candidate drug and a pharmaceutical giant with the marketing and organizational assets to take the drug through clinical trials and sell it).

Another sort of soft infrastructure is the provision of information about the investments other people are making. If intangible investments can be combined to create unexpected synergies, then it can be valuable for businesses to know where other firms are investing in potentially relevant projects and ideas. A well-established way of providing this sort of information is through talking to people and working in clusters, where there are lots of opportunities to talk to different people and convivial places where you are likely to meet them. But more formal sources of information can be useful as well. Anyone who has attended a big trade show[5] can attest that trade shows are not just about companies exhibiting to their customers; they are just as much about companies finding out what one another is doing, getting ideas, and discussing partnerships and deals. The same can be said of industry directories and maps, which make new and emerging sectors readable, both to outsiders and to firms within the sector.

The Softest of Soft Infrastructure: Trust and Social Capital

In this chapter we have gradually moved from the most tangible, most physical types of infrastructure, like transport and housing, to infrastructure that is itself intangible, like institutions, rules, and information. Continuing in this vein, let us finish by considering the least physical, least programmatic form of infrastructure: trust, and what sociologists have called social capital—the strength, number, and quality of the relationships among people in a society.

Trust among people and firms is an important precondition for intangible investment in two ways. First of all, it encourages the kinds of interactions that create synergies between different intangibles: people are less likely to share ideas in closed and demarcated societies. (Other social characteristics, like openness to experience and low levels of hierarchy, both of which are occasionally measured at a population level, probably matter too.)

Second, trust helps provide certainty around the rules for investing in intangibles. We saw earlier that uncertain rules are bad for investment: if a company is unsure whether it can gather data on its customers and whether it can use such data for commercial purposes, it is less likely to spend money gathering the data in the first place; indeed, even knowing that it specifically cannot use the data for certain things may be a better basis for investment than total uncertainty. Higher levels of trust and social capital may make it easier to reach stable consensus on these kinds of rules, which makes the rules themselves more reliable.

Conclusion: Infrastructure in an Intangible World

The death of distance has failed to take place. Indeed, the importance of spillovers and synergies has increased the importance of places where people come together to share ideas and the importance of the transport and social spaces that make cities work.

But the death of distance may have been postponed rather than cancelled. Information technologies are slowly, gradually, replacing some aspects of face-to-face interaction. This may be a slow-motion change, like the electrification of factories—if so, the importance of physical infrastructure will radically change.

Soft infrastructure will also matter increasingly. The synergies between intangibles increase the importance of standards and norms, which together make up a kind of social infrastructure for intangible investment. And standards and norms are underpinned by trust and social capital, which are particularly important in an intangible economy.

We will touch more on these policy issues in chapter 10.

8

The Challenge of Financing an Intangible Economy

A common critique of the financial system is that it is unsuited to the task of business investment. Financial markets, the argument goes, are short-termist, poorly understand risk, and place perverse incentives on managers. In this chapter we ask whether the current financial system is appropriate for an increasingly intangible-based economy, in light of the economic properties of intangibles described in chapter 4. *We argue that, while some populist critiques of the business finance system are overblown, the properties of intangibles pose particular challenges for financing businesses.*

When asked what is wrong with capitalism today, many people point to financial markets. One particularly widespread concern is that the financial system does a bad job of serving the needs of the real economy, in particular, of providing businesses with the financing they require to invest.

This critique is in some ways an old one: it was back in the 1930s that Keynes made his famous complaint that the "capital development" of countries was being delegated to the casino mentality of their stock markets.[1] But it has taken on a new urgency in the last decade, since the systemic failure of the financial system came close to collapsing the global economy.

The populist concern over business finance has a common script. Banks, it is said, are uninterested in business and starve companies of the financing they need to thrive. Equity markets are seen as both overly short-termist and, as managers pay more and more attention to their company's stock price, increasingly influential. So, managers cut R&D spending to try to please short-term investors out for a quick buck.[2] These concerns drive public policy across the developed world: most governments to some extent subsidize or coerce banks to lend to businesses, and they give tax advantages to companies that finance using debt. Many countries are considering measures to make equity investors take a longer-term perspective, such as imposing taxes on short-term shareholdings or changing financial reporting requirements. And most governments have spent money trying to encourage alternative forms of financing, particularly venture capital (VC), which is regarded as providing a big potential source of business growth and national wealth.

Some of these arguments are not as clear-cut as their proponents imply. For example, it is not always clear that managers who cut R&D spending are doing the wrong thing. It's perfectly possible that the projects they are cutting might not be working out. Would it really be better for them to keep spending on projects with no potential for success? And shareholders who sell might also be perfectly justified: maybe the prospects for the company have gotten worse. Likewise for share buybacks, the subject of much criticism in recent years: it is not obvious why they are so bad—maybe the company has matured, opportunities have shrunk, and giving money back to shareholders is a worthy reward for their commitment to the firm.

Rather than rehash these long-running arguments in detail, although we shall touch on them somewhat, in this chapter we shall do something different. We shall instead concentrate on whether the gradual change in the capital base of the "real economy" from tangible to intangible assets has implications for the functioning of the financial sector. We will argue two main things. First, that the gradual shift to intangibles helps explain many of the perceived problems that the financial sector is accused of. The reason for this can be traced back to the economic qualities of intangible assets that we outlined in chapter 4: scalability, sunkenness, spillovers, and synergies, and the broader characteristics that emerge from them, uncertainty and contestedness. Second, we argue that a better understanding of the challenges of financing an intangible economy suggests a new course of action, both by governments looking to improve what Keynes called the capital development of the country, and by financial investors looking for higher returns.

We will look, in turn, at three types of financing with a significant bearing on business investment: bank financing, public equity, and risk capital. In the first two cases we will look at the challenges these forms of finance face in funding business investment in an intangible economy. In the case of risk capital, we will look at how the venture capital industry has evolved in response to an intangible-rich economy, and how well it meets the needs of intangible-rich firms.

Financial Markets and Business Investment: An Old but Topical Problem

But first, let's recap the received wisdom about what's wrong with business finance and how it is getting worse.

The critique that the financial system hampers the real economy, and particularly business investment, is simultaneously very old and very current. It has two parts: first, that financial markets do a bad job of providing business financing because they are myopic and foolish; second, that this malign influence is getting stronger as more and more aspects of business are "financialized."

The idea was already well established before the Second World War, when Keynes asserted that stock markets were essentially casinos and had no place in determining business investment; when the British government launched the 1929 Macmillan Committee to investigate whether Britain's financial system was meeting the needs of its economy; and when Keynes, the driving force behind the committee, articulated his views on the link between financial capital and the nation's poor capital development.

Indeed, much government policy around the world is predicated on the idea that the financial system serves business poorly. For all that the financial services sector is thought of as a bastion of laissez-faire capitalism, most developed countries intervene deeply and widely in the market for business finance. Germany's Kreditanstalt für Wiederaufbau (founded in 1948) and the US Small Business Administration (SBA, founded in 1953) both guarantee or underwrite business financing; in 1945 the UK set up the Industrial and Commercial Finance Corporation to provide growth capital. A search of the UK government website in summer 2016 yielded 319 finance-based schemes.

A more recent concern relates to "financialization" and associated short-termism. Financialization is the growing importance of norms, metrics, and incentives from the financial sector to the wider economy. Some of the concerns expressed are that, for example, managers are increasingly awarded stock options to align their incentives with those of shareholders; companies are often explicitly managed to increase short-term shareholder value; and financial engineering, such as share buybacks and earnings management, has become a more important part of senior managers' jobs. The end result is that rather than finance serving business, business serves finance: the tail wags the dog. What John Kay described as "obliquity," the idea that making money was a consequence of, or a second-order benefit of, serving one's customers and building good businesses, is driven out (Kay 2010).

A third aspect of finance is the perception that venture capital will be very important for the economies of the future. It is hard to think of a major developed country whose government has not spent taxpayers' money in an attempt to build or grow its VC sector. Most developed countries have put in place coinvestment schemes or tax breaks to try and stimulate a venture capital sector like that of the United States. Some of these schemes, such as Israel's Yozma program, have even worked— indeed, the US venture capital sector itself was kick-started by the SBA's Small Business Investment Companies program. Some governments invest directly in company equity (such as Germany's High-Tech Gruenderfonds or Finland's TEKES Venture Capital), and some innovation scholars like Mariana Mazzucato (2015) argue they should do this far more often. There have also been periodic government-backed attempts to start new stock exchanges for earlier-stage companies, making it easier for businesses to access public (in the sense of publicly traded), rather than public sector equity.

As mentioned above, some of these arguments are much less clear-cut than they at first appear. But reflecting on the increasingly intangible nature of the economy helps to cast light on these concerns and to understand how we might respond to them. To do this, let's unravel the finance around business investment into (a) banking, (b) equity markets, and (c) venture capital.

Banking: The Problem with Lending in a World of Intangibles

A topic that seems to unite most small business owners is the mulishness and unreliability of banks. Banks, they argue, are slow to lend, ignorant about business realities, bureaucratic, and risk-averse.[3] It's perhaps no wonder that the idea of setting up a government bank more willing to lend to businesses regularly appears in political manifestos in the UK and, indeed, is to some extent a reality in countries like Germany, France, and the United States. It's commonly thought that intangibles make this problem worse. In this section, we will look at why this is thought to be so, and what it means for the future of bank business financing.

Hamlet's priggish uncle Polonius said "neither a borrower nor a lender be, for loan oft loses both itself and friend," but he would have been taken aback by the modern economy.[4] Most external financing that most businesses receive takes the form of debt. Banks, or more rarely bondholders, lend money for a fixed period of time and expect it back at the end, with interest in the interim. If the debt isn't repaid, say, because the business fails, the creditor usually has recourse to some of the business's assets; this may not make up their entire loss, but it significantly reduces the financial risk the lender is taking.

This is fairly straightforward if a business's assets are tangible things. Consider buses. In 1986 Britain deregulated its long-distance bus market. A hopeful start-up called British Coachways took the opportunity to try to compete with National Express, the incumbent. But this was one disruption that wasn't to be: British Coachways gave up the ghost two years later. What happened after their failure is instructive for our purposes: they returned the buses to their leasing company. Even though the business failed, their biggest investment, a fleet of coaches, retained quite a lot of value. Similarly, when Maxjet, a discount business-class airline, went bust in 2007, its five Boeing 767s reverted to a leasing company and lived on to fly another day.

Assets like buildings, machines, or particular plots of land can be valued too, and financiers will set up asset-backed loans secured against everything from aircraft engines to oil tankers. Loans do not have to be asset-backed to benefit from the recyclability of tangible assets: lenders often take a general charge (known in the United States as a negative lien) against a business with assets than can be liquidated, or even lend on the security of assets outside the business. Indeed, much business lending done by British (and US) banks, for example, is a disguised form of mortgage lending, since banks typically take a lien on the business owner's house (Fraser 2012; Black, de Meza, and Jeffreys 1996). These established systems help get around Polonius's warning: loans may still oft go wrong, but if your debtor has tangible assets, your money will not be lost and, while you may no longer be friends with your deadbeat debtor, you can at least treat them with equanimity.

Businesses that own mainly intangible assets, however, look a lot more like the world of Polonius's imagination. As we saw in chapter 4, intangible investment is often *sunk*: many intangible assets are hard to sell if for some reason you find you don't need them, especially if your business fails. Toyota invests millions in its lean production systems, but it would be impossible to separate these investments from their factories and somehow sell them off. Starbucks codifies its operations into a voluminous handbook that its branches and franchises follow, and the homogeneity and customer experience it engenders seem to increase its profitability, but it's hard to imagine the handbook would be as valuable to someone else.

Even those intangibles that can be sold, like patents or copyrights, present problems to creditors: they are typically difficult to value because a patent or a copyright is unique in a way that a van or a building or many types of machine tools are not. The liquid markets that exist for assets like vans and office blocks, or the professional advisers who will value your mine or your chemical tanker, have fewer equivalents in the world of intellectual property: it is a newer and less developed field and is conceptually more difficult. The result is that it is much harder to offer even well-specified intangibles as security on a loan.

We see this discrepancy in typical leverage ratios among large businesses in different industries: industries with mostly tangible assets have high leverage—that is to say, they are funded more by debt than by equity—while intangible-intensive industries have less debt and more equity.

This problem becomes worse if the economy as a whole becomes more intangible-intensive. If banks are less willing and less able to lend to intangible-intensive businesses, but intangible-intensive businesses are becoming more common, we would expect to see complaints that banks refused to finance viable businesses becoming more common. And current regulation disallows (almost all) intangible assets as part of capital reserves that banks must hold in case of a banking crisis.[5]

A preponderance of unsaleable intangible assets could even, in due course, present a gradual problem for the stability of a banking system. Because bank runs are economically catastrophic, regulators require banks to hold a certain amount of reserves against every loan on their books. The amount of reserves depends on the type of loan: on the whole, loans secured against valuable assets that are easy to sell require less reserves; loans with little security require more. Now, given that many bank business loans are unsecured (the bank has a claim over the assets of the firm as a whole through a negative lien, but not over a particular asset), we might expect the riskiness of banks' unsecured business loan books to increase over time: specifically, the value of the loans would fall if there was widespread business failure and need to liquidate assets.

In practice, there are three ways to fix the problem of reduced bank lending in an intangible-rich economy. The first is a traditional one: government action. As we have seen, pressuring banks to lend more or using taxpayer money to cofund or guarantee bank loans has a decades-long tradition in most developed countries. The idea that the government should do more in this vein is a mainstay of the British left and can be heard elsewhere on the political spectrum too. But in an increasingly intangible-rich economy, this approach faces a challenge: if each year the country's capital stock becomes more intangible, the gap the government is trying to fill will become larger. To be effective, a national investment bank or loan guarantee program would need to be larger and larger each year. This is not inherently impossible, but it is certainly not what most supporters of government lending programs propose, expect, or support.

The second way to address the problem is by devising new types of lending. Financial innovation has been something of a dirty word since the financial crisis—former Federal Reserve Chairman Paul Volcker went so far as to say the only beneficial financial innovation of the decades prior to the financial crisis was the automated teller machine—but, in fact, lenders have over the years come up with novel ways to use at least some types of intangible assets as security. One recent working paper (Mann 2014) suggests that 16 percent of patents registered at the US Patent and Trademark Office have been pledged as collateral at some point. A couple of studies have looked at the impact of US banking deregulation on investment in innovation: one showed that the deregulation of interstate banking saw an increase in lending to innovating companies (based on the number and quality of their patents), implying that greater competition pushes banks to be more willing to lend to businesses making (at least one type of) intangible investment (Amore, Schneider, and Zaldokas 2012).

There are also a growing number of specific financial innovations focused on lending against intangibles. When David Bowie died in 2016, there were plenty of tributes to his musical innovations, but rather fewer to the contribution he made to intangible finance by raising a $55 million bond against his future royalties. The governments of Singapore and Malaysia (working together with UK organizations such as the Intellectual Property Office), for example, have begun programs to subsidize or guarantee bank loans against intellectual property, in the hope that these subsidies will increase the availability of intangible-backed loans.

On the whole these types of lending are most appropriate for intangibles that have associated intellectual property rights, such as patents or copyrights—this will generally be a minority of the intangible investments most businesses make. But more developed institutions for financing these types of intangibles will be increasingly in demand in a more intangible economy and will benefit both the lenders who design and offer them and, to quote Keynes again, the capital development of the nation.

The final way to respond to the difficulty of lending against intangibles is the most radical. It is for businesses to change their finance mix: specifically, to rely more on equity and less on debt. Should a business fail, equity owners have no recourse—they get nothing—so can afford to be relatively insouciant about the liquidation value of a business's assets. This makes equity a better way of funding businesses with few tangible assets.

But increasing the amount of equity finance in an economy is easier said than done: it is a project that would take decades rather than years. Some of the barriers are institutional: outside of the very small world of venture capital (of which more later) and the even smaller and newer field of equity crowdfunding, most businesses do not raise equity, and most financial institutions do not provide it. There are established agencies that can rate the creditworthiness of even quite small businesses, and algorithms to allow banks to quickly and cheaply decide whether to lend to them. Nothing similar exists for equity investment, and the equivalent analytical task (working out a company's likely future value, rather than its likelihood of servicing a fixed debt) is more complex. And cultural factors stand in the way too: despite a very elegant financial economics theorem that shows that business owners should be indifferent between equity and debt finance, for many small business owners there seems a cognitive and cultural bias against giving away equity.[6]

There is one big regulatory barrier that could be removed, however. Most developed countries' tax systems favor debt finance over equity finance: a firm can claim interest on a loan as an operating expense and reduce its tax liability, but not the cost of equity capital. Fixing this distortion (for example, by allowing a tax deduction for the cost of equity, or removing the favorable tax status of debt and lowering overall rates to compensate) has long been a goal of tax experts. The influential Mirrlees report on the UK tax system by the Institute for Fiscal Studies recommended it (Mirrlees et al. 2011), but it has so far proved about as difficult as any other major corporate tax reform—which is to say, very difficult indeed, because there are lots of vested interests at stake.[7] However, with the growing importance of intangibles, the need to make this change may be increasing over time. Now would be a good time for policymakers to bite the bullet and do it.

Myopic Markets

It is not just banks that stand accused of hampering business investment. Stock markets and equity owners are also widely seen as a part of the problem. Consider the case of the chemical company ICI, once the flagship of the British chemical industry. ICI's plants in Billingham, Runcorn, and Blackley were industrial landmarks of the north of England, and its shares were a mainstay of the London Stock Exchange. For decades it invested in research and bringing to market a wide variety of innovative products, from Crimplene to tamoxifen to Perspex. It pioneered new ways of doing business that other firms profitably adopted, and ICI-trained chemists, engineers, and managers filled the ranks of British industry. But things began to change in the 1990s: frightened by a takeover threat from an activist investor, ICI began to focus on the pursuit of short-term shareholder value. To this end, it plunged enthusiastically into the M&A market, divesting or selling billions of dollars' worth of divisions, and acquiring several others. The pursuit of focus and efficiency proved tough, and the company faced a growing debt burden and problems integrating its acquisitions. By the 2000s ICI's decline was obvious, and few were surprised when what remained of the company was bought by Akzo Nobel in 2008 for a mere (relative to its past value) £8 billion.

For critics like the economist John Kay (2003), ICI is an example of the malign effect that equity markets now have on business investment. In ICI's glory days the company, in Kay's words, "treated securities markets with disdain." When it started to take its share price seriously, it failed in two ways: it generated fewer profitable innovations and less value for its own shareholders, and it relinquished its wider role in the UK's business landscape as a nursery of managerial and scientific talent, as the lynchpin of industrial supply chains, and as a voice for good governance.

The ICI example encapsulates all the elements of the core critique of equity markets: that they reward short-term financial results over long-term investment, and that financialization—the growing power and salience of financial markets in business life—makes managers overly responsive to the impatient whims of shareholders. A host of troubling data back up these concerns: research by Rachelle Sampson and Yuan Shi (2016) suggested stock markets are increasingly discounting US firms' cash flows; research by Andrew Haldane (R. Davies et al. 2014), the Bank of England's chief economist, and Richard Davies, a Chairman of the UK government's Council of Economic Advisers, found similar results in the UK, as did the economist David Miles (1993). A study by Graham, Harvey, and Rajgopal from 2005 suggested this view is not unusual: it found that 78 percent of executives said they would sacrifice long-term value to meet earnings targets.

Critics further allege that instead of investing, there are signs that companies are giving money back to shareholders: in 2014 companies in the US S&P 500 Index spent almost as much on share buybacks as they received in profits.[8] The end result is that publicly quoted companies refrain from making investments they otherwise would, preferring to keep their cash or to give it back to shareholders.[9] The innovation economist Mariana Mazzucato has made this argument, for example (2013; 2015).

Policymakers and pundits propose a number of remedies to the problems of market short-termism, including trying to encourage investors to hold stocks for longer through differential tax rates on share sales, reducing financialization by limiting or banning share buybacks or restricting the terms of options, or simply calling on owners of equities to be more responsible.

However, as we shall see, the growing importance of intangible investment changes the nature of the short-termism problem: it appears that the unusual characteristics of intangibles accentuate certain problems of underinvestment, but also create new problems that require different solutions.

What We Talk about When We Talk about Short-Termism

There are two important details of this critique of equity markets. First of all, unlike the critique of bank finance we discussed earlier, it is a critique of the indirect impact of the financial system on business decisions, not the provision of financing. Bank lending is a direct source of finance: a bank's decision not to lend stops a company investing by directly depriving it of the money it needs to make the investment. Equity markets, on the other hand, are secondary markets: the movement of a company's stock price does not directly affect the amount of money the company has; rather, markets might encourage managers to forego investments if they fear the investment will lower the company's short-term share price, especially if senior managers own shares or share options.

Second, companies that are overly influenced by equity markets have two distinct failure modes. In the first, the company's own shareholders lose out in the long run because the company turns down investments that it could reasonably expect to make it money. (In financial economics terms, they pass up projects that would have had a positive net present value.) ICI's decision to stop investing in new materials would be an example of this, according to John Kay, if we believe that those projects were genuinely likely to make money for ICI.

The other failure mode occurs if the pressure of the equity markets discourages a company from investing in things with a wider public benefit—such as ICI not training the managers or engineers who'll go off to run other businesses in the future, or not doing basic research that others use. The two failure modes have an important difference: in the second, although the company is not acting in the interests of the wider economy, it may well be acting in its own shareholders' best interests (in the short term, at least). In the first example, it is not even doing that. This distinction is especially relevant in the context of intangible investment, as we shall see.

When Equity Markets Meet Intangibles

Those who criticize equity markets for being too short-termist sometimes argue that this problem is even worse for companies that rely on intangibles. R&D, for example, is a long-term investment whose benefits are hard to predict in advance and whose costs generally are expensed on a company's income statement rather than capitalized on its balance sheet. Cutting R&D (and most other intangibles) increases a company's profits without any immediate obvious balance-sheet impact.

What's more, as we saw in chapter 4, even successful R&D can slip through a company's fingers and end up benefiting its competitors. Research shows that businesses cut R&D spending when stock markets turn against them. There is also a particularly strong correlation between R&D investment and cash flow. That is, at least in the 1990s when much of this research was done, when firms had higher cash flow, they invested more in R&D. That is consistent with the idea that businesses lack access to outside funds and so when they have the funds internally, only then can they invest (see, for example, B. H. Hall and Lerner 2010).

Equity markets seem to deter some other types of intangible investment too. William Lazonick argued that the pressures of financial markets discouraged modern companies from investing in training and employee retention, comparing the life-long careers of software engineers in the heyday of companies like Hewlett Packard and IBM with the roaming of the modern techies, who might move regularly between Facebook, Google, and start-ups, with the result that their bosses feel disinclined to invest in training them. Alex Edmans (2011) looked at the share price performance of companies that won a place on lists of the best companies to work for—these lists are compiled by researchers and journalists and tend to reflect the kinds of investments in management and processes that we would classify as organizational development and training. Edmans found that their shares persistently outperformed those of other companies, and that it is employee satisfaction that causes superior performance, rather than the reverse. This is a surprising result: if markets fairly valued the kind of organizational capital resulting from good management and workforce practices, the benefits of winning a place on this sort of list (and revealing to the market that your company is well managed) ought to be reflected in a firm's share price straight after it wins. The fact that there is a long-term increase in price suggests that, while good management practices improve firm performance (hence the long-term share price increase), equity markets undervalue the benefits of this type of intangible (since equity analysts should be able to recognize good management at the time the award is given, rather than waiting for its results to show up on the income statement).

But, of course, correlation is not causation: just because a publicly listed firm invests less in R&D, training, or other intangibles does not mean it is being led astray by equity markets. Managers might choose to invest less because they know the investments available to them are unlikely to be profitable or, more narrowly, that they might be profitable for someone, but not necessarily for them. The business pages are full of companies that have launched new products or set up new service lines only to regret their over-optimism. If equity markets are stopping this type of intangible investment, that may be no bad thing.

To be sure of what is happening, we need data that allows us to correct for the quality of intangible investment that a public company may be making, or that allows us to compare similar companies with similar investment prospects, some of which are publicly owned and some of which are not.

Fortunately, there has been a recent flourishing of just these kinds of papers. The findings are mixed. One study, by Edmans, Fang, and Lewellen (2013), offers up what looks like a smoking gun. It looks at how firms' R&D varies with the vesting period of senior managers' equity. Managers at public companies are often paid in equity (shares or options), which can only be exercised after a period of years (the "vesting period"); once options vest, managers often exercise the options and sell the shares, which makes the managers particularly sensitive to their employer's share price at that moment. It turns out that managers are unusually likely to cut R&D spending in a quarter when they have a lot of equity vesting. Since equity vesting periods are set years in advance, this seems like prima facie evidence that managers are cutting intangible investment to improve earnings to give their stock price a boost when it matters most to them.

A second study by Bernstein (2015) is also revealing, but in a different way. Bernstein began by observing that, when a private company decides to go public, it takes time—and there's many a slip between start-up and IPO. For some companies, economic times are smooth and they go public. But for others, the stock market might collapse just before they launch. Generally, these companies don't go public. This creates a natural experiment between other similar firms, some of which are publicly traded and some of which aren't; more importantly, their status is generated by something beyond the firm's control. From this, we can infer the causal effects of being public not by comparing two firms that are public or that are both private, but by comparing a firm that is public with one that is private due to an adverse shock beyond their control.

He finds two interesting things. First, the private-to-public transition does not affect a firm's patenting—one indicator of successful intangible investment, in this case in R&D. A public firm has the same number of patents relative to its nonpublic "twin." But, second, the types of patents the public firm files tend to change. The patents of a public firm have fewer citations than those of private firms, and many of the public firm's scientific staff tend to leave. But the public company buys many more patents of higher quality. This is consistent with the open innovation model we discussed in chapter 4. So, Bernstein's research suggests that the public firms might change their innovation strategy, rather than their innovation effort, at least as measured by patents.

So what is going on here? Market short-termism when it comes to intangibles seems to be real: managers cut R&D. But publicly quoted firms seem to end up with higher quality patents. One way to perhaps reconcile this is via a different strand of research, pioneered by the finance economist Alex Edmans, that suggests that *who* a company's investors are may make a difference.

When you ask managers of public companies why it is important to meet earnings targets, they often talk about sending the right signals to investors and giving them confidence. Much of what managers do when they are planning investments is both difficult to explain to outsiders and commercially sensitive, but whether or not a company makes the profits it promised is relatively easy to report and to check. A shareholder might well need to be very informed and expert to know whether a company's new product was likely to be a success, but anyone who can read an income statement can see whether it met its earnings target. You might expect informed and expert shareholders to give companies more scope to invest in risky and complex things, like intangibles.

How would you measure the expertise of a firm's shareholders? Various researchers have used proxies: in particular, they have looked at how many of a company's shares are owned by institutions (rather than individuals) and how concentrated these hold-

ings are. The logic is that financial institutions tend to be more sophisticated than ordinary punters, and that the incentive to study
and understand a company and its business increases the more
of its shares any one institution owns. (Research is a scalable intangible investment for stockbrokers, just like anyone else!) An
investor who spends time and resources to collect information will
benefit if they hold one share. But they need spend no more time
and resource to get much greater benefit if they own one million
shares. This suggests that dispersed shareholders have a poor incentive to gather information, an argument showed formally by
Alex Edmans (Edmans 2009).[10]

It seems that having more institutional investors and having
more concentrated investors both encourage investment in R&D.
Aghion, Van Reenen, and Zingales (2013) compared firms just
outside the S&P 500 with those that just scraped in. On the whole,
these firms had similar characteristics, but with one big difference:
being in the index encouraged more institutional shareholding.
They found that greater institutional ownership led to more investment in R&D. Edmans (2014) summarizes evidence showing that concentrated ownership has a similar effect: companies
with shareholders who control relatively large shareholdings (so-
called blockholders) invest more in R&D than ones with dispersed
ownership.

This suggests that the effects of equity markets on intangible
investment are mixed. There is some evidence that markets are
short-termist, to the extent that management can sometimes boost
their company's share price by cutting intangible investment to
preserve or increase profits, or cut investment to buy back stock.
But it also seems that some of what is happening is a sharpening of
managerial incentives: publicly held companies whose managers
own stock focus on types of intangible investment that are more
likely to be successful. And the extent of market myopia varies:
companies with more concentrated, sophisticated investors are
less likely to feel pressure to cut intangible investment than those
with dispersed, unsophisticated ones.

The argument that having concentrated shareholders or blockholders improves outcomes makes logical sense. After all, if
shareholders buy and sell shares we cannot just accuse them of

short-termism: the prospects of the company might genuinely have changed. So, it is not the duration of the shareholding that matters; rather, it is the information base upon which buyers and sellers are acting. Blockholders have a sharper incentive to find out about the company's long-term prospects, which nowadays are built on their intangible assets. So they are more likely to trade on the basis of long-term information, thus supporting managers who are making sound long-term investments and penalizing managers with a short-term horizon. The alignment of shareholder and manager incentives that blockholding brings is all the more important with intangible assets, since they are so often hidden from outside investors' view and so effort is needed to unearth them. We'll discuss further why they are hidden from view in chapter 9.

The Usefulness of Venture Capital, and Its Limits

Given the limitations of bank financing for intangible-intensive businesses, and the problems of underinvestment that affect public companies, it is no surprise that many people look to venture capital to finance the new economy.

After all, VC is a form of financing that developed alongside some of the world's fastest growing intangible-intensive businesses. Most of the intangible-rich businesses of Silicon Valley, and many high-growth businesses beyond, got their earliest investments from the venture capital firms on Sand Hill Road. This form of financing has evolved together with businesses like Intel, Google, Genentech, and Uber, whose competitive advantages depend on intangibles: valuable R&D, novel product design, software, and organizational development.

Indeed, like the beaks of Darwin's Galapagos finches that evolved to feed on particular cacti, many of the distinctive features of venture capital relate directly to the unusual characteristics of intangible investments that VC-funded businesses tend to make.

But this adaptation is not perfect: while the best venture capital–backed businesses have grown rapidly and expanded around the world, venture capital as a form of funding has spread much more tentatively. Many governments have tried to foster indigenous VC sectors, but very few have succeeded; some sectors where the venture capital model has been applied amid great hope, such as greentech and energy, have so far shown disappointing results. Spectacular successes have so far been pretty rare. Thinking about intangibles also helps us understand the limits of VC, and why it is wrong to view it as a panacea.

The Finch's Beak: Why VC Works for Intangibles

VC has several characteristics that make it especially well-suited to intangible-intensive businesses: VC firms take equity stakes, not debt, because intangible-rich businesses are unlikely to be worth much if they fail—all those sunk investments. Similarly, to satisfy their own investors, VC funds rely on home-run successes, made possible by the scalability of assets like Google's algorithms, Uber's driver network, or Genentech's patents. Third, VC is often sequential, with rounds of funding proceeding in stages. This is a response to the inherent *uncertainty* of intangible investment. The nature of uncertainty in start-ups is that it tends to reduce over time. When Peter Thiel made the first external investment of $500,000 in Facebook in 2004, the company's fortunes were considerably more uncertain than when Microsoft invested $240 million in 2007. Funding in rounds helps resolve uncertainty by working through the development of business in stages. For investors, it creates an "option value," that is, a value to delaying follow-on investment until information is revealed. These options are particularly valuable for businesses whose cost of innovating is relatively high.

One way to understand VC is to look where it does and doesn't work. Biotech has many VC firms that provide much funding: it seems to work. Because of the sunkenness theory, financing risk is higher for industries that have to go back to the capital market again and again and have no assets or products that can be sold at each stage. However, in biotech the process has a number of distinct stages, and there have developed institutions that can at every stage of the process sell part-approved patents, etc. In addition, intellectual property rights (IPRs) have developed that enable knowledge at the various stages to be appropriated and so marketed. By contrast, green energy has much smaller VC activity.

But this is an area with massive uncertainty, few distinct stages, and poorly established property rights.

The nature of intangible investment can also explain how venture capitalists add value to the businesses they invest in. One of the odd things about venture capital is the persistence of strong performance among funds—that is to say, the fact that the best 25 percent of venture capital funds tend to be the same funds, year after year and even decade after decade. This is far from usual in financial markets. A recent UK study found in the mutual fund industry that the best-performing 20 percent of fund managers were among the worst performing 20 percent a year later (Vanguard 2015). Private equity funds show similar variability over time. But high-performing VC firms tend to do well in fund after fund year after year.

One might think this is because venture capitalists are professional, highly remunerated people who are good at picking investments or at sitting on company boards. But then again, the people who run mutual fund businesses and private equity funds are professional and highly paid too, and the superior performance of these funds does not persist.

One possibility is that this persistence stems from the characteristics of the intangible assets that VC-backed businesses invest in. We have seen that intangibles often have significant *synergies* with one another: for example, combining Google's search algorithm with an e-mail application gave rise to Gmail, which was radically better and more profitable than its competitors when it launched in 2004. We have also seen that intangibles are often *contested*: it is harder for Uber to "own" its network of driver-partners than it is for a cab company to own a fleet of cars, and the value of the Uber asset is up for grabs in a way the fleet of cars is not.

When we look at successful VC funds and their partners, we see people who are highly networked and personally credible in their fields of investment. In the 1980s, before the Japanese economy became unfashionable, the veteran venture capitalist John Doerr used to say that his firm, Kleiner Perkins, built American "keiretsu," the interlocking business networks that used to dominate Japanese industry; to put it another way, the firm built informal links between its portfolio companies, allowing them to exploit synergies of intangibles.[11] Few people praise Japan's keiretsu nowadays, but Silicon Valley boasts a VC firm called Keiretsu Capital, and the best funds in the United States, Israel, London, and Stockholm all strive to nurture stables of businesses and exploit commonalities among them.

The social connections and reputation that the best VC firms enjoy help them not only to build networks to exploit synergies, but also to increase the value of *contested* assets. Particularly in fields like software and Internet services, the value of an intangible investment depends heavily on how it fits into a wider technological ecosystem: a new app may be worth a lot more if it integrates with Google Calendar; an analytical software business may be worth more if it can develop a partnership with an online ad distribution business. Well-connected VC firms also ensure their start-ups are plugged into open innovation networks. This has a direct financial benefit for the VC funds to the extent that it makes it easier for companies to be sold to trade buyers, thus earning a return for the fund; it also helps limit the amount of capital the fund itself needs to raise to get to an exit. The connections and reputations of VC funds and their partners add value to the intangible investments of the companies they invest in. What's more, it is plausible that this advantage persists over time, since it depends not only on the networks of partners but also on the portfolios of companies a firm is invested in.

Indeed, the recurrent critiques of the lack of diversity of Silicon Valley's VC sector and the companies that it backs can be seen as a reflection of the importance of social capital. We might speculate that the reason VCs can seem like a clique is not because the venture capitalists are unusually bad or cliquish people, but because the underlying model of the VC business thrives on dense social networks, which will always tend to gravitate to cliquishness in the absence of countervailing effort, and perhaps even then.

What Venture Capital Can't Do

So there is a strong case for saying that venture capital is well suited to investing in intangible-rich businesses and should be rightly held up as a positive type of financial innovation. But VC is not a panacea for business investment, and on its own VC will struggle to solve the problem of how to finance the capital development of an intangible economy.

There are three problems that face VC firms and VC-backed companies, some of which arise from the nature of intangible investments themselves.

The first is the problem of spillovers. The managers of VC-backed firms have strong incentives to create valuable companies— really successful founders can, after all, become very rich. But as we saw in the context of publicly owned companies, strong incentives on managers make them less willing to invest in intangibles whose returns will more likely than not go to other companies. So expecting VC-backed firms to do Bell Labs–style basic research is unrealistic. More often than not, Silicon Valley (and other tech ecosystems, like Israel's) relies on publicly funded university research for these basic intangibles.

The same is true where the size of intangible investment required is very large and very uncertain: developing commercially viable fourth-generation nuclear reactors or new green energy processes, for example, requires investments much larger than most VC funds will make, with high spillovers.

Finally, it turns out that the remarkable ability of VC funds to manage contestedness and spillovers is, unlike an algorithm or a brand, very hard to scale up. Silicon Valley's VC sector took four decades to mature, in the presence of considerable public subsidy, both direct (from Small Business Investment Companies) and indirect (from defense contracts that provided revenue streams for VC-backed companies). Part of what took so long was the process of embedding venture capital in the ecosystem of the tech industry, such that entrepreneurs sought out funds, large companies bought start-ups, and generations of entrepreneurs and venture capitalists mentored one another. Replicating this in a new industry, even with the help of an open-handed government, takes time. It is no surprise that of the many developed countries that have spent decent slugs of taxpayer money over the past thirty years trying to create their own equivalent, most, as Josh Lerner points out in his aptly titled book *The Boulevard of Broken Dreams*, have had limited success.

If venture capital is well tailored to some aspects of intangible investment, but very hard to scale, where does this leave policy-makers? On the one hand, they should moderate their expectations about what VC can do for capital development in the short term in countries and places that do not already have a globally significant VC sector: growing a VC sector is a twenty-year project, not something that can be achieved between elections; and while public subsidy is helpful, it cannot substitute for time.

We should also be cautious about the potential for VC to transform established sectors where it currently has little traction. Again, the social ties on which VC depends seem to take time to establish in new industries. The challenge is an order of magnitude harder in sectors where innovation involves much larger capital investment, such as energy generation. It would be presumptuous to say that VC cannot work in a field like nuclear energy, but it would require funds of a scale not seen before, with plenty of opportunities for pioneers to lose money along the way. Even in a well-functioning VC sector, then, the need for government to fund spillover-rich intangibles and the need for established larger companies to find a separate way to finance them will persist. The government might do that funding directly, or maybe through other publicly funded institutions: universities perhaps.

Conclusion: The Capital Development of an Intangible Economy

Let's conclude by thinking about the longer term. If we assume that intangible investment will become increasingly important for businesses, what sort of financial institutions and funding mechanisms will be required to support it, and what opportunities will this create for investors?

First of all, we would expect to see a shift away from bank lending as a means of financing businesses. Some of this slack would be taken up by the creation of new debt products secured against intellectual property, but for the most part there would be a shift toward the use of equity as a means of financing small and medium-sized businesses. This would rely on significant further tax reform—ending the favorable tax treatment of debt, for example, and introducing more tax advantages for start-ups—and on the evolution of new financial institutions to enable small-scale equity investment and to facilitate due diligence.

We would expect to see public equity investment dominated more by institutions, some of which would commit to taking large stakes in intangible-rich companies, enabling greater investment. This would require removing some regulations that discourage blockholding, and it would also rely on better tools for institutional investors to appraise and value intangible investments. Some of these tools may in time give rise to changes in financial accounting standards, so that public companies' balance sheets better reflect their (by now mainly intangible) investments (Lev 2001; Lev and Gu 2016). Given that at least some intangible investments currently seem to be undervalued, there would for a time be the opportunity for funds to make excess returns by buying and holding stock in intangible-rich companies and supporting management plans for further intangible investment. We might also expect to see an increase in the number of large privately held companies, as certain companies with large blockholders decide the benefits of being public are exceeded by the disclosure cost—which, in an age of spillover-rich intangibles, may be higher.

There may also be a different strategy available to the largest institutional investors: to invest broadly across an ecosystem, to such an extent that it is worth approving management plans for intangible investments even if they have large spillovers, since these large investors will benefit from the investment even if a different firm takes advantage of it because they have a stake in the industry as a whole. This tactic of investing across a particular industry (such as energy) could be applied more broadly perhaps—especially by very large investors such as sovereign wealth funds. This seems to be the most likely way that a latter-day generation of Bell Labs might arise under private finance.

We will probably also see an expansion of venture capital, though whether serious VC sectors will arise in many places, or break through into entirely new sectors, is less certain. Either way, they will continue to rely on close relations both with established firms and with publicly funded intangible investments (such as long-run scientific research and development) to thrive.

VC coevolved alongside a particular type of intangible-intensive business, so we might expect them to be well adapted to one another. This link between intangible investment and both the advantages and challenges of VC is not just a matter of idle curiosity. It is of practical importance because it provides clues to what sort of financial system we might expect in a world where intangible investment becomes the norm, and what sort of institutions might be required to invest in other intangible-rich businesses.

Finally, if public subsidies to private sector institutions cannot generate enough public spillovers then maybe there will be growth in the importance of publicly subsidized knowledge generators: universities. But for support to be forthcoming, they would have to be truly public knowledge-generating institutions, and experiments in organizational form are probably necessary. Perhaps that is best done by research institutes rather than conventional universities and, perhaps paradoxically, the research that should be supported should explicitly not be immediately commercializable, since that can be left in private hands.

9

Competing, Managing, and Investing in the Intangible Economy

What will successful companies look like in an intangible-rich economy, and how can managers and investors create and invest in them? In this chapter we'll look at what people thought the new economy might mean for companies and managers, and how it hasn't quite worked out that way, due, we think, to the characteristics of intangibles. We'll then look at whether the rules for sustaining competitive advantage have changed (they haven't), if management is becoming more important (it is), and how suited current accounting measures are for investors to identify such advantage (they aren't).

Back in the heady days of the late 1990s, when pundits began to be excited en masse about a new economy, there was something of a shared vision of what businesses would need to do to succeed in the new economy, and what that would mean for management and working life.

Charles Handy's 1994 book *The Future of Work* forecasted, presciently, a future of portfolio jobs and careers for the well-educated and precarious subcontracting for others. Charles Leadbeater's *Living on Thin Air*, published at the height of the dot-com bubble, begins with a portrait of the author as a portfolio knowledge worker and then identifies eight characteristics that successful new economy companies would have: they would be cellular, self-managing, entrepreneurial, and integrative; they would offer their staff ownership stakes; and they would need deep reservoirs of knowledge, public legitimacy, and collaborative leadership. The view of how businesses succeed blends Japanese management theory such as Nonaka and Takeuchi's concept of the "knowledge-creating" company (in a book of the same title, 1991) with studies of entrepreneurial innovation observed from the Silicon Valley firms of the day.

Like many of the things in Handy's and Leadbeater's books—both of which have aged rather well—all of these predictions have to some extent come to pass. Drop into a coffee shop in any of the world's major cities, and you will see peripatetic knowledge workers of the type that Handy described in the early 1990s. Look at the way people talk about the world's most admired businesses ("What Would Google Do?"), and you will see praise for the kind of knowledge-intensive, collaborative, networked business innovation that would not have seemed out of place in 1990s California or Japan.

But some things have turned out somewhat differently, either because they buck the trend of knowledge-intensive, modular businesses and the nomadic, entrepreneurial knowledge workers, or simply because they were less obvious back in 1999.

A graphic illustration of this is the Amazon warehouse. Sarah O'Connor, writing in the *Financial Times* in 2013, painted a vivid portrait of working and managing in the Amazon warehouse in Rugeley, in the UK's West Midlands.[1] The word "autonomous knowledge work" is unlikely to figure on the employees' job description. Warehouse staffers have GPS trackers that optimize their route to package an order: relatively straightforward if the order is just a book, but a formidable technical achievement if the order is a book, a vacuum cleaner, Junior Monopoly, and a pair of skis. Of course, the tracker also enables managers to keep an eye on where the workers are and how fast they are moving. O'Connor describes managers sending text messages to employees to speed up and advising them to put Vaseline on their feet to prevent blisters from all the walking (up to 15 miles per shift is quoted). So in the actually existing new economy, not everyone turned out to be a "self-facilitating media node" (as late 1990s knowledge workers were sarcastically described by satirist Charlie Brooker). The intangible economy is as much about Amazon warehouses and the Starbucks operating manual as it is about hipsters in Shoreditch and Williamsburg, or empowered Kanban production workers in Japanese-inspired factories.

Perhaps a second way that the new economy has turned out unexpectedly is the emergence of the cult of the manager. Endless management hagiographies adorn airport bookshelves. Managers get invited to Davos. Jack Welch, the former CEO of General Electric, has an institute named after him. And, of course, CEOs are famously highly rewarded. Now this has been supplanted by the new cult of "leadership." Figure 9.1 sets out by decade the number of times "leadership," as against "management," is mentioned as a subject in an article in the *Harvard Business Review*. References to management have grown steadily. But references to leadership have exploded since the 2000s.

This idolatry is in many ways a huge puzzle. Don't we live in a much less deferential age? Aren't we less willing to take instructions and less trustful of authority figures? Surely changes in social norms would appear to bias people *away* from these reverential attitudes to managers and leaders?

A third way that the new economy has turned out, perhaps not quite as expected, is what might be called a "rush for scale." Alongside the small portfolio contractors and lean, networked businesses we see some behemoths: new multi-billion-dollar companies with big scale and bigger ambitions. As we have seen in chapter 5, the leading firms seem to have become even more leading: more profitable, more productive. Peter Thiel, the cofounder of PayPal, has

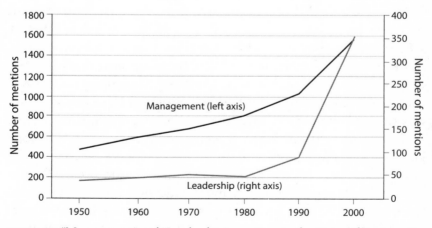

Figure 9.1. "Management" and "Leadership" mentions in the *Harvard Business Review*. Source: authors' calculations from HBR title subjects.

written engagingly on these issues in his book *Zero to One*, stressing that commercial success is built on exploiting network effects and economies of scale: as he points out, Twitter can easily scale up but a yoga studio cannot.

We shall argue that these seemingly contradictory changes all arise from the essential economic characteristics of intangible assets. To tell this story, we start by arguing that the evolution of work and the cult of management come not only from changes in social norms and the like, but also from the evolution of companies. In turn, these companies are trying to compete in their market. Thus we start by setting out the pressures companies are under to compete and how the growth of intangibles changes what companies have to do. As we shall see, in an intangible-rich economy, the pressure to compete pushes companies toward large scale and an emphasis on management. This not only changes how companies compete and manage but also where investors should look for returns, so we conclude with some advice for them.

Competing

One of the most important practical questions put to experts in business strategy, management, accounting, and economics is *"How can my firm get ahead?"* Not surprisingly, such a question has elicited many answers.

The starting point is to refine the question, since it all depends on what you mean by "getting ahead." One way to get ahead is short-term manipulation of accounting aggregates. As we observed in chapter 8, cutting R&D, for example, cuts current spending, and, if the firm already has a good stream of revenues from previous R&D, this may have no negative effect on revenues for years. Revenues the same, costs down, hey, presto: profits up. As we shall see later in this chapter, and as Baruch Lev and Feng Gu have pointed out (2016), accounting conventions make it very hard for outside investors to see if firms are doing this. But, for the moment, let us take from this observation that a more sophisticated version of "How can firms get ahead?" is to ask *"How can firms improve performance that is sustainable?"*—that is, not via short-term manipulation.[2]

The easiest way to see how firms might create sustained competitive advantage is to start by thinking about a world where they
cannot. According to the US Department of Agriculture, in 2016
there were around 25,000 farms in Idaho, cultivating almost 12
million acres, with an average farm size of 474 acres (of which 60
percent were below 100 acres).[3] That means that each single farm
area is about 0.004 percent of total cultivated area. Despite the
geographical advantages of Idaho, especially in potato production
(southern Idaho has warm days and cool nights during the potato growing season), it's pretty unlikely that any individual farm
is going to have much advantage over another. Their outputs are
going to be the same, and their inputs, the machines, soil, and expertise, are likely the same too.

All this suggests that sustainable competitive advantage comes if
a company can do something distinctive, or if it owns a distinctive
asset. An Idaho farmer cannot do better than their neighbor, but
can do better than a farmer in Canada, since they own the distinctive asset of land in Idaho. Of course, a distinctive asset might not
necessarily be an input, but it might be reputation or a network
of customers (Swiss watches, say, or Facebook). The management
literature calls these distinctive assets "strategic resources" and says
they have three characteristics. They are (a) valuable (e.g., a patent), (b) rare (e.g., a landing slot at a busy airport), and (c) hard to
imitate (e.g., Swiss watch reputation).[4]

So the advice to managers has always been: build and maintain
distinctive assets. And to investors: look for firms that have these
types of assets. Does that advice change in an intangible world?
No. But the intangible-rich world is precisely a reflection of firms
that are increasingly taking this advice. Why?

It's pretty unusual that a tangible asset is going to be a source
of distinctiveness. Perhaps a specially customized machine might
be. But for the most part tangible assets are not going to be distinctive. A bank might build a grand head office with a soaring
atrium, colorful fish-tanks, and minimalist desks in the lobby. But
any other company can do that too. It's much more likely that
the types of intangible assets we have talked about in this book
are going to be distinctive: reputation, product design, trained
employees providing customer service. Indeed, perhaps the most

distinctive asset will be the ability to weave all these assets together; so a particularly valuable intangible asset will be the organization itself.

These insights are implicit in Peter Thiel's book *Zero to One*. His view is that commercial success is built on four characteristics: building a proprietary technology; exploiting network effects; benefiting from economies of scale; and branding. These recommendations are firmly in line with the strategy for an intangible-rich business, based on the four S's that we discussed in chapter 4. So, for example, he rightly points out that Twitter can easily scale up: a prime example of economies of scale in action. By contrast, he uses a yoga studio as an example of a business that cannot scale up and so is destined to stay small. As we have seen, Les Mills International had to adopt a very different business model from traditional gym businesses in order to grow to the size it did.

The emphasis on network effects is an insight of Thiel's that suggests that governments might become more important to company success in the future. One of Peter Thiel's PayPal cofounders, Elon Musk, is currently involved in what might become one of the ultimate network businesses: self-driving, battery-powered cars. The network effect would be familiar to any nineteenth-century entrepreneur. Horses and carts needed a gigantic network of stables to feed and water the horses and repair the carts. Then gas-driven cars needed a gigantic network of garages and gas stations. Now, electric cars will need a network of charging stations. To implement all this requires state help, and Musk has been as much an entrepreneur in getting the support of governments as he has been in driving the technology in the business. The legal travails of Uber and AirB&B are similar examples.

But one characteristic of successful businesses that Thiel seems to omit is building a good organization. Wal-Mart and K-Mart are in the same industry, have more or less the same types of trucks and fixtures in their stores, and stock very similar goods. Yet even to the everyday observer, they are vastly different. What makes them different is in part their reputation, but also the very organization itself. So let us turn to the organization and, in particular, the role of management and leadership.

Managing

One reason for the celebrity status of managers is offered by the consistently fascinating blogger Chris Dillow,[5] namely, the cognitive bias of "fundamental attribution error." As we discussed in chapter 6, if people tend to relate the success of a company to its hero manager, rather than to general progress of technology or the state of the economy or the organizational capital embodied in the company itself, they may reward the manager too highly. Thus the manager or leader becomes the subject of a cargo cult. Boards, cowed by the social norms of the age, grant managers excessive salaries, which inattentive shareholders are apparently willing to put through on the nod. Outside observers fulminate as top managerial salaries, even in the public sector, become multiples of what a prime minister or president gets paid.

As the brilliant economist-educator Russell Roberts (2014) points out, chroniclers of the cult of celebrity have an extensive pedigree. Writing in *The Theory of Moral Sentiments* in 1759, Adam Smith points out, "We frequently see the respectful attentions of the world more strongly directed towards the rich and the great, than towards the wise and the virtuous." This perfectly anticipates the modern day cult around Z list celebrities. He argues that a fascination with others who are loved is part of our natural desire to be loved ourselves. So a natural obsession with celebrities is funneled toward managers, regardless of their virtue.

Management and Monitoring

We've seen that the intangible economy will build more assets that are sunk, have synergies, can be scaled, and potentially confer spillovers. Can these characteristics explain the rise of reverence for management? To answer this question we need to step back and ask a much more basic question: What are managers for?

Maybe everyday life provides the answer: they manage. They provide leadership and strategic direction to companies. They inspire and motivate. They plan and execute. A moment's reflection, however, makes one not so sure. They spend time in pointless meetings. They award themselves pay increases and don't take the blame when things go wrong.

These observations are unhelpful because they are not answers to the question: they describe what managers *do*, but not what they are *for*. To begin to get an answer, let's think about your relationship with your window cleaner. When the window cleaner comes around to your house, it's a fair bet that you do the same thing as everyone else. You ask the price. The cleaner does the windows. You have a quick look at the windows and, if they are clean, you hand over the money.

Where is the management, leadership, and strategic direction in this transaction? Where are the management consultants? What about the financial, legal, and health and safety advisors? The answer, to economists, is that they aren't needed because the market has taken care of the entire process: you have agreed on a price, the seller has delivered, the buyer pays.

But engaging a window cleaner seems different from running a firm. It's true that workers in the firm have agreed on a price for their labor, but there is no (or there shouldn't be) hour-by-hour haggling about prices and responsibilities. Instead managers within a firm have something else: they have *authority*. That is, they have the right to instruct their colleagues what to do in the execution of their tasks and to remove them if they don't perform. Of course, you can refuse to pay your window cleaner if the task isn't performed satisfactorily and get them out of your house, but that just says you can choose to stop any commercial relationship. But firms are different. In firms, managers have the authority to choose whether their workers work with the firm's assets, using the firm's machines or transacting on behalf of the firm, and so working with the firm's reputation. You can't stop your independent window cleaner from using their bucket since you don't have the authority, but if you managed a firm of window cleaners you would be able to.

So to an economist, the question *"What are managers for?"* hides a deeper question: *"What's the role of authority in an economy?"* Actually, this is a much harder question than it appears. To see why, start with an economy where we know the answer: North Korea. In a centrally planned economy authority decides everything: who

gets food, when they get electricity, what jobs people do, is all decided by the planners. So authority simply decides.

So who decides in a noncentrally planned economy? Friedrich von Hayek was awarded the Nobel Prize for Economics
in 1974 for coming up with a brilliant answer: nobody. To buy
a pencil in a market economy, one simply goes into a shop to
get it. Purchasers of pencils don't know those who made the
pencil—who mined the graphite, cut down the trees, or transported the pencil to the shop—so can hardly issue them with
instructions. Those engaged in its production, the miners, the
tree-fellers, and the truckers, take instructions not from the individual pencil buyers but via the price system. If pencil prices
rise, more graphite is mined, more trees are felled, and more
wood is transported. No personal authority is required, since
the price system issues the instructions.

In light of this, in 1937 Ronald Coase (another Nobel laureate) asked a deceptively simple, but very profound, question: Why
then do firms exist? If markets do a pretty good job coordinating
the economy, what's the need for firms? Coase's answer was that
firms did a cheaper job of coordination than markets. Inside a firm,
Coase said, coordination by internal markets would be very costly
since you would have to (a) discover what the market prices are
and (b) negotiate a contract for each and every transaction.

This is where managers come in. If the market cannot coordinate activity but authority can, then someone has to exercise the
authority. That person is the manager, where managers are defined
as people in a firm who have authority. That's quite a neat definition and is, indeed, used by statistical authorities when they run
occupational questionnaires and ask people to self-report if they
are managers.[6]

So, costs are avoided inside the firm via authority. Rather than
haggling all the time, an employer tells an employee what to do
and the employee does it. Hence, the role for managers. They perform the coordination activity within a firm that a market cannot,
and they do so via authority.

Coase's reasoning has considerable power. In 2014 the California courts delivered their verdict on whether FedEx drivers are
contractors for FedEx or employees.[7] Had Coase been alive (he

died the year before, aged 102) he would have been the perfect expert witness. They decided that FedEx was an employer precisely because they told the drivers what to do: exactly Coase's reasoning.

The exercise of authority seems like a good description of the Amazon warehouse above. A lot of careful process engineering has combined to allow a system where the optimal route around the warehouse can be computed very efficiently. As the economist Luis Garicano has pointed out (2000), enhancements in information technology have improved the flow of information around the organization. A fall in the price of information might lead to less authority: the breakdown of hierarchies, with autonomous workers e-mailing ideas up to the boss. However, monitoring has also become more efficient with the growth of IT, so, in the Amazon case, IT has reinforced a "command and control" type of organizational design.

Thus, part of the reason for the perhaps unexpected growth in this type of very nonautonomous work is that the intangibles of organizational development and software enable more and more effective monitoring. Thus they are substitutes for autonomy. Under the right circumstances (or should that be the wrong circumstances?), it automates autonomous labor in the same way a machine automates physical labor. Marxist economists have a name for this additional monitoring role: "power-biased technological change" (see, e.g., the discussion in Guy 2014). Other examples are the cash register and the tachometer in a truck (the "Spy in the Cab"). All in all, how work changes and, therefore, how the nature of management changes depends on where you sit in the intangible value chain.

Management in an Intangible-Rich World?

If management is just monitoring, then, of course, changes in monitoring technology, such as IT, change management. Indeed, there might be *less* need for management if authority can be exerted by anyone with tracking software. There doesn't seem to be any special role for intangible assets and no reason why the cult of management and managerial rewards would get bigger. So, is there more or less need for management and authority in an intangible-rich firm than in a tangible-rich firm?

In a second wave of work following Coase, economists like Oliver Williamson thought harder about the haggling problems that Coase had said could be solved by monitoring and authority within firms. In particular, Williamson observed that haggling would be particularly costly where parties sink costs. Once a railway firm, let us say, has laid some track, the firm has committed capital to the business in general and the route in particular. This potentially puts such workers in a powerful bargaining position. The anticipation of such a disadvantageous position might then deter the firm from making an initial investment: known in economics as the hold-up problem.

Now, if intangible investments are particularly significant for a firm, and if those investments are sunk, then the opportunities for hold-up are potentially substantial. That puts the costs of haggling potentially very high. If managers of those firms can exert authority and avoid this potentially costly, wasteful haggling, those managers will be potentially very valuable. So, maybe one reason for the emergence of highly rewarded managers is that in the intangible economy, the stakes are much higher, so there's a much higher demand for them.

The other features of intangibles would also raise the demand for internal coordination by managers. Much the same reasoning goes for synergy. If intangibles have lots of potential synergies, then to capture them effectively requires transacting within a firm and encouraging interactions with others who are similarly sinking costs. And if those combinations of intangibles can yield scale, then firms will get very large too, and their managers will be in high demand.

So even if all firms might need authority and coordination, the move to an intangible-rich firm will raise the demand for such coordination and so raise the demand for managers. But what will those managers *do* exactly?

One way to answer this question is to pose another: If the intangible economy will put a premium on good coordination by star managers, why isn't the whole economy taken over by these great managers? Intangibles do indeed predict giant firms, as measured by revenues, since intangibles can be scaled (think of Facebook's revenues). But what about giant firms, as measured by the number of employees? After all, if exploiting intangibles needs synergies then surely one needs giant firms with many employees to internalize all those benefits.

One answer is that intangibles, like routing software, make monitoring easier and so firms can get bigger. The countervailing force is that managing large firms is hard, and managing large intangible-intensive firms is even harder. Of course, the natural limitations of attention span and bandwidth make authority over giant firms very hard to manage, be they tangible or intangible. But in intangible-intensive businesses there are two particularly hard challenges.

The first arises from the synergies that are endemic in intangibles. Information-sharing is going to be very valuable, for when intangibles are combined with each other, the whole can be more than the sum of the parts. Is authority the way to organize these combinations? It depends on the structure of information in the firm: In other words, do managers or workers know better what's going on?

The usual response for many firms is that the workers know what's going on, since managers are remote and out of day-to-day touch. But with synergistic firms, precisely the opposite might hold. Maybe only the managers know what's going on, since only the managers can see the big picture and realize how the synergies might link up. All this suggests that both sides need each other, and it's not clear if authority is going to be the right way to organize information-building.

The second problem with managing an intangible business is that, as employment gets increasingly knowledge-intensive, the importance of key knowledge workers to the firm rises if their knowledge is tacit. And keeping those assets is harder than keeping physical assets. Tangible assets can be secured by lock and key: intangible assets not so.

All this means that in intangible-intensive firms there will be a premium on managers who can share information both up and down the organization and keep loyal workers sticking to the firm. That means using authority in a way that builds a good organization.

Building a Good Organization

Anyone who has spent time in more or less any workplace will probably recognize Milgrom and Roberts's observations on the near-universal reputation of personnel departments as representing everything that's bad about an organization:

> In every organization with which we have been associated, and in most of those of which we have heard, the Personnel Department is viewed by line managers and employees as unresponsive, rule-bound, and bureaucratic. It takes forever to get a decision from Personnel, and the decisions seem aimed more at maintaining the Personnel Department's precious rules, procedures, and job classification/earnings and experience/earnings curves than at attracting, rewarding, and retaining the best people for the organization. Moreover, protests fall on deaf ears: Personnel people are always in meetings when you try to reach them, and they do not return your calls. (Milgrom and Roberts 1988, S176)

If personnel departments are the problem, not the solution, what about star managers? Boris Groysberg, Andrew McLean, and Nitian Nohria studied twenty managers who left GE between 1989 and 2001 to become CEOs of other companies (Groysberg, McLean, and Nohria 2006). As it turns out, there are a lot of CEOs of major US companies who were from GE over their sample period: James McNerney at 3M and Robert Nardelli at Home Depot, for example. They studied profits (relative to a sensible comparator) in companies following three years of the new CEO's tenure. The result was disappointing for the reputation of managers as uniform superstars—they found that the managers were by no means uniformly successful. In nine out of the twenty cases firms did much better than their competitors (on their measure, annualized abnormal returns, by 14.1 percent) but in the other eleven, firms did substantially worse (by −39.8 percent).

So, what makes a good organization? The Amazon warehouse suggests one answer: more coordination. Issue more instructions, write tighter employment contracts, and enforce noncompete clauses when workers leave the firm. Despite its overtones, one might see how this might be a good way forward for some firms, or divisions within firms. Amazon, for example, might take the view that their reputation for fast delivery needs close supervision of their dispatch workers. Starbucks might argue that their reputation for coffee means telling baristas exactly what to do.

And some systematic evidence supports this view. The economists Nicholas Bloom and John Van Reenen and their coauthors have extensively surveyed firms to ask about the quality of their management. Such quality is very hard to measure, and they use a series of questions, building on work by McKinsey, about management practices (see www.worldmanagementsurvey.org). This divides into monitoring (monitoring the firm and improving); targets (setting targets and acting upon them); and incentives (rewarding employees based on performance). As they nicely summarize: "Our methodology defines a badly managed organization as one that fails to track performance, has no effective targets, and bases promotions on tenure with no system to address persistent employee underperformance. In contrast, a well-managed organization is defined as continuously monitoring and trying to improve its processes, setting comprehensive and stretching targets, and promoting high-performing employees and fixing (by training or exit) underperforming employees." (Bloom et al. 2011, 7)

But this might not be good management in all circumstances. Consider a firm that sets stretching targets, as in the Amazon warehouse, for example. For workers in it for the short term, maybe to earn extra cash for Christmas, they will work really hard and then stop. (Indeed O'Connor mentions that many workers are let go after the Christmas rush.) Good for them and good for Amazon. But what about workers in it for the long term? If they move fast around the warehouse before Christmas, their managers will crank up the target and require them to move even faster after Christmas. This is known as the "ratchet effect," discussed by Weitzman (1980), who credits it to Berliner (1957), writing about Soviet planning. Thus dispatchers work *less* hard initially, defeating the object of the incentive scheme. Maybe not such good management after all.[8]

Another problem with having managers do lots of target setting, performance reviews, and the like is politicking. Suppose workers realize that they can do better for themselves by spending time not producing or innovating or helping, but by trying to persuade their manager. Maybe the manager might be persuaded that the task is very hard, and so setting relaxed targets is good. Or that a bonus is really needed. Or that performance really was very good. This time spent on what the economists Paul Milgrom and John Roberts politely call "influence activities" is time spent away from productive activity (Milgrom and Roberts 1988). Again, maybe not such good management after all.

In both of these examples, a good organization is about *commitment*. In the ratchet effect example, the organization benefits if it commits not to punish good performance now with over-stretching targets in the future. One way to do this is *not* gear high reward on day-to-day performance, but instead promise a steady trajectory of reward over the longer term. Likewise, re-ducing politicking means committing to *not* making minute-by-minute adjustments of terms and conditions, but, again, to look at performance over a longer run. And in Milgrom and Robert's view, this design of the (caricatured) personnel department is one form of that commitment. If personnel bends rules instantly in response to any demand from any employee, everyone will spend their time lobbying. Having rules and being unresponsive commits to not being swayed by influence activities and so dis-suades employees from them.

So how can managers build a good organization in an intangible-intensive firm? One answer to that question is to choose the right organizational design, and that choice depends on whether your organization predominantly uses or produces intangibles.

So, if you are predominantly a *producer* of intangible assets (writing software, doing design, producing research) you prob-ably want to build an organization that allows information to flow, helps serendipitous interactions, and keeps the key talent. That probably means allowing more autonomy, fewer targets, and more access to the boss, even if that is at the cost of influence activi-ties. This seems to describe the types of autonomous organizations that the earlier writers, like Charles Leadbeater, had in mind. And it also seems to describe the increasing importance of systemic innovators. Such innovators are not inventors of single, isolated inventions. Rather, their role is to coordinate the synergies that successfully bring such an innovation to market.

Similarly, the skills to manage the innovation process will be different than before. As we have seen, the rise of the intangible economy makes the innovation process itself more important. The management scholars Mark Dodgson, David Gann, and Ammon Salter (2005) describe how it has changed from what was the traditional taxonomy of "research" and "development" to a functional description of the process of "Innovation Technology," as needing "thinking," "playing," and "doing," stressing the new scope for easier exchange of ideas, experimentation, and faster implementation of ideas.

What if, by contrast, you are more a *user* of intangible assets: say, the Amazon warehouse, using the knowledge of the routing algorithm, or Starbucks, using the franchise book? For these firms, the organization and so management would look different. You probably want to have more hierarchies and short-term targets, since you are less worried about information flows from below and more concerned about low performance and stopping influence activities.

Leadership

If many of the visions of earlier writers on the knowledge economy have come to pass (such as organizations with peripatetic, autonomous workers), one thing they did not foresee is the seemingly growing importance of leadership. And as we have seen, management by authority may have some weaknesses such as not encouraging information flow or commitment. We shall argue that leadership is important in an intangible-intensive firm since it complements authority relations and organizational forms.

Why is leadership different from management? One approach is to try describing what a "good" and "bad" leader does: are they kind or heartless, tough or gentle, family-friendly or not, and so on. Since social norms and management fads change faster than most CEOs turn over, this approach is just endless speculation.

So it's better to get to the heart of the matter, which is the simple observation that leaders have followers. In the military, the most obvious example of leaders and followers, followers follow as a matter of compulsion, so that is easy to explain. What's much more interesting is when followers *voluntarily* stay loyal to their leaders.

Having voluntary followers is *really* useful in an intangible economy. A follower will stay loyal to the firm, which keeps the tacit intangible capital at the firm. Better, if they are inspired by and empathize with the leader, they will cooperate with each other and feed information up to the leader. This is why leadership is going to be so valued in an intangible economy. It can at best replace, and likely mitigate, the costly and possibly distortive aspects of managing by authority.

A good example of the importance of leadership in an intangible age can be seen in the phenomenon sometimes called systems or systemic innovation. Elon Musk is sometimes described as a systems innovator, aspiring to develop new products in a number of related fields (electricity storage, solar power, electric cars) or in complex systems (space procurement, carbon credits). Systems innovation is also widely discussed in the not-for-profit sector, particularly as large-scale funders such as the Gates Foundation and Bloomberg Philanthropies seek to change whole systems at once, such as public health in developing countries or city government. Since even rich organizations are not usually big enough to directly control major economic systems, systems innovation relies on leadership: the ability to convince other organizations, networks of partners, and even competitors to do what the systems innovator wants. We would expect to see this kind of systemic leadership becoming more important in an age in which most investment is intangible. One reason is that in an intangible economy, there are plentiful synergies to be exploited between different investments—a leader who can convince the battery industry to develop products and design systems in sync with the electric car industry will prosper. Similarly, if the difficulty of appropriating the spillovers of intangible investments ends up being resolved by greater public investment (as we suggest in chapter 10), then the ability to interact effectively with the complex systems of the public sector will be a commercial advantage too. The systems innovators who can do these things demonstrate an example of the importance of leadership in an intangible economy.

Thus the question is: How do leaders get followers to follow them? The precise answer depends on how you think followers think. As we mentioned in the introduction, if celebrity worship is common in your employees, your employees might follow you regardless. Another view is that followers are much more hard-nosed and will only follow if they think it's in their interests to follow. The economist Benjamin Hermalin (1998) has shown that this might lead to a number of interesting features.

First, the leader will have to know more than the followers. Perhaps this explains the importance of the growth of mission statements. In some cases this is, perhaps, sheer puff. But it could be of great value if it convinces potential followers that the leaders know more than they do.

Second, leaders don't just have to know more, but to convince followers that they know more. Leaders can do so in a number of ways. Of course, they will have to be good communicators. But more interestingly, followers will be more convinced if they see commitment by leaders. Hermalin suggests that leaders can show commitment in two ways. First, by example. If a leader stays really late at the office, or invests their own money, followers will have been shown commitment. Second, by sacrifice. Want to find out if the leader thinks that a project is going to succeed? See if they buy pizza for those who work late on it. If they do, that's a signal the work is worth it.

Summary: Managers and Leaders
in an Intangible Economy

What are the lessons for managers in all this? First, the intangible economy itself will place a premium on good organization and management. With more sunk costs, spillovers, and the opportunity for scale and synergies, the need for additional coordination rises, and so good organization and management will be in higher demand.

Second, what kind of organizations will this economy demand? The economic insights of wanting coordination and knowledge flows without encouraging influence activities suggest that different types of organizations will emerge, matched to the parts of the intangible economy they specialize in. Are you creating intangible assets (writing software, doing design, producing research)? If so, you probably want a flat organization with more autonomy, fewer targets, and more access to the boss. That will cost you time on influence activities, but will build an organization that allows information to flow, helps serendipitous interactions, and keeps the key talent. Are you using intangible assets (say, the routines in the Starbucks franchise book)? Then you probably want more control and authority to use the asset to its fullest advantage and stop influence activities.

Finally, the intangible economy will demand leaders in addition to managers. Management, in the simple sense of authority, will likely not be enough in most intangible-rich firms. To exploit synergies from knowledge-intensive workers and to scale up operations in these firms is too hard to manage by simply exerting authority. Leadership, in the sense of motivating loyalty and effort, will be needed.

If sufficient numbers of employees are convinced by puffery and conceit, then some leaders will gladly supply it. But we suspect that more enduringly successful leaders will have to earn respect by making sacrifices. They will have to work hard and show commitment to the company. And those leaders will, in turn, match the right organizational form to their needs.

All this suggests that the increased interest in management and leadership that we documented at the start of this chapter is real. It's a consequence of fundamental shifts in the economy and not only attitudinal changes and social acceptance. But if the increasing demand attracts both the sincere and the charlatan, both the able and the huckster, then attitudes might change. Just as unworthy leaders are being rejected in politics, maybe the social acceptance of leaders in business might be attenuated if the perception is that such positions are dominated by the unworthy. That will make leadership of the good managers harder to earn but easier to sustain.

Investing

What about investors? As discussed above, returns are to scarcity. And scarcity, for firms, comes from building advantages that are distinctive and cannot be easily replicated. Little of that will come from tangible assets: anyone can rent a machine or delivery truck. But much might come from intangible assets. So the first question to ask is: How can an outside investor detect if a firm is building its intangible assets?

Accounting for Investment: Some General Principles

In a series of books and papers, the accounting scholar Baruch Lev and his coauthor have asked the very important question: Can investors get information about intangibles from accounting data? The answer to this question is hinted at strongly in the title of their most recent book, *The End of Accounting* (Lev and Gu 2016).

In compiling the profit and loss accounts (also known as an income statement), accountants are concerned with reporting the flows of revenues and their associated costs over the course of a financial period. And indeed, financial analysts spend an awful lot of time looking at profits or earnings—broadly, the difference between revenues and the various measures of costs.

Quite reasonably then, accountants try to *match* the revenues, in the last year, to the costs that have been incurred in generating them. For example, the cost of leather to produce shoes—that is, the cost of raw materials used up in production—are quite sensibly allocated as costs ("cost of sales").

What about matching revenues with costs incurred when spending on assets? This is trickier, since, by definition, benefits will arise over more than the particular year in which the costs are incurred and so do not match with revenues of that year. How then does one achieve the matching of this spending with revenues? The answer is to capitalize these costs: that is, to recognize that tangible spending creates an asset. Once that is done, the expense of that asset can be reflected in its depreciation or amortization: that is, a year-by-year amount is treated as an expense, and that year-by-year amount reflects a charge for the using up over time of the long-lived asset.

The alternate to capitalization of spending on assets is to "expense" them, that is, charge the entire cost of the asset in one year to costs, rather than the implicit smoothing of costs in capitalization. As is well known, and as Baruch Lev has forcefully pointed out in a long series of books and papers (see, e.g., Lev 2001), expensing the cost of long-lived assets leads to distortions in profits, resulting from the "mismatch" of revenues and costs. In the year of incurring these costs a firm looks very unprofitable, as its costs are very large but revenues unchanged. But if the asset is useful and helps generate revenues (a truck, R&D leading to a successful patent, an increased consumer network, etc.), then in the future the firm appears to be highly profitable on the basis of very little costs incurred and very few assets acquired.

Accounting Treatment of Intangibles: Expensing versus Capitalization

All this matters crucially if investors are very interested in detecting spending on intangibles. So how are they treated?

Accounting rules are broadly the same internationally in this case. If the intangible is purchased outside the company—for example, buying a patent outright or a customer list—it is an asset, not an expense, and so is capitalized. By contrast, if it is internally generated—an internal design or software, for example—it is treated not as buying an asset, but as an expense. There are exceptions to these general rules, but they tend to be rare. Internally generated software or R&D spending can be treated as asset investment but under special circumstances: essentially when such spending is on a proven process, such as the last development stages of an already-proven R&D project or software tool.[9]

It is remarkable that these rules are so asymmetric. One might reasonably object that the value of an intangible asset is so uncertain that it should not be capitalized, but that would mean not capitalizing it whether it is internally generated or bought.[10] British American Tobacco reported in 2015 that it had almost £10bn worth of intangible assets (it had only £3bn of tangible assets, that is, property, plant, equipment). Most of the increase that year had come via the value of goodwill from purchases of other companies—for example, the brand name from buying Rothmans. A very small amount had come from internally written software. But if they had invested in building trademarks in-house, the additions to intangible assets would have been zero.[11]

As a consequence, much (at least internal) investment in assets is hidden from view. Does that matter? Three tests suggest it is important. The first test is very broad brush, but revealing. Lev and Gu (2016) looked at companies that went public over each decade from the 1950s to the 2000s. For each of those decades/groups of companies, they asked: How correlated are book values and earnings to market values? Their results are very striking and set out in figure 9.2. The histogram bars show a very clear decline in the correlations over the decades, suggesting that financial accounts have indeed become much less informative of company earnings. This has occurred as R&D and SG&A (selling, general, and administrative expenses) as a percentage of sales has risen (see the solid line): the point being that many intangible investments, such as design, are allocated by accounting rules to SG&A.

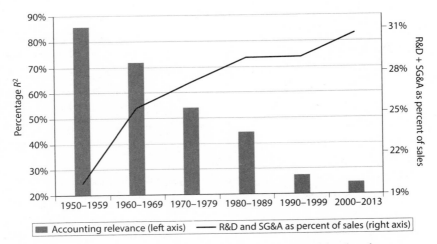

Figure 9.2. The declining informativeness of earnings and book value reporting. Bars show fraction of variance in market values accounted for by earnings and book values for companies entering stock market in successive decade. Line shows average R&D and selling, general, and administrative expenses as a share of scales for companies. Source: Lev and Gu 2016, figure 8.2.

Second, Mary Barth, Ron Kasnik, and Maureen McNichols (2001) find that analysts are much more likely to cover firms with high intangible spending (measured by R&D and advertising). This too suggests that the accounts in intangible-intensive firms and industries are less informative, since it requires analysts' know-how to ferret out additional information.

Third, the accountants Ester Chen, Ilanit Gavious, and Baruch Lev (2015) look at a sample of 180 Israeli firms over time that report using two different rules. The US-based GAAP compels firms to report R&D as expenses, but the IFRS, which is the norm for most European firms, allows the "D" in R&D to be capitalized. Thus the authors can do a direct test of whether the additional information on "D," hidden from view under the GAAP rules, is informative. Sure enough, that additional information helps predict share prices.

What Should Investors Do?

In light of all this, equity investors have a couple of choices.

The first is to avoid the problem of finding out the information altogether, which is to buy shares in every company—that is, to diversify. That avoids an additional problem of spillovers. Consider the case of EMI and the CT scanner. If you were an EMI shareholder and cared only for your returns, you would have gladly seen investment in the CT scanner stopped—from EMI's point of view, it was a colossal waste. But if you had also owned shares in General Electric and Siemens, the companies that got the spillover benefits of EMI's research and came to dominate the CT scanning market, you would have been more than happy for the project to go ahead.

We can extend this example to a general principle. If shareholders owned stock in every company in the economy—in other words, if they were perfectly diversified investors—we would expect them to be totally tolerant of companies making investments with high spillovers. They would know that what they lost on swings, they would make up on roundabout, as the British saying goes. That is, what losses they incurred would be made up with offsetting gains.

But it seems there is a dilemma here. Diversified investors are the opposite of concentrated investors: if an institution owns stock in every company on an index, it will own much less stock in each company than if it owns stock in only a few companies. And, as we have seen, institutions whose shareholdings are concentrated in particular companies have a stronger interest in becoming knowledgeable enough about the business of those companies to know the difference between bad investments and good ones and, therefore, are more likely to back profitable but long-term investments by management. And this is the dilemma, from the point of view of anyone who is eager to see public companies making more long-term investments in intangible investments. On the one hand, investors with more concentrated stakes are a good thing, but on the other, so are diversified investors. Without concentrated investors, companies are less likely to invest in tamoxifens and Gigafactories; without diversified investors, they are less likely to invest in the CT scanner or in Bell Labs.

An alternative strategy arises if, as it seems, certain types of intangible investment tend to be systematically undervalued. This suggests there are opportunities for investors who can identify good intangible investments and back companies that make them over the medium term. What's more, it suggests that time spent measuring and understanding the potential of various types of intangible investment may be worthwhile. While this might be too hard for individual investors, it seems like a possibility for asset managers in the future. They can serve investors by being much more canny about a firm, going beyond the information in the accounts. They are going to have to systematically gather much more information about the intangible-asset building that the firm is doing and the conditions for its success. Indeed, the demand for such expertise that understands the deep innards of the company and the way that external conditions will allow it to use its intangible assets will make these skills highly valued.

This vision is very much in line with the views of the economist John Kay in his book *Other People's Money* (2015). As he says, stock markets, when first started, were the vehicles for raising finance often for large infrastructure projects (typically railways) from many dispersed shareholders. But markets no longer provide this function. Almost no new projects are financed via the stock market. (Indeed, the observation that few early-state companies come to the stock market for financing rather confirms the hypothesis that stock markets have significant problems dealing with them.) Rather, stock market trading is dominated by large asset managers trading with each other. In Kay's view, they are searching for returns over and above those available to the market as a whole (searching for "alpha") by trying to anticipate what others are thinking about the value of assets rather than the value of the underlying assets themselves.

A changed role for the financial sector, Kay argues, would be for finance to return to its core function of allocating capital via what he calls "search" and "stewardship." Search is the finding of new opportunities and stewardship the monitoring of the long-term assets in the economy. Thus asset managers of the future, Kay suggests, might do much more of these functions for investors. Asset managers would do so by building trust and long-term relationships in the industries where they chose to make their expertise. With the building of intangible assets and the lack of information in company accounts, the pressures for this change are there.

Conclusion: Competing, Managing, and Investing in an Intangible Economy

The growth of intangible investment has significant implications for managers, but it will affect different firms in different ways. Firms that produce intangible assets will want to maximize synergies, create opportunities to learn from the ideas of others (and appropriate the spillovers of others' intangibles), and retain talent. These workplaces may end up looking rather like the popular image of hip knowledge-based companies. But companies that rely on exploiting existing intangible assets may look very different, especially where the intangible assets are organizational structure and processes. These may be much more controlled environments—Amazon's warehouses rather than its headquarters. Leadership will be increasingly prized, to the extent that it allows firms to coordinate intangible investments in different areas and exploit their synergies.

Financial investors who can understand the complexity of intangible-rich firms will also do well. The greater uncertainty of intangible assets and the decreasing usefulness of company accounts put a premium on good equity research and on insight into firm management. This will present a challenge to investors, partly because funding equity analysis is becoming harder for many institutional investors as regulations are tightened, and partly because of the inherent tension between diversification (which allows shareholders to gain from the spillover effects of intangible investments) and concentrated ownership (which reduces the costs of analysis).

10

Public Policy in an Intangible Economy: Five Hard Questions

The fact that intangible investments have different characteristics from tangible ones means that governments that want economic growth in an age of intangible investment may need to pursue different policies. This chapter looks at what this might mean for intellectual property rules, new markets and institutions, the financial system, and public investment.

If there is one thing that seems to come naturally to politicians and governments, it is reacting to dramatic events. The crisis meeting, the emergency response, the national challenge: these are the kinds of situations that politicians are primed to respond to. Sometimes these responses are highly effective; sometimes they are counterproductive; but one thing you can count on is that when something dramatic happens, politicians will respond.

Slow, gradual change, on the other hand, is something that politicians find *very hard* to respond to. The rise of an intangible economy is one such change: as we have seen, intangible investment has increased steadily over thirty or more years. There was no sudden shock, no excuse for an urgent news conference, or a package of emergency measures. Despite periodic attempts by some pundits and commentators to frame it as a "revolution," as revolutions go, it is too slow and subtle to make it onto most policy agendas.

This is unfortunate, to say the least. Intangible investment has distinctive economic characteristics (the four S's, outlined in chapter 4), and it plays an important role in pressing and important economic issues, from productivity stagnation to rising inequality.

So there's a strong prima facie case that government policy should change to take account of it.

This chapter sets out five priorities that governments need to address to deal with an economy in which intangible investment is increasingly important. We are sorry to say that this is not a list of policy wheezes and quick wins. On the contrary, it's a collection of dilemmas and hard problems, the answers to which are not known. We do not pretend that this offers easy pickings for writers of manifestos; but we are confident that these issues will be increasingly important to the politics of the coming decade, and that governments that can make progress toward solving them will enjoy greater prosperity than those that ignore or fudge them.

Policy Challenges in an Intangible Economy

Over the course of this book, we have identified a number of features of an intangible-rich economy that present challenges and opportunities for government policymakers. Let us recap five of the most important.

First, intangibles tend to be *contested*: it is hard to prove who owns them, and even then their benefits have a tendency to spill over to others. This problem has traditionally been addressed by intellectual property rules and norms. We would expect an economy increasingly dependent on intangibles to put a premium on good intellectual property frameworks. But working out what "good" looks like in intellectual property is very hard.

Second, we saw that in an intangible economy, synergies are very important. Combining different ideas and intangible assets sits at the heart of successful business innovation—and is what marks out the world's most successful companies, from Google to Disney to Tesla Motors. Creating the conditions for ideas to come together should be an important objective for policymakers. This is partly a matter of solving familiar policy questions, like how to encourage effective urban development, and partly about tackling new challenges, such as how to encourage research into new forms of collaboration and communication.

The third challenge, which we outlined in chapters 8 and 9, relates to finance and investment. As we saw, businesses and financial markets seem to underinvest in scalable, sunk intangible investments with a tendency to generate spillovers and synergies. Our present system of business finance makes this problem worse. Taken together, this leads to lower productivity. So we would also expect a thriving intangible economy to make significant changes to its financial architecture to make it easier for companies to invest in intangibles. We might also hope to see cultural changes in the business world that make this kind of investment more likely.

But even if governments of the future manage to clarify ownership rights over intangibles, create a productive ferment of ideas, and spur the development of financial markets that encourages business investment, a fourth economic challenge is likely to remain. All other things being equal, it is likely that it will be harder for most businesses to appropriate the benefits of capital investment in the economies of the future than in the tangible-rich economies we are familiar with. This is an important change: successful capitalism depends on the idea that private firms have a reasonable expectation of receiving some of the returns from their investments. Where this is not the case, firms have less incentive to invest, and governments may feel obliged to step in. This is already the case with some important intangibles, such as basic research, which in most countries is significantly funded by governments. So we might expect to see successful intangible-rich economies undertake more public investment in intangibles (including, but not limited to, scientific research and development). As intangibles become more important to the economy as a whole, it may be that a greater proportion of the economy's investment will be publicly funded.

Such an increase would mark a significant change from forty years of deregulation and declining government involvement in the economy. What is more, it would make big demands both on the effectiveness of government (its competence and impartiality) and on its popular legitimacy; we will explore these demands in more detail at the end of the chapter.

Finally, governments must work out how to deal with the dilemma of the particular type of inequality that intangibles seem to encourage. On the one hand, as we saw in chapters 5 and 6, the growth of intangible investment seems to increase inequality and social divisions. But as we saw in chapter 8, making the most of the spillovers and synergies of intangibles requires good social institutions and trust.

In the rest of the chapter, we will look at these five issues in order. To make it more concrete, we invite you to imagine the economy in ten or so years, when, if trends continue, intangible investments in developed countries might plausibly represent three-fifths or two-thirds of annual business investment. We will attempt to describe the kinds of policies we would see in two hypothetical countries: the Republic of Foo, which has responded effectively to the shift in capital from tangibles to intangibles, and the Kingdom of Bar, which has not. (We will later take a brief detour in box 10.1 to a third country, Ruritania, to look at an alternative set of policies that a small country might use to profit from the rise of intangibles.)

Clearer Rules and Norms about the Ownership of Intangibles

A time-honored way to encourage investment in intangibles is to make rules to allow people and businesses to own them. The classic examples are patents and copyrights; indeed, such rules even get their own clause in the US Constitution. This mitigates the problem of spillovers by making it illegal for anyone but the rights-holder to use the asset without permission.

One option for a government committed to reducing the spillovers of intangible assets is to tighten and extend these laws. It could allow broader, longer-lasting patents, IP rights over intangibles like design, and a tolerance of noncompete clauses (which help firms reduce the spillovers of training, by making it harder for trained workers to leave for other firms). At the margin, it could also make it cheaper to obtain IP protection.

All of this would certainly increase companies' ability to appropriate the intangible investment they make. But there would be a high price to pay. Strong IP rights reduce the opportunities for other firms to realize the synergies between intangibles; so while it may increase the incentive to invest, it reduces the productivity gain from investments. As Bronwyn Hall has pointed out, interlocking suites of interlocking patents sometime act as a barrier to competition (Hall, Helmers, and Graevenitz 2015). In some cases, the potential productivity gain from synergies is sufficiently strong that there is a good case for weakening rather than strengthening IP rights—such as software patents, or telecoms, where there are a lot of interlocking patents that make it too hard for an innovating firm to bargain with all the relevant patent-holders. A further danger of strengthening IP laws is that it's possible to do so in uneven and partial ways that favor incumbent rights-holders and patent trolls (both of which groups often devote significant resources to lobbying), while doing little to encourage new intangible investment.

There is, however, a good case for *clearer* IP rights. Well-run patent offices are equipped to reject vague patents that create uncertainty. Clear legal processes give IP owners confidence that their rights do what they think they do and discourage vexatious lawsuits and the kind of legal shopping-around that has brought so many patent cases to the notoriously troll-friendly Eastern District of Texas court.

PROPERTY RIGHTS

The Republic of Foo's high-intangible-investment economy has clear intellectual property laws, consistent IP courts with clear jurisdiction, and well-run patent and copyright authorities that reject confusing or overly broad IP claims.	The Kingdom of Bar, on the other hand, has an unwholesome mix of very strong IP laws in particular areas where rights-holders have lobbied effectively, and unclear and poorly administered IP laws in other areas, resulting in lots of low quality and disputed IP rights. The adjudication of these laws varies wildly, with some courts leaning toward rights-holders and others toward defendants.

There is more to rules around intangibles than intellectual property law itself: markets and norms matter too.

Let's consider markets first. As we saw in chapter 4, part of the reason tangible assets are less likely to be sunk costs is that they are tradable and people know what they are worth. Valuing a patent or a copyright will probably never be as easy as valuing a used van, but establishing markets like the Digital Copyright Exchange proposed in the UK by Ian Hargreaves in 2011 may help this process; patent pools, in which firms coinvest in research and agree to share the resulting rights, have been used in a variety of industries since the early twentieth century.

Given sufficient advances in technology and infrastructure, these kinds of markets and institutions need not be limited to major intangible assets like patents or copyrights. They may also be applicable to the tiny elements of user-generated data that collectively make up the vastly valuable databases and networks of firms like Google and Facebook. Jaron Lanier, the philosopher and computer scientist, called for a system that would allow the creators of user-generated content—that is, you and me every time we interact online or often offline—to charge a very small fee for the use of our data. Establishing these kinds of exchanges is a major undertaking, requiring significant coordination between rights-holders, content platforms, collection agencies, and governments. But it may be worth the effort: efficient markets and platforms for exchanging IP will be economically valuable in an intangible economy.

Because intangibles often have valuable synergies, they rely on norms, rules, and standards about how to bring them together. Some of these norms are technical, like technological protocols that allow different pieces of software to interact; some of them are professional norms, like the phasing of rounds of venture capital; some of them are regulatory, like rules about what data websites can gather and what they can do with it, or the regulations that govern relationships between firms (for example, between platforms like YouTube and the owners of copyrighted video content). Most of them are underpinned by social consensus about how things should work (the belief among developers that software should be compatible, not proprietary and closed off, for example, or the beliefs about the balance between personal privacy and the rights of businesses that inform data protection law).

To maximize effective intangible investment, an economy needs carefully thought-out rules, based on informed and somewhat stable social consensus. This, in turn, requires investment (developing standards is not free) and social capital. Divided, fractious, or incurious societies, those with insufficient social capital, are more likely to have unstable and ever-changing views on what the rules on things like privacy should be trying to achieve—and when it comes to encouraging investment, stability may be more important than the precise norm that is adopted. Establishing and enforcing these norms is costly: they require appropriately funded patent offices and regulators, and they require government to expend political capital to regulate fairly (rather than simply implementing the will of the most expensive lobbyists).

THE FUTURE: INTELLECTUAL PROPERTY

The Republic of Foo's high-investment, intangible-based economy has deep markets for various intellectual property rights, perhaps including patents and copyrights. It is noted for its effective rules and standards on everything from privacy to medical research; these rules are not the most liberal or the most conservative in the world, but they are notable for their clarity and stability. This stability derives in part from a mature and informed public debate on issues like privacy and data use, and partly from a strong technical and practical skill base.

The Kingdom of Bar, by contrast, lacks effective markets, and its standards are poorly defined, inexpertly designed, and often unreliable, being subject to knee-jerk shifts as public opinion changes.

Helping Ideas Combine: Maximizing the Benefits of Synergies

Good public policy should be just as assiduous about creating the conditions for knowledge to spread, mingle, and fructify as it is about creating property rights for those who invest in intangibles.

Despite frequent predictions that the Internet will lead to the death of distance, for the time being the spillovers between intangibles happen in specific places where people congregate, especially in cities. This makes good urban planning and land-use policies extremely important. There is of course a vast literature on what constitutes good policy for cities, but in the context of intangibles, there are two important principles.

On the one hand, city rules should not make it hard to build new workplaces and housing. Cities should have freedom to grow to make the most of the ever-increasing synergies arising from intangibles.

On the other hand, cities need to be connected and livable. Synergies are more likely to be realized if people meet each other and interact than if urban life is atomized and siloed. Getting this right involves striking a balance; it takes a combination of Jane Jacobs–style liberalism, tolerating messy and diverse areas rather than building multilane highways through them, and of some benign planning, providing enough infrastructure for people to get around and places for them to meet. The kinds of cities that attract what Richard Florida called the "creative class," or the "innovation districts" that Bruce Katz observed emerging across the United States, involve a mixture of judicious planning and organic growth.

There are inevitably tensions in this kind of policy. In intangible-intensive cities like New York and London, liberalizing planning rules to allow more housing to be built is criticized for causing the destruction of important public spaces and cultural venues where people congregate. Good development, especially in an age of intangibles, involves providing both for the basics of housing and transport and for conviviality.

A skeptical reader might at this point ask what is new about the need for good town planning and land-use rules. After all, liberalizing planning rules is one of those policies that academic economists have been demanding for decades, but that is generally thwarted by other factors, from the desire to reduce sprawl and unsightly development to existing homeowners' defensiveness about the value of their properties. It is true that this is a well-trodden issue. But the significance of the rise of intangibles is that with each year that goes by, the economic cost of bad urban policy, of protecting greenbelts, of restricting building heights, or of protecting lot sizes, will go up: the more reliant the economy is on intangibles, the more the economy will lose out by restricting the opportunities for intangibles to cross-fertilize.

To get a sense of the changing costs of planning restrictions consider the geographer Christian Hilber's (2016) dramatic example from London. If you go to King Henry VIII's Mound, Richmond Park, ten miles southwest of St. Paul's Cathedral in London, you will find an avenue of trees, planted in the early 1700s, that creates a "keyhole" view of the dome of St. Paul's. That view has been the same since 1710. How has it survived so long? It is protected by planning regulations, namely the *London View Management Framework*.[1] These regulations prohibit tall buildings in the sight line between Richmond Park and St. Paul's. They also don't allow tall buildings *behind* St. Paul's, which the planners have decided would constitute an unacceptable backdrop to that view. As the LVMF (2012, para. 175) says: "In determining applications [for new buildings], it is essential that development in the background of the view is subordinate to the Cathedral and that the clear sky background profile of the upper part of the dome remains." As Hilbers says, "while this view is certainly enjoyable for those living nearby or for hikers, it arguably imposes an astronomic and ever growing economic 'opportunity cost.' . . . The protected vista, through limiting supply, raises housing costs of all Londoners and adversely affects the capital's productivity."

THE FUTURE: LAND USE AND PHYSICAL INFRASTRUCTURE

The Republic of Foo, our high-investment, intangible economy of the future, has significantly overhauled its land-use rules, particularly in major cities, making it easier to build housing and workplaces; at the same time, it invests significantly in the kind of infrastructure needed to make cities livable and convivial, in particular, effective transport and civic and cultural amenities, from museums to nightlife. In some

The cities of the Kingdom of Bar have chosen one of two unfortunate paths: in some cases, they have privileged continuity over dynamism in its towns—creating places like Oxford in the UK, which are beautiful and full of convivial public spaces, but where it is very hard to build anything, meaning few people can take advantage of the economic potential the place creates.

cases, this involves rejecting big development plans that destroy existing places. It has faced political costs in making this change, especially from vested interests opposed to new development or gentrification, but the increased economic benefits of vibrant urban centers have provided enough incentive to tip the balance of power in favor of development.

Other cities resemble Houston, Texas, in the 1990s—a low-regulation paradise where an absence of planning laws keeps home and office prices low, but where the lack of walkable centers and convivial places makes it harder for intangibles to multiply. (To Houston's credit, it has changed for the better in the last twenty years.)

The worst of Bar's cities fail in both regards, underinvesting in urban amenities and making it hard to build. In all three cases, the economic disadvantage of not having vibrant cities that can grow have become larger and larger as the importance of intangibles has increased.

But creating the infrastructure for spillovers is not just about physical space. Currently, the most effective collaborations happen face-to-face, despite the dizzying variety of digital technologies for socializing and collaboration, from Skype and e-mail to Facebook and Slack. But just because the widely predicted death of distance has not come to pass, doesn't mean that it will never do so. It seems very likely that at some point people will discover better ways to interact meaningfully with one another at a distance using IT, as new applications develop and the workforce becomes populated by people who grew up with online social lives and hobbies.

The question of how people use technology to boost what some call "collective intelligence" has a long history: it lies behind the famous "mother of all demos," the 1968 presentation in which Douglas Engelbart demonstrated the world's first instances of videoconferencing, dynamic file linking, revision control, and electronic collaboration. Collective intelligence is intimately entwined with the development of Internet phenomena like Wikipedia, and it continues to evolve in the form of platforms like Slack and GitHub.

An economy that can develop technologies and ways of working that replicate the social power of face-to-face interaction at a distance will be transformed, particularly when it comes to land use. Freedom from the tyranny of ever more expensive city center property is a big economic win. So while the death of distance may be a long shot, the kind of thing that is promised long before it is delivered, the economic rewards are very large.

There are a few things governments could do to help this along the way. The government of Foo, our intangible-friendly state, could follow the example of DARPA in the 1960s and 1970s and fund experimental development into the use of technologies to foster collective intelligence and effective collaboration. (Indeed, the European Union currently funds several research programs into this under the Horizon 2020 program; in the United States, programs by not-for-profit organizations such as the MacArthur Foundation Research Network on Opening Governance play a similar role.) More ambitiously, Foo might experiment with tools for distance working and collaboration in its own business. This could involve making government departments lead users of distance working tools; it could also involve using digital collaboration tools to run public consultations, democratic deliberations, and other engagement exercises that only governments tend to do.

A Financial Architecture for Intangible Investment

We saw in chapter 8 that financial markets are designed to meet the needs of businesses that invest in tangible assets, not in intangible ones. Changing how financial markets work is not easy, but most governments already do it to some extent, whether by offering government loan guarantees, tax breaks for certain types of finance like venture capital, or, most significantly, by treating debt interest but not the cost of equity financing as a tax-deductible expense. What would a country do differently if it wanted to create the conditions for intangible-intensive businesses to get the capital they need to thrive?

First of all, governments should encourage new forms of debt finance that make it easier for companies to borrow against intellectual property—intangible assets to which property rights can be attached. Government cannot usually make financial innovation happen, but it can make it easier. As we saw, the governments of Singapore and Malaysia have put in place schemes to encourage intangible-backed loans, partly by subsidizing the loans and partly by instructing government bodies responsible for IP (such as patent offices) to work with banks to reduce legal and technical barriers.

In the longer term, the government should create the conditions for a shift from debt to equity financing. As we have seen, it is often hard to raise debt financing against intangible investments because they are sunk: the bank can take a charge or lien on your fleet of vans or your office in the event you can't repay your loans, but it's harder to do the same with a proprietary process or a brand. Because companies can claim tax relief on interest payments but not on the cost of equity, debt is cheaper than equity for any given level of risk. As intangible investment becomes more important, this distortion will hold back investment more and more.

Creating a tax credit for equity financing—that is, reducing a company's tax liability by an amount reflecting the cost of equity—is one way to correct this; another is to tax debt interest payments but lower overall tax rates to compensate. It is a proposal with a respectable pedigree: a credit exists in Belgium, and various versions of the credit were analyzed and recommended by Nobel laureate James Mirrlees in his canonical 2011 review of the UK tax system (Mirrlees et al. 2011). Governments should not be under any illusions about the difficulty of this kind of plan: it is the equivalent of open-heart surgery on a central part of the corporate tax system, and it will be opposed by any number of vested interests whose business models depend on cheap debt. And such a plan would require the emergence of new institutions for providing equity financing to small and medium-size businesses, which would also take a lot of time to emerge. But as the importance of intangibles grows, the rewards for making the change, in terms of increased investment and productivity, will grow ever greater.

We would expect to see public equity investment dominated more by institutions, some of whom would commit to taking longer-term stakes in intangible-rich companies, enabling greater investment. Government has a few roles that it can play here. First, it can remove regulations that discourage blockholding (these include disclosure requirements, rules on what information companies may provide blockholders, and rules about which shareholders may vote with borrowed stock). Second, it can reexamine standards of financial accounting to identify better ways of reflecting intangible investments (following the lead of the designers of California's planned Long-Term Stock Exchange or of accounting scholar Baruch Lev's reform agenda set out in *The End of Accounting*).

There may also be a different strategy available to those governments fortunate enough to run sovereign wealth funds or large, endowed state pension funds. As we have seen, the largest institutional investors may be able to invest broadly across an ecosystem, knowing that they can benefit from spillovers of intangible investments even if an individual company they have backed does not. These larger national funds could be deployed to invest in particular ecosystems (in the way that Fidelity is reported to have invested across Elon Musk's intangible-intensive business empire).

Alongside these regulatory changes, we might cautiously hope for a cultural shift among the managers of large companies and institutional investors. The UK's *Purposeful Company* project (Big Innovation Centre 2017) and the international initiative *Focusing Capital on the Long Term* have both argued for managers and large shareholders to be more willing to make long-term investments, particularly in intangible investments like R&D and organizational and human capital. Skeptics might argue that fine words and good intentions are not enough to change the behavior of big businesses. But in combination with other policy measures, they may prove effective; it certainly seems that the behavior of those companies that are willing to make large, long-term investments in intangibles is at least partly a matter of culture.

While we might expect to see venture capital develop further in an increasingly intangible economy, it is not clear that governments can or should do much more to promote it than they already do. As Josh Lerner showed in *The Boulevard of Broken Dreams* (2012), once tax breaks or subsidies for venture capital get beyond a certain level, they tend to encourage dumb investment (since the tax gain on its own is enough for the investors to profit); since the entire point of venture capital is smart investment, very large tax breaks are self-defeating. For a country to grow its venture capital sector, time and favorable framework conditions are more important than additional subsidies.

THE FUTURE: FINANCIAL ARCHITECTURE

The Republic of Foo, our intangible-savvy jurisdiction, implemented many of these recommendations. Over a period of years, it managed to radically change its tax system to equalize the corporate tax status of debt and equity, in the teeth of significant political opposition and administrative difficulty. Foo is now known as a center of equity investment, with increasingly deep equity markets for smaller businesses, as well as an innovative IP-backed debt finance market. It has been helped by the commitment of several large domestic institutional investors to take larger, longer-term interests in public companies, a move that seems to have helped encourage more investment among large quoted companies and reduced the volume of buybacks.

The Kingdom of Bar, by contrast, continues to struggle: the financing of its smaller businesses is still as dominated by debt as it ever was, partly because it continues to be favored by the tax system and partly because so few institutions can provide equity financing to smaller firms. Following international fads, it has spent millions trying to develop an indigenous venture capital industry, but frequent changes of policy and the unattractiveness of the wider conditions for investing in intangibles mean that there is little to show for their efforts.

Solving the Intangible Investment Gap

So far we have suggested that governments should mitigate the underinvestment problem posed by an intangible economy in three ways: strengthening ownership claims to intangibles, where possible; creating the conditions where businesses can make the most of intangible spillovers and synergies; and encouraging financial reform so that companies face fewer incentives to underinvest. These are all worth doing, but it seems unlikely that they will entirely solve the underinvestment problem. After all, the underlying incentives for companies to hold back from investments with high spillovers will still remain. And to the extent that intangibles look set to become more and more important to the economy each year, the underinvestment problem will get worse and worse.

There are two actors in the economy that have an interest in making intangible investments, despite the risk of the benefits spilling over.

The first is the small number of large, dominant firms that seem to have an ability to not only gain from their own investments but also to appropriate the benefits of other firms' investments. This is one interpretation of what firms like Google or Facebook are doing when they back moonshot-style R&D programs, or when they spend liberally on supporting "start-up ecosystems" in major cities—if you are a big and diverse enough firm, these kinds of investments may be in your enlightened self-interest.

The second is the government and other public interest bodies such as large not-for-profit foundations, both of which are meant to take a wider perspective.

It is theoretically possible that large, dominant firms might over time invest more and more in intangibles, making up the short-fall from the rest of the business sector. This would effectively be a return to the days of large, Bell Labs-style investments. It may even be that some of the same underlying dynamics encourage them: just as the public-good research of Bell Labs was in some ways a quid pro quo for the US government's willingness to tolerate AT&T's telecoms monopoly, perhaps big tech companies of the future that enjoy effective monopolies due to networks will be encouraged to invest in R&D and other intangibles as part of their license to operate. But, on the whole, this seems unlikely: the relationship between government and business in most developed countries has changed so much since the 1960s and 1970s that it is hard to imagine this kind of corporatism being re-created on a significant scale, and it is hard to imagine that it would not have other negative effects that would lower productivity.[2] (A smaller scale version of this might emerge, however, if more companies follow the pattern of Microsoft, which generated great personal wealth for its founders, who then went on to fund intangible investments for the public good. Examples are Bill Gates, whose Gates Foundation funds research into tropical diseases, and Nathan Myhrvold, who backs nuclear and geoengineering research. But this seems unlikely to make up the difference.)

This leaves government as an investor of last resort. It is hard to escape the conclusion that if intangible investment is harder for businesses to fund, and if it is becoming more important to the economy, then unless we are prepared to see a shortfall in investment, the role of government as an investor will have to grow.

This ought not to be a totally alien concept in developed countries, whose governments already make significant investments in intangibles that firms use, especially in the form of public R&D and subsidized training. In the UK, about a third of all R&D, and a much greater proportion of early-stage R&D, is funded by the government. But anyone with a passing familiarity with public sector software projects will know that not all government-funded intangible investment works well. How then can a country increase publicly funded investment in intangibles without leading to widespread malinvestment? There are a few practical options.

Public R&D Funding. The first is to increase government spending on R&D: spending more on university research, public research institutes, or research undertaken by businesses. Paying for research is one of the least ideologically controversial types of investment a government can make to promote growth: it is popular with Jeremy Corbyn and Bernie Sanders on the left, Peter Thiel on the right, and a significant number of politicians and pundits in between. The rationale harks back to one of our four S's of intangibles: spillovers. Because returns on R&D are not always captured by the person or business investing in it, businesses do less R&D than is optimal for the economy as a whole, and therefore government has a legitimate role in stepping in, either funding research in universities or institutes or paying firms to do R&D with grants or tax breaks. In total, in 2013 OECD countries spent about $40bn on publicly funded R&D and another $30bn on R&D tax breaks (Appelt et al. 2016).

The evidence for the economic benefits of public research turns out to be harder to evaluate than you might think, but such evidence as we possess looks quite positive. Research by one of the authors together with Alan Hughes, Peter Goodridge, and Gavin

Wallis suggests that extra investment by the UK government in research in universities increases national productivity by 20 percent (Haskel et al. 2015). (There were substantial swings in government support for universities over the 1990s and 2000s, and those ups and downs are well correlated with productivity ups and downs, with around a three-year lag.)

As we have pointed out, correlation does not prove causation. For example, many universities are in economically fortunate areas. But does this mean having a good university raises local economic fortunes? Or do rich areas open universities? One needs a strategy to identify the causal link, if there is one, from university spending to local prosperity.

One clever way to get at the answer to this question of linkage is by studying more or less an experiment arising from a unique custom of US university finance. The economists Shawn Kantor and Alexander Whalley (2014) pointed out that many universities in the United States spend a fairly fixed amount (about 4 percent) of their endowments each year. (This practice has a name, the Bengen rule, after the financial adviser who calculated that this was a sustainable annual drawdown or spending rate from an endowment or pension fund.) So, when stock markets boom or collapse, university spending tends to rise or fall with the market values of their endowments, independently of local economic conditions. Kantor and Whalley looked at whether there was a correlation between changes in university spending per capita (caused by these shocks) and local economic conditions (measured as nonuniversity wages in the local area).

Using a sample of 135 colleges and universities located in 85 US counties, they found that, when there was a stock market boom leading to higher drawdowns, the increases in university activity (mostly increased research output) did indeed raise local incomes. So there is a spillover link from university research to local economic success, and it lasts for a long time (at least five years, based on their data), but on average it is modest. Interestingly, the strength of the link varies. The links are larger if (a) the university is research-intensive and (b) conditions in the local area are more conducive to absorbing that research. Those conditions are that firms in the local area are more high skilled and are technologically closer to the university's research (e.g., they cite university patents).

One thing we can infer from this is that science policy can be a complement with regional policy and not a substitute for it. The benefits to providing science funding to a university in a disadvantaged town will be substantially muted unless that local community has the capacity to absorb the results of the increased research (for example, high-skilled workers and local industries that can make use of research outputs).

There is a lively debate on what specific methods—from funding public research to mission-oriented programs, competitions, tax credits for private R&D—work best. (In the UK, the mix is roughly £1 on R&D grants to businesses to £3 in tax breaks for business R&D to £10 of publicly funded academic science.) But the idea that we would expect to see more public money spent on R&D in one form or another seems a logical consequence of the growing importance of intangible investment.

R&D is not the only sort of intangible that governments can fund, though. The public sector has historically played an important, if largely unheralded, role in funding the other intangibles needed to bring products to market. Sometimes this happens through tax breaks or direct funding. The government of Singapore subsidizes business investment in a range of intangibles through what is in effect an intangibles tax break, the Productivity and Innovation Tax Credit,[3] which covers design, automation of processes, training, and the acquisition and development of various sorts of intellectual property, alongside R&D. Some governments provide cheap or free advice on production methodologies (such as the UK's recently discontinued Manufacturing Advisory Service or the US Manufacturing Extension Partnership)—this is in practice a publicly provided organizational development or design investment. Governments are also financing intangibles when they fund the arts, to the extent that this benefits those parts of the economy dependent on design, expression, or aesthetic creativity. Nesta research suggested that over 10 percent of the economy of the UK could be classed as "creative" in this sense (Higgs, Cunningham, and Bakhshi 2008), and that publicly subsidized art in the UK made a significant contribution to the commercial creative industries.

Public Procurement. Another way government can in practice fund intangible investment is by using the lever of procurement. When the US military funded the development of the semiconductor industry in the 1950s, they did not just fund R&D. By acting as a lead customer (often paying on a cost-plus basis), they effectively funded America's businesses to invest in the intangibles needed to produce and sell chips, an investment that proved valuable when the businesses expanded into commercial markets. The Taiwanese government's support for its nascent semiconductor industry in the 1970s and 1980s (particular through its technology agency ITRI) worked similarly: ITRI did not just invest in R&D, it incubated companies like UMC and TSMC, investing in the intangibles they needed to run semiconductor foundries effectively and link them to the global semiconductor supply chain. The success rate of industrial policy in supporting infant industries is an open question; but to the extent that it works, it is an example of government investment in non-R&D public intangibles.

The innovation scholar David Mowery has studied whether "smart" public procurement works in the United States and whether the romance about US examples like DARPA, the Small Business Innovation Research program, or the Apollo and Manhattan programs is misplaced (Henderson, Newell, and Mowery 2011). He observes that the development of the US IT sector is a major success story for procurement. In the 1950s the US military procured a lot of software and semiconductors, and this demand helped Texas Instruments and other firms invest not just in R&D, but also in the other processes necessary to make and sell semiconductors. He notes that one provision of this program was that more than one supplier was needed, and this made the sharing of information and standards in the industry a common practice. By the late 1960s, however, the military was buying a very small share of IT products, and private sector demand had become very important. Fortunately, the military projects were, in fact, highly complementary to private sector needs. Over time things have changed, and the software industry has matured to a point where the military now buys software from the private sector. An attempt by the US military in the 1980s to make its own software was a failure. So ultimately the success was in developing something that was very complementary to private sector needs, and the private sector just took over the lead.

While the development of the US IT industry is an example of procurement effectively encouraging intangible investment, there have also been some failures. In the 1970s and 1980s the US Air Force invested in the development of computer-aided machine tools, but their efforts were surpassed by those of Japanese businesses. Civilian nuclear power also benefited from swathes of defense funding and procurement spending, but if anything the needs of the defense sector (such as powering submarines and creating plutonium for atomic weapons) hindered rather than helped the evolution of effective nuclear technologies.

All this shows that using procurement to encourage intangible investment is not a free lunch. There are four things governments must believe they can get right if they want this strategy to work.

First of all, there is the question of scale. Policy wonks around the world often look enviously at DARPA, the US defense innovation agency, which spends around $3 billion a year on a mixture of innovative research and challenges and has played an important role in the development of technologies from the computer mouse to the driverless car. But part of the reason DARPA works is that it is backed up by the United States' $600 billion defense procurement budget, one of the principles of which is to maintain the technological superiority of the American military.

Second, there must be a sufficient level of political commitment. Using procurement to encourage innovation involves a risk of failure. If a government cannot tolerate this and constantly tries to mitigate the risk of failure, innovation is unlikely to result. One of the reasons that defense procurement has in the past been good at encouraging innovation is that it has typically been insulated from many political pressures, freeing recipients of defense funding to take more risks.

Third, there is an inherent tension between the normal incentives of procurement—getting good value for money—and the risks and mindsets involved in promoting innovation. It is not just a question of personnel, although that is important—the kinds of officials who are good at getting value for money will often be different types of people from those who are good at fostering wild breakthroughs. More worrying is that when value-for-money procurement fails, innovation is often used as an excuse ("we lost money, but we were trying something new!"). This runs the risk that doing too much innovation procurement creates a cover for standard procurement failure.

The final question for any government considering using innovation to foster procurement is Clint Eastwood's: "Do you feel lucky?" It is very hard to know what the real odds of success in innovation procurement are partly because survivorship bias is great (How many failed attempts to use procurement to foster innovation do we simply not know about?), and partly because what made it work is so unclear (To what extent was fostering innovation in semiconductors or data communications good luck? How easy would it be to pick the next winner?).

Training and Education. We might also foresee a growing public role in financing particular sorts of training and education. Governments' involvement in training relates mainly to funding the education of young people (which has many effects and purposes, one of which is to improve the productivity of citizens as workers) and providing some subsidies for industrial training programs, such as (in some countries) apprenticeships.

Paying for citizens to go to school for longer was, for much of twentieth century, an important way that governments increased productivity; the economists Claudia Goldin and Lawrence Katz documented the vital role of education in the economic growth of the United States, pointing out, for example, that while 62 percent of the 1930 US birth cohort graduated from high school, 85 percent of the 1975 cohort did (Goldin and Katz 2008). Robert Gordon and Tyler Cowen have argued that there are diminishing returns here—children and young people can only spend so long in school or college—and that this will prove to be a major brake on US economic growth in the future (Gordon 2016; Cowen 2011).

Working out how to defy these diminishing returns has proved challenging. Goldin and Katz suggest more targeted support at all stages of education to increase the supply of educated workers: more very early stage support, lower class sizes for middle schools, and more support for college. And, of course, some people are spending longer in school, as more occupations demand degrees or even postgraduate qualifications. But the challenge of trying to fit more education into the finite number of years of a person's youth remains.

Others have argued that the answer lies in changing not how much we teach, but what we teach. In recent years, it has become fashionable to argue that particular types of education may be unusually valuable: consider, for example, the fashion for teaching coding in schools, or for encouraging children and students to learn collaborative problem-solving skills, both of which, it is argued, will give them skills that will be particularly useful in the economy of the future.

However, we should be somewhat skeptical about our ability to predict what skills the economy of the future needs and our ability to teach them. Perhaps in twenty years' time, coding will, for the most part, be automated. Perhaps collaborative problem solving cannot be inculcated by changing the curriculum.

But there is an alternative that may solve both the problem of when to teach people and the question of what to teach them: increasing the amount of training people receive in adulthood. Adult education has always been the Cinderella of the educational system, starved of prestige and of public funding. But its usefulness in an increasingly intangible-rich economy seems clear.

First of all, adult education by definition need not delay people from entering the workforce; being able to invest in a person's education throughout a person's life makes many more decades available. Second, the availability of adult education reduces the problem of trying to guess what skills will be valuable in twenty or thirty years' time. For all the excellent research done on the skills needed by the economy of the future, predicting a couple of decades out reminds one of Sam Goldwyn's advice: "never make predictions—especially about the future." But if people have the opportunity to acquire more skills during their working lives, prediction becomes less important: adult education provides people with option value. It may also help mitigate some of the problems of inequality we described in chapter 6: to the extent that the growth of intangibles disadvantages those with poor skills and makes some skills obsolete, the availability of training offers a way of redressing the imbalance.

However, anyone planning to expand adult education faces a strategic problem: how to deliver it effectively. Schools, universities, and further education/community colleges are well established organizations with long track records. They may not be perfect, but they have evolved and improved over many years, and society has evolved alongside them, such that going to school and into further or higher education is an expected part of most people's life-course, at least in the developed world. Adult education is less of a known quantity. Moreover, it seems likely that new technologies ought to make educating adults easier: digital technologies should offer ways of teaching more cheaply and conveniently. (MOOCs—Massive Open Online Courses—seem so far not to have lived up to their initial promise, but the field is still less than two decades old, and it is too early to say whether better versions could be substantially more effective.) What is needed is significant investment in innovating how we deliver adult education, to identify new models that work cost-effectively and at scale. Even if these forms of education end up being paid for by the adult students themselves rather than by taxpayers, the research to develop new models that work seems like a worthy goal of public policy.

Government funding can also help reduce coordination problems that may hold businesses back from investing. Suppose there are big economic gains to be had from developing self-driving cars and reconfiguring our cities around them (fewer car accidents, more productive commutes, freeing up parking spaces for redevelopment, and so on). But realizing these benefits requires a lot of investments to be made together (driverless car technology, urban design, new insurance policies, and so on); it may well be that no company is willing to make investments on its own unless it knows that others will make complementary ones. In this case, it is possible that government investment may not only be useful in itself (by funding high-spillover investments that others would not make), but would also encourage wider investment by increasing the likelihood that others would make complementary investments. The role of government in making these kinds of "test-bed" investments will increase in an intangible economy.

The Challenges of Public Investment

The idea that the government will need to fund a greater share of investment is not one that we suggest lightly. It raises at least three further challenges—competence and bias, how to pay for this funding, and the question of legitimacy—each of which highlights an important change that will need to take place if the intangible economy is to thrive.

Many critiques of government involvement in the economy, and particularly of attempts by government to make investments, focus on the issue of "government failure." How will governments know where to invest, and, even if they do, how can we be sure that they will not be swayed by vested interests? In the worst case, governments might back unwanted or unviable technologies, either out of ignorance or because certain businesses have successfully lobbied them. This view can overlook the extent to which governments already make rather specific investments and "pick winners," but the danger it identifies is real. This can be mitigated to some extent by honesty and knowledge. Impartial judgment can reduce the effectiveness of industry lobbying; better use of data and analytics can improve officials' ability to administer procurement schemes or run test beds.

This means that if we want to see a government willing to invest more in intangibles than governments currently do, then we would need to see a steady increase in the honesty, competence, and economic knowledge of policymakers. Good governance would be at an increasing premium for a government in an intangible economy, since the opportunities for malinvestment and enabling rent-seeking will increase.

The second problem is one of public finance. Spending more money on university research, research grants, or innovative procurement generates another call on public budgets, which are stretched all over the developed world. One way or another, it would need to be paid for. One proposal to fund this kind of spending is for governments to take equity stakes in businesses benefiting from public R&D funding and plow the returns into the next generation of intangible investment (this recommendation was made by Mariana Mazzucato in her best-selling *The Entrepreneurial State*). But it is not clear if this proposal gets around the problem of intangible spillovers: the precise reason government is funding intangible investments is because the benefits do not reliably accrue to the firm making the investment; simply taking a stake in a firm alongside which government invests will not provide a reliable source of funding. What is more, making the government dependent on the performance of particular firms for its future operating budget is likely to increase its conflicts of interest, making it harder for the government to make investments in an impartial way, which, as we have seen, becomes more important the more investment decisions the government itself makes. In fact, the most reliable way for the government to fund intangible investments is from general taxation: this allows the government to benefit from the spillovers of intangible investment wherever they arise and reduces government dependence on a subset of firms in which it holds equity. So, increasing public investment in intangibles implies an increase in the tax burden or a reduction in other areas of public spending.

This leads to a third implication: to obtain approval for more public spending funded either by raising taxes or by reducing other areas of spending, democratic governments will need to make a stronger case for why it is necessary. Traditionally, science and technology policy (the banner under which most government intangible investments in R&D have been made) has been technocratic, rather than democratic. The goals of scientific research were set by scientists or nonpolitical funding agencies; the question of how much to fund science has rarely been a controversial political hot topic. The vision of funding research based on scientific merit alone rather than to advance specific aims was set out in the United States by Vannevar Bush in *Science: The Endless Frontier* and in the UK formed the basis for what became known (somewhat mythically) as the Haldane Principle. While there were exceptions (the space race and the funding of DARPA in the United States were both highly mission oriented), for the most part public science investment made an unspoken deal with democratic politics: science funding decisions would be done by technocrats, not voters; but in return, it would be a relatively small budget line in the government's spending plans. For democratic governments to commit to a significant increase in intangible investment, a different political settlement may be needed. One possible way to achieve this is by winning greater public buy-in to the intangible investments that government plans to make: by showing that they contribute to specific goals that voters value, for instance. (Opinion research suggests that, at least in the UK, aligning science funding to specific missions is the key to building a supportive coalition of over 50 percent of the population.) There is, of course, a tension here: greater democratic control of things like research funding could lead to more malinvestment—the public may be worse at directing funding than technocrats or scientists. But in a democracy, increasing the legitimacy of the funding process may be the most effective way to build the case for greater public funding.

To see how public coinvestment in intangibles might turn out, let's turn back to our two imaginary countries, the Republic of Foo and the Kingdom of Bar. Despite the sensible measures it has taken to codify IP rights, manage the spillovers of intangibles, and create an intangible-friendly finance system, Republic of Foo businesses still invest less in intangibles than is optimal for the economy. While some of the slack has been taken up by not-for-profit foundations (set up with the windfall profits from some of the Republic's successful intangible-based businesses), the shortfall would still persist had not the government over time stepped in to make some of these foregone investments. This change has been the source of considerable political stress and strain: the idea that the government should fund more investment in things like science and training was initially not popular among voters, most of whom had other priorities for public spending and thought these investments should be left to businesses. Making the change was only possible because successive governments were able to present public investment in research, training, and procurement as the answer to pressing national challenges, and such investment gradually won popular support for greater funding. The Republic has been helped in this by the quality of its political culture, which frequently is near the bottom of league tables for corruption and near the top of tables for the quality of public administration. Despite this, there have been occasional scandals of malinvestment and even bribery relating to public investments—but so far, thankfully, on a small scale. The luckless Kingdom of Bar, by contrast, has done nothing to increase public investment in research, training, or other intangibles; together with its other failings, this has resulted in a significantly lower level of investment and a decade of disappointing productivity growth. Even faced with the example of other countries whose governments invest and whose economies seem to be thriving, no one has been convinced that more public investment would help the Kingdom, partly because most voters still see investment in research as a narrow, technocratic concern and partly because the regular corruption scandals that plague the government give no one the confidence that public investment would be allocated sensibly or impartially.

Box 10.1. An Opportunity for Small Nations: or, What Should Ruritania Do?

Most economic changes bring opportunities to those countries quick enough to respond to them. The shift to intangibles is no exception. There may well be a first-mover advantage to countries able to adapt quickly to the needs of an intangible economy. The policies required are most easily implemented in small, open economies with sufficient political cohesion and administrative competence to agree on goals quickly and execute them effectively—we have called our exemplar of this sort of country Ruritania.

Unlike most of the recommendations in this chapter, the ideas that Ruritania adopt tend to be zero-sum games: they are based on the principle of attracting economic activity from other countries, and, to the extent that Ruritania gains, other countries lose out. That is not to say that governments may not want to try them.

Let's consider some policies Ruritania has adopted that have given it a significant economic boost.

Become an Arbitration Center for Intangible Claims

Investors in intangibles like certainty over what they own, but this is often unclear, partly as a result of legal uncertainty and partly because of the variability of different jurisdictions in enforcing the law. Ruritania invested in up-to-date, clear laws on ownership of IP and on effective, well-funded courts to administer them. As a result, businesses in many nearby countries chose to draft their contracts according to Ruritanian law.

Offer Favorable Tax Rates on Intangible Capital

Intangible capital is often more mobile than tangible capital: it is hard to move a factory or a shopping mall, but relatively easy to move a patent, a brand, or the location of a set of operating procedures. Ruritania capitalized on this by designing a very intangible-friendly tax code, providing significant deductions for profits relating to intangible assets. This might not have been a good idea from the point of view of Ruritania's own businesses (there is limited evidence that big tax breaks like patent boxes do much to encourage new intangible investment), but the code did an excellent job of attracting other countries' intangible-intensive businesses to establish themselves, or their local branches, in Ruritania, generating jobs and, often, follow-on investment.

Develop Financial and Intellectual Clusters

Once Ruritania had managed to attract regional head offices and had made itself a local center for contracting and dispute resolution on intellectual property, it built on these attributes by fostering a financial services sector well geared to the financing of intangible-intensive businesses (with an emphasis on IP-backed loans and venture capital); it also invested in public research alongside the intangible-intensive companies that had located there to take advantage of its tax and legal framework. (Both of these would have been good tactics for any country, as we have seen, but Ruritania's status as an intangible hub makes them more likely to succeed.)

Strengthen Social Capital

Ruritania, being a small and relatively wealthy country, had always been quite socially cohesive. This advantage served it well as it sought to thrive in the intangible economy: these social networks made it easier for ideas to spread around the economy and made it more politically feasible to mitigate through government policy the potential increases in inequality arising from the intangible economy.

Clearly, not every nation can imitate Ruritania, since not everyone can be a hub, and widespread tax competition is counterproductive. But for an individual small, nimble country looking for a way to respond to changes in the economy, it may represent a viable path. Observers of Singapore and Ireland may notice familiar aspects of Ruritania's strategy in the recent development of those two countries.

Coping with Intangible Inequality

The final big issue that governments will need to address in an intangible age is how to deal with the particular types of inequality that arise from an economy reliant on intangibles.

As we saw in chapter 5, an intangible-rich economy has a tendency to create a small number of highly profitable firms, partly because valuable intangibles can be scaled across a very large volume of business, and partly because the best firms seem to be profiting from their own intangible investments and from appropriating the benefits of other firms' intangibles. In chapter 6 we saw that this tendency for firms to divide into leaders and laggards was partially responsible for long-run increases in income inequality. We also speculated that the psychological and cultural characteristics of workers who prosper in an intangible economy might be at odds with the mindsets of those whom the intangible economy leaves behind, with the result that the economic inequality fostered by the growth of intangibles is intertwined with a social schism.

Chapter 7 showed that a successful intangible economy depends a lot on what we called soft infrastructure: the norms, values, and social capital that allow people and firms to share spillovers, exploit synergies, and work collaboratively.

This creates a particularly vexatious double dilemma for governments. For a start, it seems that the dominant mode of production in the economy of the future is more likely to give rise to inequality, which many voters find problematic in itself. But in addition, governments find that the particularly divisive forms of inequality that the intangible economy appears to give rise to in fact threaten the social institutions on which a thriving intangible economy depends. There are a number of metrics that researchers have devised that might help us predict which countries and places will do better, and these include trust, power distance (how hierarchical the society is), and openness to experience (how interested and tolerant people are of new things). Some of these are deep-seated cultural traits; but other important factors may be influenced by government policy. Very unequal societies are likely to exhibit lower trust; very conservative ones will be less open to experience. Recent research by Alex Bell and his colleagues (2016) found that early exposure to technology made Americans much more likely to be inventors in later life, and that this early exposure tended to be influenced by wealth and class. One implication of this is that creating more opportunities for school children to be exposed to technology may increase the pool of people who can share ideas, thus increasing the possibility of positive synergies between intangibles in a country.

Inequality can also be economically counterproductive at the level of firms. And powerful intangible-rich businesses have an incentive to lobby government for unfair advantages, which again deters others' incentives to invest.

All of this creates a deep challenge for governments. To help the intangible economy thrive, policymakers will want to encourage trust and strong institutions, encourage opportunity, mitigate divisive social conflict, and prevent powerful firms from indulging in rent-seeking. But at the same time, an effective intangible economy seems to exacerbate all of those problems, creating particularly socially charged forms of inequality, threatening social capital, and creating powerful firms with a strong interest in protecting their contested intangible assets.

We would like to tell you we have a solution to this problem, but, like most politicians in the developed world, we do not. It is not even clear what a world in which these problems had been successfully resolved would look like. But we are confident that this tension will dominate the political economy of the years to come, and that whichever country can resolve it will pave the way for great prosperity.

11

Summary, Conclusion, and the Way Ahead

This book is about the change in the type of investment observed in more or less all developed countries over the past forty years. We have looked at *investment*, the spending that businesses and governments undertake to build future productive capacity. Investment used to be mostly *physical* or *tangible*, that is, in machinery, vehicles, and buildings and, in the case of government, in infrastructure. Now, much investment is *intangible*, that is, in knowledge-related products like software, R&D, design, artistic originals, market research, training, and new business processes. We have explored how an intangible-intensive economy looks very different from a tangible-intensive economy because intangibles have different underlying characteristics. And we have used the logic of these underlying characteristics to try to understand slowing growth and secular stagnation, inequality, and the challenges to finance and public policy.

Along the way, we've tried to illustrate these changes with a combination of real-world business examples and macroeconomic data (the data are in chapters 2 and 3). Our examples have taken us to the gym (chapter 2), where Les Mills has transformed modern-day gyms to rely on not just the tangible assets of weights and treadmills, but also on the intangibles of branded exercise regimes and instructor training; innovation and innervation. We've looked at the EpiPen (chapters 4 and 5), and how a good that is seemingly very simple to copy has nonetheless remained a market leader by the use of intangible investments in branding and training. And we've looked back in history from a period of few intangibles (the eleventh century, chapter 1) to microwave ovens, body scanners, and the Beatles (chapter 4). We've tried also to clarify the (sometimes confusing) terms in the field: investment, capital, assets (chapter 2); knowledge, information, ideas (box 4.1); productivity and profitability (box 5.1); income, earnings, and wealth (box 6.1).

Our argument has several parts:

1. There has been, and continues to be, a long-term shift from tangible to intangible investment.
2. Much of that shift does not appear in company balance sheets and national accounts because accountants and statisticians tend not to count intangible spending as an investment, but rather as day-to-day expenses.
3. The intangible, knowledge-based assets that intangible investment builds have different properties relative to tangible assets: they are more likely to be *scalable* and have *sunk costs*; and their benefits are more likely to *spill over* and exhibit *synergies* with other intangibles.
4. These characteristics have consequences for the economy. In particular, we argue that they contribute to:
   a. Secular stagnation. Investment appears too low since some is unrecorded; scalability of intangibles allows large and profitable firms to emerge, raising the productivity and profits gap between the leaders and laggards; the slowed pace of intangible capital building after the Great Recession has thrown off fewer spillovers and enables less scaling, thus slowing total factor productivity.
   b. Inequality. Income inequality rises as synergies and spillovers increase the gap in profitability between competing companies, raising the demand for managers and leaders with coordinating skills; wealth inequality rises as cities, where spillovers and synergies abound, become increasingly attractive, driving up the property prices; esteem inequality rises as psychological traits like openness to experience become more important.
   c. Challenges to the financial system, specifically relating to the financing of business investment. Debt finance is less appropriate for businesses with more sunk

assets; public equity markets appear to undervalue at
least some intangible assets in part due to underre-
porting of such assets but also due to the uncertainty
around intangibles; venture capital, a response to the
sunkenness and uncertainty around intangibles, is currently hard to scale to many industries.

   d. New requirements for infrastructure. In particular, the
shift from tangible to intangible assets has increased
the need for IT infrastructure and affordable space
in large cities, while making greater demands on our
"soft infrastructure": the norms, standards, and rules
that govern collaboration and interaction among
people, government, and firms.

5. This shift has implications for management and financial
investing. Firms using intangibles become more au-
thoritarian; those generating intangibles will need more
leadership; financial investors will have to find information well beyond the current financial statements that
purport to describe current businesses.

6. The shift also changes the public policy agenda. Policymakers will need to focus on facilitating knowledge
infrastructure—such as education, Internet and communications technology, urban planning, and public science
spending—and on clarifying IP regulation but not necessarily strengthening it.

It is worth reviewing in what respect these points are
controversial—and where the balance of proof lies. The first point,
that there has been a shift from tangible to intangible spending, is
relatively widely accepted. The most controversy surrounds how
to measure investment in business processes, which is intrinsically
very hard, but even if we entirely disregard these types of intangibles, the increasing relative importance of intangible investment
still holds. Likewise the second point, that much of this intangible
spending is unrecorded, is acknowledged by those who design the
accounting conventions that govern the treatment of intangibles.

The third point, namely the properties of intangibles, is more
conceptual. Scalability and spillovers follow from the fundamental

properties of knowledge as a good (it can be used over and over again, and it might be hard to prevent others from using it). To a certain extent sunkenness (the inability to get the specific intangible investment back after it is spent) is a consequence of the lack of markets for intangible assets and may be mitigated as markets for intangibles develop. And synergies between intangibles seem like a natural property of the power of ideas in combination.

The fourth point, the consequences for the economy, is inevitably speculative. Our aim in this book has been to propose how this important change in the capital stock of the economy could help explain certain topical economic problems and puzzles. It is unlikely that the shift to intangibles is the only cause of any of these widespread and complex phenomena, but we hope that we have shown that it may play a role—a role that for the most part has not been widely recognized.

Points five and six, the implications for management and investment, and public policy, respectively, include a range of recommendations that will be familiar to some. We do not pretend that the idea of publicly funding R&D or of paying attention to leadership in businesses is new. But we do argue that the steady, long-run rise of intangible investment puts these recommendations in context and helps managers and policymakers to prioritize. Countries are faced with a dizzying range of policy choices. We hope this book makes the case that those strategies that go with the grain of the long-run rise of intangible investment, such as those we set out here, are more likely to secure prosperity than those that go against it.

NOTES

Chapter 1: Introduction

1. The Domesday Book entry for "Stansted [Mountfitchet]" is at http://opendomesday.org/place/TL5124/stansted-mountfitchet/.
2. See Office for National Statistics 2016.
3. See Microsoft's financial statement: https://www.microsoft.com /investor/reports/ar06/staticversion/10k_fr_bal.html.

Chapter 2: Capital's Vanishing Act

1. SNA 2008, para 10.32. If a producer also sells assets, then the measure is the new assets minus any assets sold. There is an additional complication to do with improvements to land arising from the particular treatment of land or, more generally, nonproduced assets, in national accounts. The same definition as in the SNA is to be found in the ESA 2010, para 3.124.
2. SNA 2008, 617.
3. Although he was not the first to use the term, Marx is perhaps the popularizer of "capitalism." For him, "capitalism" is when production is organized in society such that capital (in the sense above of machines and infrastructure) is owned privately. In *Capital*, "capital" is used variously to describe stocks and flows associated with capital in the above sense but also in other ways, for example, working capital (money in store to pay wages), constant capital (which includes depreciation), etc. See Blaug 1978 on all this. See box 6.1 for an explanation of capital, earnings, and wealth and box 6.2 for an outline of Piketty's model of capital.
4. The exact passing date depends somewhat on ongoing data improvements and revisions but the pattern of growing intangible importance is consistent in the data. (See, for example, Nakamura 2010.)

5. These are known by their acronyms COINVEST (www.coinvest.org
.uk), INNODRIVE (www.innodrive.org) SPINTAN, (www.SPINTAN
.net), and INTAN-Invest (www.intan-invest.net).

6. Beniger's book *The Control Revolution* is full of fascinating pre-IT
historical examples of intangible investment. The history of break-
fast food is one such: Henry P. Crowell's invention of Quaker Oats
in 1879 required, argued Beniger, a strenuous advertising campaign
to convince consumers that the food was not horse fodder. Crowell's
innovations in marketing included prizes, endorsements, and special
offers (Beniger 1986, 266). Likewise, in the UK, James Spratt, the first
manufacturer of dog biscuits, needed to convince skeptical consumers
in the 1860s and erected the first billboard in London. His employee
Charles Cruft set up the Cruft's dog show, and Spratt's firm advertised
its biscuits as being used by appointment to Queen Victoria.

7. A more formal exploration of this relationship finds intangible investment negatively correlated with employment strictness and product
market restrictions, controlling for other factors (Corrado et al. 2016).

Chapter 3: How to Measure Intangible Investment

1. A very helpful guide to measuring investment and GDP, packed with
data, is from Eurostat: http://ec.europa.eu/eurostat/statistics-explained
/index.php/National_accounts_and_GDP.

2. Smith, *The Wealth of Nations*, book 2, chapter 3.

3. Hence, we have Alan Greenspan's remarks in 2000 on the challenges
faced by the US Bureau of Economic Analysis in defining and calculating GDP: "It's become evident that there has been an increasing technological change within our system, which has muddied the distinction
between what we call capital investment and current expense. And
20–30 years ago when you built a steel plant, it was perfectly obvious
what it was and it was capitalized. And when you consumed coke or
ore, it was expensed. But in today's world it has become very much
more difficult to figure out whether a particular outlay is expensed
and not included in the measure of the GDP, or whether it is capitalized and it is." https://www.bea.gov/scb/account_articles/general
/0100od/maintext.htm.

4. One might argue that this is all "R&D," and we would agree: however, the
official definition of R&D relates to work to resolve scientific and technical uncertainty, which typically, in spirit at least, excludes things like design and artistic endeavors. Thus, these categories are separate from R&D.

5. An example of the survey is: http://www.ons.gov.uk/file?uri=/surveys /informationforbusinesses/businesssurveys/quarterlyacquisitionsand disposalsofcapitalassetssurvey/ft14qcastcm77375040.pdf.
6. Such changes in the value of an asset might be due to "wear and tear," which is what accountants usually mean by depreciation, or due to their value being reduced via the competitive process, which is what economists, following Triplett, call "obsolescence." See the appendix to this chapter for more on this.
7. This will not be true if, for example, the distribution of returns to spending is highly skewed so that a small number of projects are very successful. Hall, Jaffe, and Trajtenberg (2005) find that patent citations have a very skewed distribution, but less is known about the skew of returns to designs, software, and marketing spending.
8. There is some data on how time is spent in the public sector. For example, O'Mahony quotes the study by Klinke and Muller (2008), who surveyed doctors in German hospitals, in which they had to indicate the amount of time spent on six different task areas. On average doctors spent 4.3 hours per working day with medical tasks; 2.1 hours with administrative tasks; 1.4 hours talking with patients and relatives; and 1.2 hours writing medical reports. If medical tasks and patient conversations are grouped into "close-to-patient" tasks, they together took up 5.7 hours of a normal working day. If administrative tasks and the writing of medical reports are classified as "patient-distant" tasks, these together took up 3.3 hours. In this way the surveys indicated a ratio of about 2:1 between direct patient services and patient administration.
9. The rule of law might be thought of as an important factor affecting the incentives to build assets but itself is not an asset directly.
10. In a famous paper, the American economist Martin Weitzman (1976) showed that while GDP is not a measure of welfare, a closely related measure, net domestic product (appropriately price adjusted) is a useful measure, if consumers are seeking to maximize their flow of consumption. The reason that investment, which is in GDP, features in a consumption-based welfare measure is that consumers value current investment since they understand, in his model, that it will yield future consumption.

Chapter 4: What's Different about Intangible Investment?

1. Economists often call synergies "complementarities," since the presence of one asset raises the value of another.

2. Strictly speaking, in economics, scalability is a property of an input/ output relation rather than of capital itself. Economists often use "scale" when they talk about "economies of scale," by which they mean that when a firm doubles all its inputs it more than doubles output. Nonrivalry or, in our language, scalability is related. To see this suppose we re-create planet Earth and put on it all the same natural resources, labor, and capital inputs we currently have. Then suppose we double resources, labor, and capital inputs. Would we also need to double the input of ideas (re-create algebra, for example) to get the same output as the current planet? No. We can simply scale the same ideas from the original planet due to non-rivalry. So when we talk about intangible assets being "scalable," strictly speaking, it's the knowledge underlying the asset that is being used over and over again.

3. Sutton (1991) is the classic discussion of scalability and sunk costs and their effect on market structure.

4. http://www.mckinsey.com/business-functions/strategy-and -corporate-finance/our-insights/learning-to-let-go-making-better -exit-decisions.

5. Avinash Dixit (1992) points out that if investment involves some sunk costs, if there is ongoing uncertainty, and if the investment opportunity might occur again later, then waiting has some value: waiting will avoid sunk costs and will reveal more about the future. Dixit and Pindyck (1995) set out an example of a two-stage, sunk R&D investment project where stage one, which is very costly, reveals information about the profitability of the (less costly) stage two. A simple net present value calculation in their example reveals that stage one is not worth it, due to its high sunk costs. But if the return from resolving uncertainty is also counted, stage one can turn out to be very valuable, since it creates an "option," that is, the opportunity to decide whether to proceed to stage two. Thus, investing in intangibles, even if they don't directly create an asset, as in stage one, is very valuable and might be described as having what Carol Corrado and Charles Hulten (2010) call a "strategic" property.

6. *The Writings of Thomas Jefferson*. 1905. Edited by Andrew A. Lipscomb and Albert Ellery Bergh. Thomas Jefferson Memorial Association, 13:333–35.

7. Article I, Section 8, Clause 8 of the United States Constitution empowers the United States Congress: "To promote the Progress of Science and useful Arts, by securing for limited Times to Authors and Inventors the exclusive Right to their respective Writings and Discoveries."

Chapter 5: Intangibles, Investment, Productivity, and Secular Stagnation

1. Published as Summers 2015. Summers developed his views further in a Keynote Address at the National Association for Business Economics Policy Conference, February 24, 2014, published as Summers 2014. Paul Krugman has also popularized the term "liquidity trap," which refers to a position whereby interest rates can be lowered no further and so monetary policy, which works by adjusting interest rates and so changing investment and consumption, loses its power to affect activity.

2. There are a number of different measures of profits. One such measure is published by statistical agencies. They measure economy-wide company profits (often with sectors removed, e.g., banks or oil industries) that they divide by economy-wide commercial capital to produce a return on capital employed. (A related alternative is company profits divided by GDP, but this is not a return on capital employed, but rather the share of those profits in total incomes.) Other measures sometimes referred to as "profits" are from stock market valuations—for example, Tobin's Q (ratio of the market value of nonfinancial corporations to the value of their tangible capital) or the market value of equities as a share of GDP.

3. One challenge to this view comes in work by James Bessen (2016). He combines company market value with data on (i) company intangibles, using R&D, advertising, and general spending on administration costs and (ii) industry data on the extent of regulation, lobbying, and rent-seeking in that industry. Like other studies, he finds a statistically significant correlation between market values and the various intangible measures and the lobbying/rent-seeking measures. However, in his data, from the 2000s, the intangible/tangible capital ratio is falling, so he concludes that intangibles cannot explain the rise in profits in the 2000s, although they can account for the rise from 1980 to 2000. As he acknowledges, however, his regulation and R&D measures are highly concentrated in just a few industries, such as pharmaceuticals and transport. Hence, he is not measuring the broader range of intangibles we use.

4. Remember that TFP measures how well firms are using their inputs (that is, output per unit of all their inputs). If they can scale them or, better yet, benefit from inputs of *other* firms, then TFP rises.

5. See, for example, http://stumblingandmumbling.typepad.com/stum bling_and_mumbling/2016/03/barriers-to-productivity-growth.html.

Chapter 6: Intangibles and the Rise of Inequality

1. They are called mules because they were a hybrid of two earlier inventions, the water frame and the spinning jenny, a nice demonstration that the synergies between intangible investments—in this case, different types of R&D—are not a recent discovery.
2. Louis Anslow, https://timeline.com/robots-have-been-about-to-take -all-the-jobs-for-more-than-200-years-5c9c08a2f41d#.wh363gjar. See also Bakhshi, Frey, and Osborne 2015.
3. See, for example, his post: http://stumblingandmumbling.typepad .com/stumbling_and_mumbling/2011/10/the-bosses-pay-con-trick .html.
4. There's a deeper reason behind this logic, which is that taxing mobile capital ends up costing the workers. How can it be that a tax bill that capital owners have to pay ends up being paid by the workers? The answer is the difference between the legal and economic incidence of the tax. The legal incidence is the identity of the party who writes the check. The economic incidence is the identity of the party whose income changes as a consequence. So, if a government taxes capital, which can move abroad, the legal incidence does indeed fall upon the capital owner who has to pay; in this example no one pays the tax since the capital all goes abroad. But with less capital to work with, workers are less productive and so their wages fall. Thus the economic incidence falls upon them.
5. Reported in Krueger 2016.

Chapter 7: Infrastructure for Intangibles, and Intangible Infrastructure

1. John Fairley paints a vivid portrait of the 300,000 horses in 1900 in London that "were sustained by an infrastructure of extraordinary organizational complexity and sophistication . . . the Great Western Railway built an equine hostelry of stables four storeys high . . . with an attendant army just as large of stablemen, farriers, vets and feed waggoners" (*Horses of the Great War* 2016, prologue).
2. Edgerton also points out that claims on the death of distance have been going for quite a while. He quotes George Orwell, writing in 1944, "People go on repeating certain phrases which were fashionable before 1914. Two great favourites are 'the abolition of distance' and 'the disappearance of frontiers'. I do not know how often I have met

with the statements that 'the aeroplane and the radio have abolished distance' and 'all parts of the world are now interdependent.'" Orwell, "As I Please," *Tribune*, May 12, 1944.

3. Economists evaluating "place-based" policies have found two important problems. First, as ever in policy, it is hard to know what the counterfactual is, that is, what would have happened in the absence of the cluster. Second, economists have continued to find evidence of "displacement." The economists Henry Overman and Elias Einio looked at the Local Enterprise Growth Initiative, a 2006–11 UK initiative that subsidized employment in deprived areas. They found it raised employment by 5 percent in the deprived areas, but lowered it by 5 percent in the neighboring areas. Worse, when the program finished, after six years, the businesses all moved back to the original area. Thus the program spent around £418 million to move businesses temporarily about half a mile.

4. Her resignation letter is at https://shift.newco.co/letter-of-resignation -from-the-palo-alto-planning-and-transportation-commission -f7b6facd94f5#.9oa7winlu, quoted in the Marginal Revolution blog, http://marginalrevolution.com/marginalrevolution/2016/08/collective -land-ownership-in-palo-alto.html.

5. Daniel Davies and Tess Read's book *The Secret Life of Money* has an excellent chapter on the economics of trade shows (D. Davies and Read 2015).

Chapter 8: The Challenge of Financing an Intangible Economy

1. In the *General Theory of Employment, Interest and Money*, Keynes, in chapter 12, distinguishes between *speculation* as "the activity of forecasting the psychology of the market" and the term *enterprise* for "the activity of forecasting the prospective yield of assets over their whole life. [If an] investor . . . will not readily purchase an investment except in the hope of capital appreciation . . . he is, in the above sense, a speculator. Speculators may do no harm as bubbles on a steady stream of enterprise. But the position is serious when enterprise becomes the bubble on a whirlpool of speculation. When the capital development of a country becomes a by-product of the activities of a casino, the job is likely to be ill-done."

2. A more nuanced argument is that publicly available R&D is being stifled. A study by Arora, Belenzon, and Patacconi (2015) looked at

scientific publications by American companies on the US stock exchange between 1980 and 2007 and found that, while public firms are patenting more, and the value of these patents seems to be stable, they are publishing ever less of their research in journals.

3. A recent CMA/FCA report found that only 25 percent of small businesses thought that "their bank supports their business."

4. *Hamlet*, Act 1, Sc. 3, lines 75–76.

5. For United States' rules, see, for example, http://www.federalreserve .gov/bankinforeg/stress-tests/2014-revised-capital-framework.htm#f37r.

6. This seems to persist even when we adjust for the impact of taxes.

7. Some of this is discussed in the *Economist*: http://www.economist .com/news/briefing/21651220-most-western-economies-sweeten -cost-borrowing-bad-idea-senseless-subsidy.

8. http://www.bloomberg.com/news/articles/2014-10-06/s-p-500 -companies-spend-almost-all-profits-on-buybacks-payouts.

9. Ikenberry, Lakonishok, and Vermaelen (1995), it should be noted, argue that share buybacks create value in the short term and create even more value in the long term.

10. This is related to a famous argument made by the economists Sanford Grossman and Oliver Hart (1980), who pointed out that small shareholders will not devote resources to getting rid of poorly performing managers, but rather they will just implicitly rely on the work of others (in particular, corporate raiders) via the share price.

11. See his profile in *Forbes Magazine*, http://archive.fortune.com/magazines /fortune/fortune_archive/1998/10/26/250008/index.htm.

Chapter 9: Competing, Managing, and Investing in the Intangible Economy

1. Sarah O'Connor, "Amazon Unpacked," February 8, 2013, https://www .ft.com/content/ed6a985c-70bd-11e2-85d0-00144feab49a.

2. Sustained advantage should not be confused with sustainability, often referred to not as a measure of longevity but of environmental concern. In many cases, however, both will be congruent goals, since legislation and public pressure will likely ensure firms want to do both. But there will always be cases where firms can, for example, raise short-term earnings by causing environmental damage (e.g., disposing of waste improperly). Likewise, the easiest way to raise short-term earnings is to renege on promises to suppliers (and maybe customers): none of these tactics is sustainable in the long term and thus we rule them out.

3. http://data.ers.usda.gov/reports.aspx?StateFIPS=16&StateName=Ida ho&ID=10633#.U-5XxfldXzg.
4. For more discussion, see the very accessible treatment by Lev and Gu (2016) and Foss and Stieglitz (2012). Kay (1993) groups the distinctive assets firms can create under three headings: innovation, reputation, and architecture (the latter being features of the organization).
5. http://stumblingandmumbling.typepad.com/.
6. A very lively literature asks who then should have that authority, managers, workers, or owners?
7. Reported in, for example, www.sfgate.com (http://www.sfgate.com /bayarea/article/Court-to-FedEx-Your-drivers-are-full-time-5717048 .php). It is reported that although FedEx required their drivers to provide their own vans, they specified "their dimensions, shelving, and paint color."
8. And the management survey work does try to correct for this effect: so, for example, the world management survey asks about the time horizon of targets and gives a high score if "Long term goals are translated into specific short term targets so that short term targets become a 'staircase' to reach long term goals." (World Management Survey, question 10, manufacturing questionnaire, http://worldmanagement survey.org/wp-content/images/2010/09/Manufacturing-Survey -Instrument.pdf.)
9. There are, of course, a lot of complications over and above these general principles. First, in company accounts, intangible assets are often split into "intangibles other than goodwill" (such as the patent discussed) and "goodwill." Goodwill is generated only externally, when a business is combined with another, for example, via a takeover. Goodwill measures the gap between what is paid for the business and the value of its tangible assets. That measure of goodwill is treated as an asset and then amortized (or, if the value of the goodwill falls in an agreed-upon fashion, called impairment, then an expense is entered for this). For UK guidance on this, see the UK Financial Reporting Council, FRS102, chapters 18 and 19. Appendix A to Lev (2001) reports the rules for the United States, which follow the same pattern, with a series of complicated exceptions in, for example, the purchase of information in a credit card portfolio, libraries of movie and TV companies, and mineral and airport landing rights.
10. As Lev and Gu (2016) point out, in 2011 HP acquired Autonomy for $10bn, much of whose value was software; but then wrote off almost all of it the following year.

11. BAT Financial statement, 2015: www.bat.com/ar/2015/assets /downloads/BAT_Financial_Statements_2015.pdf.

Chapter 10: Public Policy in an Intangible Economy

1. The specific regulations are set out in Part 1 of the Framework, p. 89 ("London View Management Framework" 2012).
2. On the one hand, allowing some monopolies that may have generated some benefits to wag the whole competition-policy dog is unlikely to be a good policy. On the other hand, fixating on competition policy that creates a market structure with lots of small companies will not be a good policy decision since consumers will not enjoy the many benefits that come from intangible-rich (presumably big) firms. Rather, competition policy should be focused on whether a market is delivering rivalry, for example, allowing new firms or products to be introduced.
3. See https://www.iras.gov.sg/irashome/Schemes/Businesses/Productivity -and-Innovation-Credit-Scheme/#title5.

REFERENCES

Aghion, Philippe, and Peter Howitt. 1992. "A Model of Growth through Creative Destruction." *Econometrica* 60 (2): 323–51. doi:10.2307/2951599.

Aghion, Philippe, John Van Reenen, and Luigi Zingales. 2013. "Innovation and Institutional Ownership." *American Economic Review* 103 (1): 277–304. doi:10.1257/aer.103.1.277.

Allen, Robert C. 1983. "Collective Invention." *Journal of Economic Behavior & Organization* 4 (1): 1–24. doi:10.1016/0167-2681(83)90023-9.

Alvaredo, Facundo, Anthony B. Atkinson, Thomas Piketty, and Emmanuel Saez. 2013. "The Top 1 Percent in International and Historical Perspective." *Journal of Economic Perspectives* 27 (3): 3–20. http://www.aeaweb.org/articles?id=10.1257/jep.27.3.3.

Amore, Mario Daniele, Cédric Schneider, and Alminas Zaldokas. 2012. "Credit Supply and Corporate Innovations." *SSRN Electronic Journal*. doi:10.2139/ssrn.2022235.

Andrews, Dan, Chiara Criscuolo, and Peter Gal. 2016. "Mind the Gap: Productivity Divergence between the Global Frontier and Laggard Firms." OECD Productivity Working Papers.

Appelt, Silvia, Matej Bajgar, Chiara Criscuolo, and Fernando Galindo-Rueda. 2016. "R&D Tax Incentives: Evidence on Design, Incidence and Impacts." OECD Science, Technology and Industry Policy Papers, No. 32. http://dx.doi.org/10.1787/5jlr8fldqk7j-en.

Arora, Ashish, Sharon Belenzon, and Andrea Patacconi. 2015. "Killing the Golden Goose? The Changing Nature of Corporate Research, 1980–2007." Fuqua Business School, Working Paper. https://faculty.fuqua.duke.edu/~sb135/bio/w20902.pdf.

Arrow, Kenneth. 1962. "Economic Welfare and the Allocation of Resources for Invention." In *The Rate and Direction of Inventive Activity: Economic and Social Factors*, edited by Universities-National Bureau, 1:609–26. National Bureau of Economic Research, Inc. http://ideas.repec.org/h/nbr/nberch/2144.html.

Arthur, W. Brian. 2009. *The Nature of Technology: What It Is and How It Evolves*. Free Press.

Autor, David H. 2013. "The Task Approach to Labor Markets: An Overview." *Journal for Labour Market Research* 46 (3): 185–99. https://ideas.repec.org/a/iab/iabjlr/v2013i3p185-199.html.

———. 2014. "Skills, Education, and the Rise of Earnings Inequality among the 'Other 99 Percent.'" *Science* 344 (6186).

Awano, G., M. Franklin, J. Haskel, and Z. Kastrinaki. 2010. "Measuring Investment in Intangible Assets in the UK: Results from a New Survey. *Economic & Labour Market Review* 4 (7): 66–71.

Bakhshi, Hasan, Carl Benedikt Frey, and Mike Osborne. 2015. "Creativity vs. Robots." http://www.nesta.org.uk/sites/default/files/creativity_vs._robots_wv.pdf.

Bakhshi, Hasan, Juan Mateos-Garcia, and Andrew Whitby. 2014. "Model Workers: How Leading Companies Are Recruiting and Managing Data Talent." http://www.nesta.org.uk/publications/model-workers -how-leading-companies-are-recruiting-and-managing-data-talent.

Bandiera, Oriana, Luigi Guiso, Andrea Prat, and Raffaella Sadun. 2011. "What Do CEOs Do?" Harvard Business School, Working Paper, No. 11–081.

Barth, Mary E., Ron Kasznik, and Maureen F. McNichols. 2001. "Analyst Coverage and Intangible Assets." *Journal of Accounting Research* 39 (1): 1–34. doi:10.1111/1475-679X.00001.

Belfield, Chris, Jonathan Cribb, Andrew Hood, and Robert Joyce. 2014. *Living Standards, Poverty and Inequality in the UK: 2014.* IFS Reports, Institute for Fiscal Studies.

Bell, Alex, Raj Chetty, Xavier Jaravel, Neviana Petkova, and John Van Reenen. 2016. "The Lifecycle of Inventors." *SSRN Electronic Journal.* doi:10.2139/ssrn.2838018.

Bell, Brian D., and John Van Reenen. 2013. "Extreme Wage Inequality: Pay at the Very Top." *American Economic Review* 103 (3): 153–57. http://www.jstor.org/stable/23469720.

Beniger, James R. 1986. *The Control Revolution: Technological and Economic Origins of the Information Society.* Harvard University Press.

Berliner, J. S. 1957. *Factory and Manager in the Soviet Union.* Cambridge University Press.

Bernstein, Shai. 2015. "Does Going Public Affect Innovation?" *Journal of Finance* 70 (4): 1365–1403. doi:10.1111/jofi.12275.

Bessen, James. 2015. "Toil and Technology." *Finance and Development* 52 (1). http://www.imf.org/external/pubs/ft/fandd/2015/03/bessen.htm.

———. 2016. "Accounting for Rising Corporate Profits: Intangibles or Regulatory Rents?" Boston University School of Law, Law & Economics,

Working Paper, No. 16–18. http://www.bu.edu/law/faculty-scholarship/working-paper-series/.

Big Innovation Centre. 2017. "The Purposeful Company: Policy Report." http://biginnovationcentre.com/media/uploads/pdf/TPC_Policy Report.pdf.

Black, Jane, David de Meza, and David Jeffreys. 1996. "House Prices, the Supply of Collateral and the Enterprise Economy." *Economic Journal* 106 (434): 60. doi:10.2307/2234931.

Blaug, Mark. 1978. *Economic Theory in Retrospect*. 3rd ed. Cambridge University Press.

Bloom, Nicholas, Christos Genakos, Raffaella Sadun, and John Van Reenen. 2011. "Management Practices across Firms and Countries." Harvard Business School, Working Paper, No. 12-052.

Bloom, Nicholas, Raffaella Sadun, and John Van Reenen. 2012. "Americans Do IT Better: US Multinationals and the Productivity Miracle." *American Economic Review* 102 (1): 167–201. http://ideas.repec.org/a/aea/aecrev/v102y2012i1p167-201.html.

Bonnet, Odran, Pierre-Henri Bono, Guillaume Chapelle, and Etienne Wasmer. 2014. "Does Housing Capital Contribute to Inequality? A Comment on Thomas Piketty's Capital in the 21st Century." SciencesPo Economics Discussion Paper 2014-07. http://econpapers.repec.org/RePEc:spo:wpecon:info:hdl:2441/30nstiku669glbr66l6n7mc2oq.

Bower, M. 1979. *Perspective on McKinsey*. Internal McKinsey publication.

Braggion, Fabio, and Lyndon Moore. 2013. "The Economic Benefits of Political Connections in Late Victorian Britain." *Journal of Economic History* 73 (1): 142–76. doi:10.1017/S0022050713000053.

Brynjolfsson, Erik, Loren Hitt, and Shinkyu Yang. 2002. "Intangible Assets: How the Interaction of Computers and Organizational Structure Affects Stock Market Valuations." *Brookings Papers on Economic Activity* 33 (1): 137–98.

Brynjolfsson, Erik, and Andrew McAffee. 2014. *The Second Machine Age*. W. W. Norton and Co.

Chen, Ester, Ilanit Gavious, and Baruch Lev. 2015. "The Positive Externalities of IFRS R&D Rule: Enhanced Voluntary Disclosure." http://people.stern.nyu.edu/blev/files/Positive-Externalities-of-IFRS_March_30_2015_k4gn98s2.pdf.

Chesson, Adrian. 2001. "Estimation of Software in the UK National Accounts—Recent Developments." OECD STD/NA(2001)23. http://www.oecd.org/std/na/1908892.doc.

Colecchia, Alessandra, and Paul Schreyer. 2002. "ICT Investment and Economic Growth in the 1990s: Is the United States a Unique Case?" *Review of Economic Dynamics* 5 (2): 408–42. doi:10.1006/redy.2002.0170.

Corrado, Carol A. 2010. "Intangible Capital and Economic Growth." https://www.wilsoncenter.org/sites/default/files/Corrado Presentation.pdf.

Corrado, Carol A., and Janet X Hao. 2013. "Brands as Productive Assets: Concepts, Measurement and Global Trends." http://www.wipo.int/export/sites/www/econ_stat/en/economics/pdf/wp13.pdf.

Corrado, Carol A., Jonathan Haskel, Cecilia Jona-Lasinio, and Massimiliano Iommi. 2013. "Innovation and Intangible Investment in Europe, Japan, and the United States." *Oxford Review of Economic Policy* 29 (2): 261–86. http://ideas.repec.org/a/oup/oxford/v29y2013i2p261-286.html.

———. 2016. "Intangible Investment in the EU and US before and since the Great Recession and Its Contribution to Productivity Growth." EIB Working Paper, No. 2016/08. http://www.eib.org/attachments/efs/economics_working_paper_2016_08_en.pdf.

Corrado, Carol A., and Charles R Hulten. 2010. "How Do You Measure a 'Technological Revolution'?" *American Economic Review* 100 (2): 99–104. doi:10.1257/aer.100.2.99.

Corrado, Carol A., Charles Hulten, and Daniel Sichel. 2005. "Measuring Capital and Technology: An Expanded Framework." In *Measuring Capital in the New Economy*, edited by Carol A. Corrado, John Haltiwanger, and Daniel Sichel. University of Chicago Press.

———. 2009. "Intangible Capital and U.S. Economic Growth." *Review of Income and Wealth* 55 (3): 661–85.

Corrado, Carol A., M. O'Mahony, and Lea Samek. 2015. "Measuring Education Services as Intangible Social Infrastructure." SPINTAN Working Paper Series, No. 19.

Cowen, Tyler. 2011. *The Great Stagnation: How America Ate All the Low-Hanging Fruit of Modern History, Got Sick, and Will (Eventually) Feel Better*. Penguin eSpecial from Dutton.

CQ Researcher. 2016. "The Iron and Steel Industry." http://library.cqpress.com/cqresearcher/document.php?id=cqresrre1930050100.

Crawford, Rowena, Dave Innes, and Cormac O'Dea. 2016. "Household Wealth in Great Britain: Distribution, Composition and Changes 2006–12." *Fiscal Studies* 37 (1):35–54. doi:10.1111/j.1475-5890.2016.12083.

David, Paul. 1990. "The Dynamo and the Computer: An Historical Perspective on the Modern Productivity Paradox." *American Economic Review* 80 (2): 355–61.

Davies, Daniel, and Tess Read. 2015. *Secret Life of Money—Everyday Economics Explained*. Metro.

Davies, Richard, Andrew Haldane, Mette Nielsen, and Silvia Pezzini. 2014. "Measuring the Costs of Short-Termism." *Journal of Financial Stability* 12 (June): 16–25.

Dixit, Avinash. 1992. "Investment and Hysteresis." *Journal of Economic Perspectives* 6 (1): 107–32. http://www.aeaweb.org/articles?id=10.1257/jep.6.1.107.

Dixit, Avinash, and Robert S. Pindyck. 1995. "The Options Approach to Capital Investment." *Harvard Business Review* 73 (3). https://hbr.org/1995/05/the-options-approach-to-capital-investment.

Dodgson, Mark, David Gann, and Ammon J. Salter. 2005. *Think, Play, Do: Technology, Innovation, and Organization*. Oxford University Press.

Domar, Evsey D. 1961. "On the Measurement of Technological Change." *Economic Journal* 71 (284): 709–29.

Edgerton, David. 2011. *Shock of the Old: Technology and Global History since 1900*. Profile.

Edmans, Alex. 2009. "Blockholder Trading, Market Efficiency, and Managerial Myopia." *Journal of Finance* 64 (6): 2481–2513. doi:10.1111/j.1540-6261.2009.01508.x.

———. 2011. "Does the Stock Market Fully Value Intangibles? Employee Satisfaction and Equity Prices." *Journal of Financial Economics* 101 (3): 621–40. doi:10.1016/j.jfineco.2011.03.021.

———. 2014. "Blockholders and Corporate Governance." *Annual Review of Financial Economics* 6 (1): 23–50. doi:10.1146/annurev-financial-110613-034455.

Edmans, Alex, Vivian W. Fang, and Katharina Lewellen. 2013. "Equity Vesting and Managerial Myopia." NBER, Working Paper, No. 19407, 1–60. doi:10.2139/ssrn.2270027.

Forman, Chris, Avi Goldfarb, and Shane Greenstein. 2016. "Agglomeration of Invention in the Bay Area: Not Just ICT." *American Economic Review* 106 (5): 146–51. doi:10.1257/aer.p20161018.

Forth, T. 2015 "The North-South Divide: We Never Even Tried." http://www.tomforth.co.uk/wenevertried/.

Foss, Nicolaï, and Nils Stieglitz. 2012. "Modern Resource-Based Theory(ies)." In *Handbook on the Economics and Theory of the Firm*, edited by Michael Dietrich and Jackie Krafft. Edward Elgar Publishing, Inc. doi:10.4337/9781781002407.00030.

Fraser, Stuart. 2012. "The Impact of the Financial Crisis on Bank Lending to SMEs." http://mbsportal.bl.uk/taster/subjareas/smlbusentrep/bis/13799212_949_bank_lending_smes.pdf.

Freeman, Richard. 2007. "The Great Doubling: The Challenge of the New Global Labor Market." In *Ending Poverty in America: How to Restore the American Dream*, edited by John Edwards, Marion Crain, and Arne L. Kalleberg. New Press.

Fukao, Kyoji, Tsutomu Miyagawa, Kentaro Mukai, Yukio Shinoda, and Konomi Tonogi. 2009. "Intangible Investment in Japan: Measurement and Contribution to Economic Growth." *Review of Income and Wealth* 55 (3): 717–36.

Garicano, Luis. 2000. "Hierarchies and the Organization of Knowledge in Production." *Journal of Political Economy* 108 (5): 874–904. doi:10.1086/317671.

Garicano, Luis, and Thomas N. Hubbard. 2007. "Managerial Leverage Is Limited by the Extent of the Market: Hierarchies, Specialization, and the Utilization of Lawyers' Human Capital." *Journal of Law and Economics* 50 (1): 1–43.

Gaspar, Jess, and Edward L. Glaeser. 1998. "Information Technology and the Future of Cities." *Journal of Urban Economics* 43 (1): 136–56.

Giorgio Marrano, Mauro, and Jonathan Haskel. 2007. "How Much Does the UK Invest in Intangible Assets?" CEPR Discussion Papers, No. DP6287. http://ideas.repec.org/p/cpr/ceprdp/6287.html.

Giorgio Marrano, Mauro, Jonathan Haskel, and Gavin Wallis. 2009. "What Happened to the Knowledge Economy? ICT, Intangible Investment and Britain's Productivity Record Revisited." *Review of Income and Wealth* 55 (3): 686–716.

Glaeser, Edward L. 2011. *Triumph of the City*. Macmillan.

Glaeser, Edward L., Hedi D. Kallal, José A. Scheinkman, and Andrei Shleifer. 1992. "Growth in Cities." *Journal of Political Economy* 100 (6): 1126–52. doi:10.1086/261856.

Goldin, Claudia, and Lawrence F. Katz. 2008. *The Race between Education and Technology*. Harvard University Press.

Goodridge, P. R., and J. Haskel. 2016. "Big Data in UK Industries: An Intangible Investment Approach." Imperial College Business School. http://hdl.handle.net/10044/1/32279.

Goodridge, P. R., J. Haskel, and G. Wallis. 2016. "Accounting for the UK Productivity Puzzle: A Decomposition and Predictions." *Economica* (Dec). doi:10.1111/ecca.12219.

Goos, Maarten, and Alan Manning. 2007. "Lousy and Lovely Jobs: The Rising Polarization of Work in Britain." *Review of Economics and Statistics* 89 (1): 118–33. http://ideas.repec.org/a/tpr/restat/v89y2007i1p118-133.html.

Gordon, Robert J. 2016. *The Rise and Fall of American Growth: The U.S. Standard of Living since the Civil War*. Princeton University Press.

Graham, John R., Campbell R. Harvey, and Shiva Rajgopal. 2005. "The Economic Implications of Corporate Financial Reporting." *Journal of Accounting and Economics* 40 (1): 3–73. doi:10.1016/j.jacceco.2005.01.002.

Griliches, Zvi. 1992. "The Search for R&D Spillovers." *Scandinavian Journal of Economics* 94 (supplement): S29–47.

Grossman, Sanford J., and Oliver D. Hart. 1980. "Takeover Bids, the Free-Rider Problem, and the Theory of the Corporation." *Bell Journal of Economics* 11 (1): 42–64. doi:10.2307/3003400.

Groysberg, Boris, Andrew McLean, and Nitin Nohria. 2006. "Are Leaders Portable?" *Harvard Business Review* 84 (5): 92–100.

Guy, Frederick. 2014. "Technological Change, Bargaining Power and Wages." In *Our Work Here Is Done: Visions of a Robot Economy*, edited by Stian Westlake. Nesta.

Håkanson, Christina, Erik Lindqvist, and Jonas Vlachos. 2015. "Firms and Skills: The Evolution of Worker Sorting." IFAU—Institute for Evaluation of Labour Market and Education Policy, Working Paper, No. 2015:9

Hall, Bronwyn H., Christian Helmers, and Georg von Graevenitz. 2015. "Technology Entry in the Presence of Patent Thickets." NBER, Working Paper, No. 21455. doi:10.3386/w21455.

Hall, Bronwyn H., Adam Jaffe, and Manuel Trajtenberg. 2005. "Market Value and Patent Citations." *RAND Journal of Economics* 36 (1): 16–38.

Hall, Bronwyn H., and Josh Lerner. 2010. "The Financing of R&D and Innovation." In *Handbook of the Economics of Innovation*, edited by Bronwyn H. Hall and Nathan Rosenberg. Elsevier B.V.

Hall, Robert E. 2001. "Struggling to Understand the Stock Market." *American Economic Review* 91 (2): 1–11. http://ideas.repec.org/a/aea/aecrev/v91y2001i2p1-11.html.

Haskel, J., P. Goodridge, A. Hughes, and G. Wallis. 2015. "The Contribution of Public and Private R&D to UK Productivity Growth." Imperial College Business School. http://hdl.handle.net/10044/1/21171.

Henderson, Rebecca M., Richard G. Newell, and David C. Mowery. 2011. "Federal Policy and the Development of Semiconductors, Computer Hardware, and Computer Software: A Policy Model for Climate Change R&D?" In *Accelerating Energy Innovation: Insights from Multiple Sectors*, edited by Rebecca M. Henderson and Richard G. Newell. University of Chicago Press. http://www.nber.org/chapters/c11753.

Hermalin, Benjamin E. 1998. "Toward an Economic Theory of Leadership: Leading by Example." *American Economic Review* 88 (5): 1188–1206. http://ideas.repec.org/a/aea/aecrev/v88y1998i5p1188-1206.html.

Higgs, Peter, Stuart Cunningham, and Hasan Bakhshi. 2008. "Beyond the Creative Industries." Nesta Technical Report.

Hilber, Christian. 2016. "The UK Planning System: Fit for Purpose?" *Planning & Building Control Today* (July): 8–11.

Hulten, Charles R. 1978. "Growth Accounting with Intermediate Inputs." *Review of Economic Studies* 45 (3): 511–18.

———. 2001. "Total Factor Productivity: A Short Biography." In *New Developments in Productivity Analysis*, edited by Charles R. Hulten, Edwin R. Dean, and Michael J. Harper. University of Chicago Press. http://ideas.repec.org/h/nbr/nberch/10122.html.

———. 2010. "Decoding Microsoft: Intangible Capital as a Source of Company Growth." NBER, Working Paper. No. 15799. doi:10.3386/w15799.

Hulten, Charles R., and Frank C. Wykoff. 1981. "The Estimation of Economic Depreciation Using Vintage Asset Prices." *Journal of Econometrics* 15 (3): 367–96. doi:10.1016/0304-4076(81)90101-9.

Ikenberry, D., J. Lakonishok, and T. Vermaelen. 1995. "Market Underreaction to Open Market Share Repurchases." *Journal of Financial Economics* 39 (1995): 181–208. http://www.sciencedirect.com/science/article/pii/0304405X9500826Z.

Kahneman, Daniel, Dan Lovallo, and Olivier Sibony. 2011. "The Big Idea: Before You Make That Big Decision . . ." *Harvard Business Review* 89 (6): 51–60. https://hbr.org/2011/06/the-big-idea-before-you-make-that-big-decision.

Kantor, Shawn, and Alexander Whalley. 2014. "Knowledge Spillovers from Research Universities: Evidence from Endowment Value Shocks." *Review of Economics and Statistics* 96 (1): 171–88. doi:10.1162/REST_a_00357.

Kaufman, E. 2016a. "Brexit Voters: Not the Left Behind." *Fabian Review*, June 24, 2016.

———. 2016b. "It's NOT the Economy, Stupid: Brexit as a Story of Personal Values." *LSE British Politics and Policy Blog*, July 7, 2016. http://blogs.lse.ac.uk/politicsandpolicy/personal-values-brexit-vote/.

Kay, John. 1993. *Foundations of Corporate Success*. Oxford University Press. https://www.johnkay.com/1993/12/06/foundations-of-corporate-success-1993/.

———. 2003. "The High Cost of ICI's Fall from Grace." http://www.johnkay.com/2003/02/13/the-high-cost-of-icis-fall-from-grace/.

———. 2011. *Obliquity: Why Our Goals Are Best Achieved Indirectly*. Profile Books.

———. 2015. *Other People's Money*. Profile Books.

Khan, B. 2008. "An Economic History of Patent Institutions." *EH.net Ency-clopedia*. https://eh.net/encyclopedia/an-economic-history-of-patent-institutions/.

Krueger, Joachaim I. 2016. "The Personality of Brexit Voters." *Psychology Today Blog*, June 29, 2016. https://www.psychologytoday.com/blog/one-among-many/201606/the-personality-brexit-voters.

Lakhani, Karim R., and Jill A. Panetta. 2007. "The Principles of Distrib-uted Innovation." *Innovations: Technology, Governance, Globalization* 2 (3): 97–112. doi:10.1162/itgg.2007.2.3.97.

Lazonick, William. 1979. "Industrial Relations and Technical Change: The Case of the Self-Acting Mule." *Cambridge Journal of Economics* 3 (3): 231–62. doi:10.1093/OXFORDJOURNALS.CJE.A035423.

Lerner, Josh. 2012. *Boulevard of Broken Dreams: Why Public Efforts to Boost Entrepreneurship and Venture Capital Have Failed—and What to Do about It*. Princeton University Press.

Lev, Baruch. 2001. *Intangibles*. Brookings Institution Press. https://www.brookings.edu/book/intangibles/.

Lev, Baruch, and Feng Gu. 2016. *The End of Accounting*. Wiley.

London View Management Framework. 2012. https://www.london.gov.uk/file/7988/download?token=YJoKa7uK.

Lucas, Robert E. 1993. "Making a Miracle." *Econometrica* 61 (2): 251–72. doi:10.2307/2951551.

Machlup, Fritz. 1962. *The Production and Distribution of Knowledge in the United States*. Princeton University Press.

Maizlin, Zeev V., and Patrick M. Vos. 2012. "Do We Really Need to Thank the Beatles for the Financing of the Development of the Computed Tomography Scanner?" *Journal of Computer Assisted Tomography* 36 (2): 161–64. doi:10.1097/RCT.0b013e318249416f.

Mann, W. 2014. "Creditor Rights and Innovation: Evidence from Patent Collateral." Wharton Job Market Paper.

Mazzucato, Mariana. 2013. "Debunking the Market Mechanism: Organ-isations, Innovation and Inequality—A Response to John Kay." *The Political Quarterly* 84 (4): 444–47. doi:10.1111/j.1467-923X.2013.12039.x.

———. 2015. *The Entrepreneurial State: Debunking Public vs. Private Sec-tor Myths*. Anthem Press.

Miglani, Jitender. 2016. "Apple Revenues and Profits 2000 to 2015: Pre- and Post-iPhone." *R&P Research* January 4, 2016. http://revenuesandprofits.com/apple-revenues-and-profits-2000-to-2015-pre-and-post-iphone/.

Milanović, Branko. 2005. *Worlds Apart: Measuring International and Global Inequality*. Princeton University Press.

Miles, David. 1993. "Testing for Short Termism in the UK Stock Market." *Economic Journal* 103 (421): 1379–96. doi:10.2307/2234472.

Milgrom, Paul, and John Roberts. 1988. "An Economic Approach to Influence Activities in Organizations." *American Journal of Sociology* 94: S154–79. http://www.jstor.org/stable/2780245.

Mintzberg, Henry. 1990. "The Manager's Job: Folklore and Fact." *Harvard Business Review* 90 (2): 163–76.

Mirrlees, James, Stuart Adam, Tim Besley, Richard Blundell, Stephen Bond, Robert Chote, Malcolm Gammie, Paul Johnson, Gareth Myles, and James M Poterba. 2011. *Tax by Design*. Institute for Fiscal Studies. http://www.ifs.org.uk/docs/taxbydesign.pdf.

Mokyr, Joel. 2002. *The Gifts of Athena: Historical Origins of the Knowledge Economy*. Princeton University Press.

Moulton, Brent R., Robert P. Parker, and Eugene P. Seskin. 1999. "A Preview of the 1999 Comprehensive Revision of the National Income and Product Accounts: Definitional and Classificational Changes." *Survey of Current Business*, August.

Nakamura, Leonard I. 2001. "What Is the U.S. Gross Investment in Intangibles? (At Least) One Trillion Dollars a Year!" Federal Reserve Bank of Philadelphia, Working Paper, No. 01-15.

———. 2010. "Intangible Assets and National Income Accounting." *Review of Income and Wealth* 56 (s1): S135–55. doi:10.1111/j.1475-4991.2010.00390.x.

Nightingale, Paul. 2004. "Technological Capabilities, Invisible Infrastructure and the Un-Social Construction of Predictability: The Overlooked Fixed Costs of Useful Research." *Research Policy* 33 (9): 1259–84. doi:10.1016/j.respol.2004.08.008.

OECD. 2015. *Frascati Manual 2015: Guidelines for Collecting and Reporting Data on Research and Experimental Development*. OECD Publishing. doi:http://dx.doi.org/10.1787/9789264239012-en.

OECD Secretariat. 1998. "Measuring Intangible Investment: Selected Bibliography." Presented at a conference on OECD Work on Measuring Intangible Investment, Amsterdam, June 1999. https://www.oecd.org/sti/ind/1943317.pdf.

Office for National Statistics. 2016. *UK National Accounts, The Blue Book: 2016*. https://www.ons.gov.uk/economy/grossdomesticproductgdp/compendium/unitedkingdomnationalaccountsthebluebook/2016edition/unitedkingdomnationalaccountsthebluebook2015edition.

Oliner, Stephen D., and Daniel E. Sichel. 1994. "Computers and Output Growth Revisited: How Big Is the Puzzle?" *Brookings Papers on Economic Activity* 1994 (2): 273–334. doi:10.2307/2534658.

———. 2000. "The Resurgence of Growth in the Late 1990s: Is Information Technology the Story?" *Journal of Economic Perspectives* 14 (4): 3–22. doi:10.1257/jep.14.4.3.

Pardey, Philip G., Julian M. Alston, and Connie Chan-Kang. 2013. "Public Agricultural R&D over the Past Half Century: An Emerging New World Order." *Agricultural Economics* 44 (s1): 103–13. doi:10.1111/agec.12055.

Parviainen, Jaana. 2011. "The Standardization Process of Movement in the Fitness Industry: The Experience Design of Les Mills Choreographies." *European Journal of Cultural Studies* 14 (5): 526–41. http://ecs.sagepub.com/content/14/5/526.abstract.

Perez, Carlota. 2002. *Technological Revolutions and Financial Capital: The Dynamics of Bubbles and Golden Ages*. Edward Elgar Publishing, Inc.

Piketty, Thomas. 2014. *Capital in the Twenty-First Century*. Harvard University Press.

Pisano, Gary, and Willy C. Shih. 2009. "Restoring American Competitiveness." *Harvard Business Review* 2 (July-Aug).

Rauch, Ferdinand. 2011. "Advertising Expenditure and Consumer Prices." CEP Discussion Paper No. 1073. http://cep.lse.ac.uk/pubs/download/dp1073.pdf.

Ridley, Matt. 2010. *The Rational Optimist: How Prosperity Evolves*. Fourth Estate.

Roberts, Russell D. 2014. *How Adam Smith Can Change Your Life: An Unexpected Guide to Human Nature and Happiness*. Portfolio/Penguin.

Rognlie, Matthew. 2015. "A Note on Piketty and Diminishing Returns to Capital." MIT. http://mattrognlie.com/piketty_diminishing_returns.pdf.

Romer, Paul M. 1990. "Endogenous Technological Change." *Journal of Political Economy* 98 (5): S71–102.

Rosen, Sherwin. 1981. "The Economics of Superstars." *American Economic Review* 71 (5): 845–58. http://www.jstor.org/stable/1803469.

Sampson, Rachelle C., and Yuan Shi. 2016. "Evidence and Implications of Short-Termism in US Public Capital Markets: 1980–2013." *SSRN Electronic Journal*. doi:10.2139/ssrn.2837524.

Smil, Vaclav. 2005. *Creating the Twentieth Century: Technical Innovations of 1867–1914 and Their Lasting Impact*. Oxford University Press. doi:10.1093/0195168747.001.0001.

Solow, Robert M. 1957. "Technical Change and the Aggregate Production Function." *Review of Economics and Statistics* 39 (3): 312–20. doi:10.2307/1926047.

Solow, Robert M. 1987. "We'd Better Watch Out." *New York Times Book Review*. http://www.standupeconomist.com/pdf/misc/solow-computer-productivity.pdf.

———. 2014. "Thomas Piketty Is Right: Everything You Need to Know about 'Capital in the Twenty-First Century.'" *New Republic*, April 22, 2014. https://newrepublic.com/article/117429/capital-twenty-first-century-thomas-piketty-reviewed.

Song, Jae, David J. Price, Fatih Guvenen, Nicholas Bloom, and Till von Wachter. 2015. *Firming Up Inequality*. NBER, Working Paper, No. 21199. doi:10.3386/w21199.

Soto, Hernando de. 2001. *The Mystery of Capital: Why Capitalism Triumphs in the West and Fails Everywhere Else*. Black Swan.

Sutton, John. 1991. *Sunk Costs and Market Structure: Price Competition, Advertising, and the Evolution of Concentration*. MIT Press.

Summers, Lawrence H. 2014. "U.S. Economic Prospects: Secular Stagnation, Hysteresis, and the Zero Lower Bound." *Business Economics* 49 (2): 65–73.

———. 2015. "Have We Entered an Age of Secular Stagnation?" *IMF Economic Review* 63 (1): 277–80.

———. 2016. "Corporate Profits Are Near Record Highs. Here's Why That's a Problem." *Washington Post Wonkblog*, March 30, 2016. http://larrysummers.com/2016/03/30/corporate-profits-are-near-record-highs-heres-why-thats-a-problem/.

Thwaites, Gregory. 2015. "Why Are Real Interest Rates So Low? Secular Stagnation and the Relative Price of Investment Goods." Bank of England Staff Working Paper, No. 564. http://www.bankofengland.co.uk/research/Pages/workingpapers/2015/swp564.aspx.

Triplett, J. E. 1996. "Depreciation in Production Accounts and in Income and Wealth Accounts: Resolution of an Old Debate." *Economic Inquiry* 34 (1): 93–115.

van Ark, Bart, Janet Hao, Carol Corrado, and Charles Hulten. 2009. "Measuring Intangible Capital and Its Contribution to Economic Growth in Europe." *European Investment Bank Papers* 14 (1): 62–93.

Vanguard. 2015. "Can Active Funds Deliver Persistent Performance?" https://www.vanguard.co.uk/documents/adv/literature/can-active-funds-deliver-persistent-performance.pdf.

Walters, Ben. 2016. "What Are Queer Spaces for Anyway?" Not Television. http://www.nottelevision.net/what-are-queer-spaces-for-anyway/.

Weitzmann, M. L. 1976. "On the Welfare Significance of National Product in a Dynamic Economy." *Quarterly Journal of Economics* 90 (1): 156–62. http://www.jstor.org/stable/1886092.

———. 1980. "The 'Ratchet Principle' and Performance Incentives." *Bell Journal of Economics* 11 (1): 302–8.

Willetts, David. 2010. *The Pinch: How the Baby Boomers Took Their Children's Future—and Why They Should Give It Back*. Atlantic Books.

Young, Alison. 1998. "Towards an Interim Statistical Framework: Selecting the Core Components of Intangible Investment." OECD Secretariat. https://www.oecd.org/sti/ind/1943301.pdf.

accounting, treatment of intangibles in, 202–4
advertising spending, 50
Aghion, Phillipe, 41, 62, 173
AirBnB, 24, 51; contestedness and, 115; legal travails of, 187; scalability of, 67; and synergies, 82
Akzo Nobel, 167
Allen, Robert, 83
Amana, 80, 85, 183
Amazon, 111, 191, 194–95, 197
American Airlines, 49
Andreessen, Marc, 23
Andrews, Dan, 96
Angry Birds, 65
Ansari-X Prize, 85
Anslow, Louis, 127
Appert jar, 64
Apple, 23–24, 51, 87, 104; and spillovers, 72–73, 110; and synergies, 86
applied knowledge, 65
Arrow, Kenneth, 62, 147
Arthur, Brian, 62, 80
assets, definition of, 19–21
Atkinson, Anthony, 118
Atlas, Charles, 18
authority, of managers, 189
automated bank teller machines, 127

Autor, David, 123
Awano, Gaganan, 56

banking, 158–59, 162–66
Barth, Mary, 204
basic knowledge, 65
Baumol, William, 28
Baumol's Cost Disease, 28
Beatles, the, 59, 61, 240
Bell, Daniel, 4
Beniger, James, 30
Berliner, Joseph S., 195
Bernstein, Shai, 171, 172
Bessen, James, 114–15, 127
Black Cap pub, 150
Blaug, Mark, 54
blocking patents, 113–14
Bloom, Nicholas, 82, 129, 195
Bodypump®, 17–18, 21
Bonnet, Odran, 128
Bono, Pierre-Henri, 128
Boulevard of Broken Dreams, The (Lerner), 178, 220
Braggion, Fabio, 132–33, 134
branding, 49, 76
Brexit, 122, 141–42, 143
British Airports Authority (BAA), 1–2
British Airways, 49
British Coachways, 162
Brooker, Charles, 183

Brynjolfsson, Erik, 30, 82, 123
Buffet, Warren, 19
Bureau of Economic Analysis
    (BEA), 39–41, 244n3
Burroughs, Edgar Rice, 76
Bush, Vannevar, 232
business climate, changes in,
    31–34

Callaghan, James, 127
capital, 10; definition of, 19–21;
    human, 54, 119; social, 156,
    236
Capital (Marx), 126
Capital in the Twenty-First Century
    (Piketty), 19, 121, 128, 136
capitalism, 158, 243n3
capitalization, versus expensing,
    202–4
Chapelle, Guillaume, 128
Chen, Ester, 204
Chesbrough, Henry, 83
Citibank, 40
Clayton, Tony, 42
clusters, 147–48, 235–36
Coase, Ronald, 190–91, 192
Coca Cola Company, 9–10, 49
code of laws, of Ur-Nammu, 75
codified knowledge, 65
Collecchia, Alessandra, 40
collective intelligence, 217
ComCab, 82
competitive advantage, 185–87
computerized information, 43–45
Conference on Research in In-
    come and Wealth, 4, 42
contestedness, 87–88, 115, 132;
    venture capital and, 177

Cook, Tim, 51
copyright, 76–79, 165, 213
Corbyn, Jeremy, 223
Corrado, Carol, 4, 5, 42, 43, 45
cost of intangible investment, 28
Cowen, Tyler, 93, 228
Coyle, Diane, 4, 36
"creative class," the, 215
Criscuolo, Chiara, 96
crowdfunding, 166
CT scanners, 59–61, 104, 204
cult of the manager, 184
Curtiss Aeroplane and Motor
    Company, 79

DARPA, 218, 226–27, 232
data, 63
David, Paul, 151–52
Davies, Richard, 168
de Soto, Hernando, 153
Digital Copyright Exchange, 213
Digital Millennium Copyright
    Act, 76
Dillow, Chris, 110, 136, 188
disbenefits, 79
Disney, 78–79, 209
diversified investors, 205
Dodgson, Mark, 197
Doerr, John, 176
Domesday Book, 2–3
dot-com bubble, 4, 42, 145–46
Downing, Kate, 148
DunnHumby, 23

economic competencies, 43–45
economies of scale, 185
Edgerton, David, 146
Edmans, Alex, 170, 171, 172–73

education and training, 51–52, 170, 228–30

Einstein, Albert, 127

e-mail, 217

EMIDEC computer, 59

EMI Records, 59–61, 104, 204

employment strictness, 32

End of Accounting, The (Lev and Gu), 201, 220

endogenous growth theory, 62

Engelbart, Douglas, 217

Enron, 42

Entrepreneurial State, The (Mazzucato), 232

EpiPen, 85–86, 112, 239

Ericsson, 104

esteem, inequality of, 122–23, 141–42; intangibles' effects on, 129–40

expensing, versus capitalization, 202–4

Facebook, 34, 67, 170, 175, 217, 222

Fang, Vivian W., 171

fast followership, 110

Federal Reserve. *See* US Federal Reserve

FedEx, 190–91

financial assets, 20

financialization, 161, 168

Financial Times, 183

financing, 158–60, 179–81; banking industry and, 158–59, 162–66; through crowdfunding, 166; and equity markets, 169–74; for intangible investments, 218–21; and investing

in the intangible economy, 201–6; problems in, 160–79; short-termism in, 161, 168–69; stock markets and, 167–68, 205–6; through venture capital (VC), 154–55, 161, 166, 174–79

Five Star Movement, 122–23

fixed assets, 20

Florida, Richard, 148, 215

Food and Drug Administration. *See* US Food and Drug Administration

Ford, Henry, 36

Forman, Chris, 139

Frascati Manual, 38

Freeman, Chris, 39

Freeman, Richard, 124

FreshDirect, 23

Fukao, Kyoji, 42

Future of Work, The (Handy), 182

Gal, Peter, 96

Gann, David, 197

Garicano, Luis, 134, 135, 191

Gaspar, Jess, 146

Gates, Bill, 222–23

Gates Foundation, 222–23

Gavious, Ilanit, 204

GDP: A Brief but Affectionate History (Coyle), 36

Genentech, 174, 175

General Electric (GE), 51, 60–61, 184, 194, 204

General Theory of Employment (Keynes), 249n1

generational inequality, 121–22

GitHub, 29, 79, 152, 217

Glaeser, Edward, 62, 79, 138–39, 142, 146, 147
globalization, 119; and growing market sizes, 34–35
Gold, Joe, 17
Goldfarb, Avi, 139
Goldin, Claudia, 228
Goldwyn, Sam, 229
Goodridge, Peter, 25, 223
goodwill, 251n9
Google, 67–68, 73, 87, 170, 209, 222; contestedness and, 115; Kaggle and, 152; scalability of, 101–2, 105; spillovers and, 110; venture capital and, 174, 175, 176, 177
Goos, Martin, 123
Gordon, Robert, 93, 228
government: funding of training and education by, 228–30; investment by, 231–34, 234–36; and public procurement, 226–28; R&D spending by, 33–34, 55, 77, 223–24
Graham, John R., 168
Great Depression, 36, 127
"Great Doubling, The" (Freeman), 124
Great Invention: The Story of GDP, The (Masood), 36
Great Recession, 103, 108, 116
Great Stagnation, The (Cowen), 93
Greenspan, Alan, 40, 244n3
Greenstein, Shane, 139
Griliches, Zvi, 38, 62
gross domestic product (GDP), 3, 20, 42; difficulty in calcula-tion of, 37, 244n3; government spending and, 55; human capital and, 54; and intangible investment, 35, 54, 117; IT investment and, 29–30; measurement of, 38, 40–41, 245n10; and tangible versus intangible investment, 25–27, 32
Groysberg, Boris, 194
Gu, Feng, 185, 203
Guerrero kidnapping, 74
Guvenen, Fatih, 129
gyms, commercial, 15–19

Håkanson, Christina, 131, 133
Haldane, Andrew, 168
Hall, Bronwyn, 62, 105–6, 211–12
Haltiwanger, John, 42
Handy, Charles, 182, 183
Hargreaves, Ian, 213
Harvard Business Review, 184
Harvey, Campbell, R., 168
Haskel, Jonathan, 42
Hayek, Friedrich von, 190
Hermalin, Benjamin, 199
Hewlett Packard, 170
high-intensity interval training (HIIT), 17
Hilber, Christian, 216
Home Depot, 194
Horizon 2020 program, 218
Hounsfield, Godrey, 59, 61
housing, 122, 128–29, 136–39; affordable, 148–49; creative class and, 215; planning of, 215–16
Howitt, Peter, 41
HTC, 73, 112

Hubbard, Thomas, 134, 135
Hughes, Alan, 223
Hulten, Charles, 4–5, 43, 45, 48, 56
human capital, 54, 119

IBM, 39, 170
ICI, 167, 169
income, 119–20, 127–28; implications of an intangible economy for, 143; intangibles, firms, and inequality of, 130; intangibles' effects on, 129–40; scalability and, 133–34
industrial commons, 84–85
Industrial Revolution, 126
industrial structure, 30–31
inequality, 118–19; accumulation of capital as reason for, 124–25; and differences in wages between firms, 129; of earnings, 120–21, 127–40; of esteem, 122–23, 129–40, 141–42; field guide to, 119–23; between the generations, 121–22; in an intangible-rich economy, 130–32, 135–35, 236–38; measures of, 119–20; of place, 122, 128–29, 136–39, 249n3; as result of improvements in technology, 123–24, 126–27; role of housing prices in, 122, 128–29, 136–39; standard explanations for, 123–25; symbolic analysts and, 133–34; and taxes, 139–40; trade and, 124; of wealth, 121, 128–40; worker screening and, 134–35

influence activities, 196
information, definition of, 64
infrastructure, 144, 157; definition of, 144–45; enabling character of, 145; hype and false promises surrounding, 145–47; institutional, 153–56; physical, 147–51; role of norms and standards in, 154–55; soft, 156; telecommunications, 151–52
innervation, 18
innovation districts, 215
innovative property, 43–45
Institution of Cleveland Engineers, 83
Institution of Mechanical Engineers, 83
intangible economy, the, 182–85, 206–7; competition in, 185–87; cult of the manager and, 184, 188; financing of (see under financing); inequality in (see under inequality); investing in, 201–6; managing in, 188–200; public policy and (see under public policy); R&D in (see under R&D [research and development])
intangible myths, 135–36
intangibles, 10–11, 201–6, 239–42; accounting treatment of, 202–4; banking industry and, 162–66; changing business climate and, 31–34, 239–40; contestedness of, 87–88, 115, 132; cosmopolitanism versus conservatism and, 141–42; depreciation of, 56–57;

intangibles (*continued*)
  differences between tangibles
  and, 7–10, 58; effect on GDP
  growth of, 117; effects of
  institutional infrastructure on,
  153; effects of low levels of
  investment in, 102–3; effects
  on income, wealth, and esteem
  inequality of, 129–40; emergent characteristics of, 86–88;
  equity markets and, 169–74; as
  explanation for secular stagnation, 101–16; financial architecture for, 218–21; the four
  S's of, 8–10, 58, 61–63, 88;
  future challenges of measuring,
  52–55; globalization and growing market sizes and, 34–35;
  in gyms, 15–19; and income
  inequality, 130–32; industrial
  structure and, 30–31; measurement of, 7–8, 46–49; mobile,
  139–40, 248n4; properties
  of, 8–10; public procurement
  and, 226–28; as real investment or not, 49–52; reasons
  for growth of investment in,
  27–35; research on, 5–7; and
  secular stagnation (*see under*
  secular stagnation); solving
  underinvestment in, 221–30;
  steady growth of investment in,
  23–27; types of, 21–22, 43–46;
  venture capital as well-suited
  for, 175–77; worker screening
  and, 134–35. *See also* investment; scalability; spillovers;
  sunkenness; synergies

Intel, 174
intellectual property rights (IPRs),
  45, 165, 175–76; clearer rules
  and norms about, 211–14
Intellectual Ventures, 152
interdisciplinarity, 85
interest rates, 92–93
International Monetary Fund
  (IMF), 93
Internet of Things, 85, 152
investment: definition of, 19–21;
  examples of changing nature of,
  15–19, 239–40; government,
  231–34, 234–36; importance
  of, 3, 15; in intangibles, 3–5,
  21–22, 49–52, 202–6, 239–42;
  measurement of, 36–43; and
  secular stagnation, 92–93
investors, choices for, 204–6
IPOs, 171–72
Israeli Statistical Bureau, 56
iTunes, 18

Jacobs, Jane, 138, 142
Jacobs spillovers, 138
Jaeger, Bastian, 141
Jaffe, Adam, 105–6
Jarboe, 54
Jefferson, Thomas, 72
Jobs, Steve, 87, 110
John Deere, 76
Jones, Arthur, 16
Jones, Chad, 62
Joy, Bill, 84

Kaggle, 152
kaizen system, 51
Kanban system, 29, 183

Kantor, Shawn, 224
Kasnik, Ron, 204
Katz, Bruce, 215
Katz, Lawrence, 228
Kaufmann, Eric, 141
Kay, John, 161, 167, 169, 205–6
keiretsu system, 176–77
Keynes, John Maynard, 158, 160, 165, 249n1
Khan, Zorina, 75–76
Kleiner Perkins, 176
K-Mart, 187
knowledge: definition of, 63, 64; embodied versus disembodied, 64–65; propositional versus prescriptive, 64–65; scalability of, 66
knowledge-creating companies, 182–83
Knowledge and the Wealth of Nations (Warsh), 62

labor productivity, 96
land use policies, 214–17
Lazonick, William, 127, 170
Leadbeater, Charles, 4, 182, 183, 196
leadership, 197–99
left-behind communities, 122, 141–42
Lerner, Josh, 62, 178, 220
Lev, Baruch, 41, 43, 62, 185, 201–4, 220
Lewellen, Katharina, 171
Lindqvist, Erik, 131
Litton, 80, 85
Living on Thin Air (Leadbeater), 182

LMUK, 23
London View Management Framework, 216
Longitude Prize, 85
Lucas, Robert, 41

MacArthur Foundation Research Network on Opening Governance, 218
Machlup, Fritz, 38, 43
management: authority of, 189; and building a good organization, 194–97; in an intangible-rich world, 191–93; leadership and, 197–99; monitoring and, 188–91; roles of, 189–90
management consulting, 134–35
Manning, Alan, 123
Marrano, Mauro Giorgio, 42
Marshall, Alfred, 62, 147
Marshall-Arrow-Romer spillovers, 62, 138
Marx, Karl/Marxism, 126–27, 191, 243n3
Masood, Ehsan, 36
Massive Open Online Courses. *See* MOOCs
Matthews, Colin, 1–2
Maxjet, 162
Mazzucato, Mariana, 161, 168, 232
McAfee, Andrew, 30, 123
McDonald's, 67
McKinsey & Company, 73, 135, 195
McKinsey Global Institute, 81
McLean, Andrew, 194
McNerney, James, 194

McNichols, Maureen, 204
measurement, of intangibles,
    36–43, 46–49; and different
    types of investments, 43–46;
    future challenges in, 52–55
Mickey Mouse Curve, 78–79
Microsoft, 4–5, 7–8, 40, 175,
    222–23; scalability of, 67, 102,
    105
microwave ovens, 80, 81, 85, 239
Milanovic, Branko, 120, 124
Miles, David, 168
Milgrom, Paul, 194, 196
Mills, Les, 17–18, 21, 187, 239
Mills, Philip, 17
Mintzberg, Henry, 53
Miyagawa, Tsutomu, 42
mobile intangibles, 139–40,
    248n4
Mokyr, Joel, 64
monitoring and management,
    188–91
monopolies, 76, 78
MOOCs (Massive Open Online
    Courses), 230
Moore, Lyndon, 132–33, 134
Moore's Law, 30
Mowery, David, 226
Mukai, Kentaro, 42
mule-spinners, 126–27
multi-factor productivity, 98–101
Musk, Elon, 187, 198, 220
Myhrvold, Nathan, 152, 223
Mylan, 112, 113

Nakamura, Leonard, 41
Napster, 18
Nardelli, Robert, 194

national accounts, 20–21, 43, 51
National Bureau of Economic
    Research (NBER), 38
National Institute for Health and
    Clinical Excellence, 154
Nature of Technology, The (Arthur),
    80
neoliberalism, 119
network effects, 66
New Growth Theory, 66
Nightingale, Paul, 155
NIMBYs, 139, 150
Nohria, Nitian, 194
Nokia, 104
nonexcludable ideas, 72
non-rivalry, 66

obliquity, 161
Ocado, 23
Occupy Wall Street, 120
O'Connor, Sarah, 183
Office for National Statistics
    (ONS), 46
Oliner, Steve, 39
open innovation, 83–84, 103–4, 110
openness to experience, 141–42
option value, 72, 87, 175
oral rehydration therapy (ORT),
    66, 67
Organisation for Economic Co-
    operation and Development
    (OECD), 5, 38, 41, 43, 52; on
    employment strictness, 32; on
    productivity gap, 96; on qual-
    ity adjustment figures, 40
organizational development,
    50–51
Other People's Money (Kay), 205

Oulton, Nicholas, 41
ownership, of intangibles, 211–14

Parlophone records, 59, 61
Pasteur, Louis, 64
patents, 76, 153, 165, 213; blocking, 113–14
patent trolling, 78–79
Patientslikeme, 152
PayPal, 78, 184–85, 187
pensioners, 121–22
Pepsi Co., 49
Perez, Carlota, 146
Pets.com, 42
Pfizer, 31
Piketty, Thomas, 19, 118, 121; on capital accumulation, 124–25; on housing, 136–37, 139; on the income gap, 127–28
Pinch, The (Willetts),121
Pisano, Gary, 84–85
place, inequality of, 122, 128–29, 136–39, 249n3
populism, 122–23
Porter, Michael, 148
post-Fordist economy, 4
post-industrial future, 4
prescriptive knowledge, 64
Presley, Elvis, 61
Price, David, 129
producers, 20; and profitability explained, 97–101
production, 20–21
Production and Distribution of Knowledge in the United States, The (Machlup), 38
productivity: of intangibles, 28–30, 95–96; labor, 96; profits and, 97–101, 103–7; and the ratchet effect, 195–96; total factor, 96, 98, 102, 107–9
profitability, 97–101, 103–7, 247n2
profits, and secular stagnation, 94–96
property rights, 153, 212
propositional knowledge, 64
public investment: challenges of, 231–34, 234–36; and public procurement, 226–28; in R&D, 33–34, 55, 77, 223–24; in training and education, 228–30
public policy, 208–9; challenges for, 209–11, 231–34; and cultivating synergies, 214–18; and financing for intangible investments, 218–21; and government-funded investment in intangibles, 223–30; and intangible inequality, 236–38; and ownership of intangibles, 211–14
public procurement, 226–28
Pumping Iron, 16, 17
purchases of investment assets, 47
Purposeful Company project, 220

Quarterly Acquisitions and Disposals of Capital Assets Survey, 46

Radio Taxis, 82
Rajgopal, Shiva, 168
R&D (research and development): accounting treatment of, 202–4; cost of, 28, 41, 71;

R&D (*continued*)
  definition of, 244n4; effect on
  GDP of, 38, 43; government
  spending on, 33–34, 55, 77,
  223–24; in-house, 47; as intan-
  gible investment, 7, 22, 28, 43,
  44, 49; investment in, 169–74;
  Microsoft's investments in, 5;
  returns on, 29, 31; scalability
  and, 60; and spillovers, 72–73
ratchet effect, 195
*Rate and Direction of Inventive
  Activity, The* (conference), 38
Rauch, Ferdinand, 49
Raytheon, 80
Reich, Robert, 133, 134
rent-seeking, 113
Ridley, Matt, 81
*Rise and Fall of American Growth,
  The* (Gordon), 93–94
Roberts, John, 194, 196
Roberts, Richard, 126
Roberts, Russell, 188
Rognlie, Matthew, 128, 137
Rolls-Royce, 31
Romer, Paul, 41, 62, 63, 66, 147
Rosen, Sherwin, 130
Rowling, J. K., 131
rules and norms, 211–14

Sadun, Rafaella, 53, 82
Salter, Ammon, 197
Sampson, Rachelle, 168
Samsung, 73, 112
Sanders, Bernie, 223
Santa Fe Institute, 80
scalability, 9–10, 58, 60, 87,
  101–2; definition of, 246n2;

importance of, 67–68; income
  inequality and, 133–34; and
  increased investment, 110;
  and intangibles, 65–67; secular
  stagnation and, 103–5
Schreyer, Paul, 40
Schwarzenegger, Arnold, 16
Science: The Endless Frontier
  (Bush), 232
Second Machine Age, 30
secular stagnation, 91, 116;
  explanation for, 101–16; and
  intangibles investment, 102–3;
  profits and productivity differ-
  ences and, 103–7; relationship
  of scalability and spillovers to,
  109–16; symptoms of, 92–96
Shankar, Ravi, 61
Shi, Yuan, 168
Shih, Willy, 85
Shinoda, Yukio, 42
short-termism, 161, 168–69
Sichel, Dan, 4, 5, 39, 42, 43, 45
Siemens, 60–61, 204
single-factor productivity, 98–101
Six Sigma, 51
Skype, 217
Slack, 152, 217
smartphones, 72–73, 81
Smil, Vaclav, 146
Smith, Adam, 36, 188
social capital, 156, 236
soft infrastructure, 156
solar energy, 85
Solow, Robert, 39, 125
Song, Jae, 129, 131, 135
South Wales Institution of Engi-
  neers, 83

speculation, 249n1

spending, 46–47, 54; on assets, 20; rent-seeking, 113

Spenser, Percy, 80

spillovers, 9, 58, 61, 87, 102; contestedness and, 87; importance of, 77–79; and intangibles, 72–77, 109–16; Jacobs, 138; Marshall-Arrow-Romer, 62, 138; physical infrastructure and, 147–51; secular stagnation and, 103–4; slowing TFP growth and, 107–9; venture capital and, 178

Spotify, 18

Stack Overflow, 29

Stansted Airport, 1–2, 3–4

Starbucks, 34, 52, 65, 140, 183, 195, 197; scalability of, 67

start-up ecosystems, 222

Statute of Anne (1709), 76

stock markets, 167–68, 205–6; IPOs and, 171–72

stock of intangible assets, 56–57

Summers, Larry, 93

sunkenness, 8–9, 58, 60, 87, 246n5; as characteristic of intangibles, 68–70; importance of, 70–72; venture capital and, 175–76

sustained advantage, 250n2

Sutton, John, 67

symbolic analysis, 132–34

synergies, 10, 58, 61, 87–88, 213; and intangible assets, 80–83, 83–86; among investments, 110; maximizing the benefits of, 214–18; physical infrastructure and, 147–51; venture capital and, 176

System of National Accounts, 20, 43, 51

systems innovation, 198

tacit knowledge, 65

tangible investments, differences between intangible and, 7–10, 58

taxes, 139–40, 235; and financing, 166, 219

technology: and cost of intangible investment, 28; inequality as result of improvements in, 123–24, 126–27; and productivity of intangibles, 28–30; and spillovers, 151–52

Tesla Motors, 24, 111, 209

Thatcher, Margaret, 127

Theory of Moral Sentiments, The (Smith), 188

Thiel, Peter, 78, 175, 184–85, 187, 223

3M, 194

Toffler, Alvin, 4

Tonogi, Konomi, 42

total factor productivity (TFP), 96, 98, 102; poor performance of, 109–9, 114

Toyota, 29, 51

trade and inequality, 124

trademarks, 76

training and education, 51–52, 170, 228–30

Trajtenberg, Manuel, 106

Trump, Donald, 122, 141–42, 143

trust, 156

23andMe, 152
Twitter, 185, 187

Uber, 24, 28, 51; building of
    driver network by, 112–13;
    contestedness and, 115; legal
    travails of, 187; scalability of,
    67, 101–2, 105; and synergies,
    82; venture capital and, 174,
    175
uncertainty, 87
Ure, Andrew, 126
Ur-Nammu, 75
US Federal Reserve, 4, 40, 41, 42,
    165
US Food and Drug Administra-
    tion, 154

Van Reenen, John, 82, 136, 173,
    195
venture capital (VC) funding,
    154–55, 161, 166, 174–75;
    problems with, 177–79; and
    intangibles, 175–77
Vlachos, Jonas, 131
Volcker, Paul, 165
von Mises, Ludwig, 38
von Wachter, Till, 129

Wallis, Gavin, 42, 223–24
Walmart, 81, 187
Warsh, David, 62

Wasmer, Etienne, 128
Watt, James, 78
wealth, 119–20, 121; housing
    and, 122, 128–29, 136–39;
    inequality of, 139–40; intan-
    gibles' effects on, 129–40
Wealth of Nations, The (Smith),
    36
Weightless World, The (Coyle), 4
Weitzman, Martin L., 195
Welch, Jack, 184
Whalley, Alexander, 224
"What Is the U.S. Gross Invest-
    ment in Intangibles? (At Least)
    One Trillion Dollars a Year!"
    (Nakamura), 41
Wikipedia, 217
Willetts, David, 121
Williamson, Oliver, 192
William the Conqueror, 2
worker screening and intangibles,
    134–35
World Trade Organization
    (WTO), 31
Wright brothers, 78, 79, 153
Wyckoff, Frank, 56

Yahoo, 68
YouTube, 213

Zero to One (Thiel), 78, 185, 187
Zingales, Luigi, 173